THE AGE OF ASTONISHMENT

THE AGE OF ASTONISHMENT

John Morris in the Miracle Century:
From the Civil War to the Cold War

BILL MORRIS

PEGASUS BOOKS
NEW YORK LONDON

THE AGE OF ASTONISHMENT

Pegasus Books, Ltd.
148 West 37th Street, 13th Floor
New York, NY 10018

Copyright © 2022 by Bill Morris

First Pegasus Books cloth edition April 2022

Interior design by Maria Fernandez

Library of Congress Cataloging-in-Publication Data is available.

ISBN: 978-1-64313-704-9

10 9 8 7 6 5 4 3 2 1

Printed in the United States of America
Distributed by Simon & Schuster
www.pegasusbooks.com

For Anne Drayton Nelson, keeper of flames.

"It would be a mistake to say that I felt guilt for the past. A person cannot be culpable for the acts of others, long dead, that he or she could not have influenced. Rather than responsible, I felt accountable for what had happened, called on to try to explain it."

—from *Slaves in the Family* by Edward Ball

CONTENTS

AUTHOR'S NOTE

This book is a mongrel. It's nonfiction, but it's a mix of numerous breeds, including biography, history, reportage, memoir, autobiography, and, when the record runs thin, speculation that flirts with fiction. I have cited the sources of quoted remarks, and when I've engaged in speculation I've announced it by inserting such markers as "it's likely" or "he might have said," or by urging the reader to "imagine" with me if it's the only way into the history or the lives of the characters. Racial slurs in speech and literature are quoted verbatim, not because I condone their use but because they are a valid part of the historical record. I am a reporter and a novelist, not a scholar or historian, so this book does not contain footnotes or an index, though there is a detailed list of sources at the end. I have done my best to stick to the facts in my pursuit of the truth. Any errors are entirely the fault of the author.

curled up under our school desks as a pathetic way of preparing for nuclear Armageddon. And, yes, I lived to see the civil rights movement, interstate highways, rock 'n' roll, the Vietnam War, a man on the moon, the flowering of feminism and gay rights, Watergate, personal computers, the internet, the smart phone, and the #MeToo and Black Lives Matter movements. These are not trifles, but my inventory led to an unassailable conclusion: not all that much has changed during my lifetime, really, and certainly not in the fundamental ways my grandfather's day-to-day life changed. The difference between a buggy and a jet is far greater than the difference between the rotary phones I grew up using and the smart phone I use today.

In 2016, a monumental new book put flesh on the bones of my theory. *The Rise and Fall of American Growth: The U.S. Standard of Living Since the Civil War* by Robert J. Gordon is guided by two central premises: that the years from 1870 to 1970, very nearly the dates of my grandfather's birth and death, comprised "the special century," a spurt of life-altering inventions and economic growth in the United States that is unmatched in human history; and that since 1970, change has been far slower, and it has been confined to the much narrower spheres of entertainment, communication, and information. The innovations and breakthroughs of the special century, Gordon argues, will never be repeated. The age was a one-off. I don't think Gordon went far enough in calling this age the "special" century; I have come to see it as the *miracle* century.

I began to wonder: Would it be possible to paint a portrait of that astonishing age by tracing the life of one man who lived through it, my grandfather, John Morris? I decided to try. This book is the result.

PRELUDE

THE MISFIT

In a black-and-white family snapshot now lost to time, an elderly gentleman with spun-sugar hair gazes at the camera through owlish round glasses. He's wearing a three-piece suit and an expression of delight mixed with terror, for on his right knee he's balancing a swaddled infant who has the bewildered, bug-eyed look of a space alien. The man is my father's father, John Morris; I am the infant.

That snapshot was taken in November 1952, the month the United States detonated the first hydrogen bomb, a weapon a thousand times more powerful than the atom bombs that incinerated Hiroshima and Nagasaki. Three years later, in the fall of 1955, my grandfather died at the age of ninety-two. I have no memories of the man, but even as a boy I found myself marveling at the changes he must have witnessed and experienced in his long lifetime. He was born into a slave-owning Virginia family during the Civil War and died at the peak of the Cold War. At the time of his birth, the dominant technologies were the steam engine, the railroad, the telegraph, and photography. He grew up in a world lit by kerosene lamps and candles, he traveled by foot and horseback and wagon on dirt roads, drank water hauled from a well, used an outdoor privy. He mastered Latin and Greek and German. He became a lawyer, a philologist, and a college professor.

Along the way he lived through Reconstruction, booms and busts, women's suffrage, urbanization, Prohibition, labor unrest, the Great Depression, two world wars, the Korean War, and the advent of nuclear weapons. He was among the original users of window screens, the telephone, modern plumbing, electric lights, typewriters, radio, automobiles, phonographs, airplanes, elevators, movies, subways, safety razors, television, penicillin, pasteurized milk, refrigeration, antibiotics, and central heat and air conditioning. He witnessed the horrors of Jim Crow, unhappily, and he was in Germany to witness Hitler's rise, also unhappily. He wrote scholarly articles for obscure journals and spent decades producing a German-English dictionary that was never published.

It seems that John Morris dealt with all this dizzying change by remaining firmly rooted in the nineteenth century, a classically educated southern gentleman who pursued willfully obscure passions. For all that, he held remarkably progressive beliefs on race relations, child rearing, women's rights, and religious freedom. Deep in the Bible Belt, he was an agnostic, possibly an atheist. He married an Irish Catholic from upstate New York at a time when Catholics, Jews, and Yankees were not warmly welcomed in the South. And in that traditionally bellicose region, he was a lifelong pacifist and opponent of capital punishment. He was, in a word, a misfit. My grandfather, who was too young to remember the freeing of the family's slaves in 1865, treated Black people with respect and did not allow racial slurs to be uttered under his roof. I'm reminded of the passage in *To Kill a Mockingbird* when Scout asks her father, "Do you defend niggers, Atticus?"

"Of course I do. Don't say nigger, Scout. That's common."

"'s what everybody at school says."

"From now on it'll be everybody less one—"

As I grew older, my boyish sense of wonder at my grandfather's world spawned an allied suspicion: I came to question the widespread belief that, as a Baby Boomer, I was living in a time of unprecedented change. Yes, we

THE AGE OF ASTONISHMENT

PART ONE
WAR AND PEACE
1863-1898

Taylor's Creek in Montpelier, Virginia.

A BIRTH DURING WARTIME

John Morris was born on June 23, 1863, at a family place called Aspenwall in Goochland County, Virginia. He would spend the first two years of his long life shuttling between Aspenwall and Taylor's Creek, his parents' home, a handsome frame house in neighboring Hanover County that had been in the family since it was built in 1732 by an immigrant from Wales named William Morris. The plantation came to cover as much as two thousand rolling acres, and it had always been worked by slaves.

John's father, Charles Morris, was not present at the birth. He was thirty miles away in Richmond, serving in the quartermaster corps, which supplied Confederate troops with food, clothing, weapons, and horses, safely removed from the escalating slaughter but plagued by torments of a different kind. Chief among them was his incessant worrying about the safety and health—indeed the survival—of his wife, Mary, and their three young sons: infant John, three-year-old James, and seven-year-old Sylvanus. Charles's fretting was not groundless. Mary had delivered one stillborn child, a niece of Charles's had recently died before her first birthday, and a neighbor's wife had just died after giving birth to a healthy child. This was, as the US Surgeon General put it, "the end of the medical Middle Ages." Infant mortality rates were shocking by today's standards—about 175 deaths per 1,000 births the year John was born, destined to peak at 215 per 1,000 in 1880, which was roughly the rate of infant mortality in Tudor England. Pasteur's revolution and the germ theory were still two decades away, so children who survived infancy were beset by an array of infectious diseases including cholera, diphtheria, yellow fever, pneumonia, and tuberculosis. Malnourished children suffered from afflictions so unheard-of today that they almost sound like foreign words: pellagra, hookworm, rickets, scurvy. Charles Morris suffered from neuralgia and chronic dysentery, and John and his brothers were constantly sick with colds, fevers, and whooping cough. Soldiers were twice as likely to die from disease as from bayonet, bullet, or shell. Because of infection, a wound to the gut amounted to a death sentence.

Lacking medicine, even relatively sophisticated people had to rely on folk remedies. Before the war, Charles Morris had graduated from college and law school, served as county attorney, taught law, and, with an inheritance from an aunt, spent five months touring Europe, roaming from Pompeii to Naples to Rome, through Switzerland, France, and Holland, and on to London, where he attended the Great Exhibition at the Crystal Palace. There he marveled at the gigantic Trophy Telescope, the Koh-i-Noor diamond, hydraulic presses, steam hammers, adding machines, Cyrus McCormick's reaping machine, Samuel Colt's revolvers, and Matthew

Brady's daguerreotypes. As he moved through the awestruck throngs, he might have brushed against Charles Darwin and Charles Dickens and Charlotte Bronte. He described the trip as "a dream of pleasure." Yet here was this worldly man's medical advice to Mary: "Take care of the children and get some camphor and snakeroot and put it in a bag around their necks to keep off the hooping [*sic*] cough." The second Industrial Revolution was, indeed, dawning at the end of the medical Middle Ages.

John Morris was born on one of the brighter days in the brief life of the Confederate States of America. The Army of Northern Virginia had rebuffed a Union assault on Richmond, eluded disaster at bloody Antietam, and scored brilliant victories at Fredericksburg and Chancellorsville. Now in the hot dry summer of 1863, with New York City poised to explode in violence against President Lincoln's new draft law, Gen. Robert E. Lee was leading 70,000 Confederate troops across the Mason–Dixon Line into Pennsylvania for the first time, hoping for a victory on northern soil that would yield cascading rewards. It might persuade England and France to support the cause and allow the South to hold on until the 1864 elections, when a war-weary US electorate might vote for a peace candidate, securing the survival of the Confederacy. Lee's army was drawn north by more than the prospect of seizing Philadelphia, Baltimore, or possibly even Washington, DC. Unlike ravaged Virginia, Pennsylvania was untouched by the war, and Lee's army was tantalized, as one southern diarist put it, by the "rich farms" awaiting them in the North. Among Lee's troops on that spirited summertime march was one of John Morris's uncles, another John Morris, his mother's twenty-four-year-old brother, a lieutenant in an artillery battalion commanded by Lt. Col. R. L. Walker.

As Lee's army was pushing into enemy territory, Charles Morris was busy juggling his duties as a quartermaster with his duties as a husband, father, and owner of "that poor old plantation," as he described Taylor's Creek during the lean wartime years. In truth, "plantation" was too grand a word for the place. The house was originally a modest one-room structure that was added onto repeatedly, most recently by Charles just before he brought his bride there to live and start a family in 1854. The place may have met the strict definition of a plantation—that is, a self-contained agricultural enterprise worked by captive labor—but Hanover County was never the Old South of legend. Taylor's Creek was a functional farmhouse, not in league with the grand mansions on the James River built by the First Families of Virginia, or the elegant presidential retreats in the Blue Ridge. Nor did it rival the pillared palaces of the rice and indigo barons of the Georgia and South Carolina Low Country, or the sugar and cotton kings of the Deep South. The house has been lovingly preserved and expanded by cousins of mine, Anne Nelson and her late husband Garnett, who have taken it from merely handsome to truly elegant. But the rooms are smallish and not particularly sunny. The doorways are barely six feet high. The house is charming, but it is not a mansion.

If life was hard for the residents of that house during the war, it was downright grim for Charles. His Richmond posting was not his first. Shortly after Fort Sumter, he had gone to war with the Hanover Troop, swept up, like so many others in both the North and the South, by patriotic fervor, a shot at glory, and the nearly universal illusion that this was going to be a brief and glorious little war. He was assigned to the quartermaster corps under Gen. John Bankhead Magruder, a handsome and flamboyant Virginian known as "Prince John." Conveniently, Charles was stationed in Williamsburg, the colonial capital of Virginia, where he was already set up as a professor of law at the College of William & Mary. In the early months of the war, as Union forces pushed up the peninsula toward Williamsburg and Richmond, Charles's letters to Mary are full of frets and complaints. From Williamsburg he writes, "I feel mightily inclined to resign at these times, when I feel how unjust is the treatment I received from many of the men here and how far in spite of all my efforts I fall short of accomplishing what is expected of me. It is a very inglorious and insidious office I hold." To make matters worse, the college announced it was suspending professors' pay for the duration of the war, which infuriated Charles. His commanding officer, who brilliantly slowed the Union advance against staggering odds, was one bright note. "Gen. Magruder has been very kind to me," Charles writes, "and I think rather likes me and commiserates my numerous troubles." Meanwhile, Charles was assigned an ancillary duty that brought out his wry sense of humor. "I suppose I told you I have been appointed a Director of the Lunatic Asylum," he writes to Mary in the fall of 1861. "I shall be thankful if I don't get into it as one of the patients."

The grinding Union advance forced the Confederates to abandon Williamsburg and pull back to Richmond, but the change of venue brought Charles little relief. "I never saw such a perfect wilderness as this place is becoming," he writes to Mary the summer before John's birth, when the vicious rolling Seven Days Battles were rattling the city's windows and its citizens' nerves, sending 15,000 wounded soldiers streaming into its overflowing hospitals, then spilling into churches, hotels, warehouses, barns, and private homes. Refugees had tripled the city's population since the war's outbreak. "Almost all 'business' has ceased," the letter continues, "and rows and rows of stores are closed and occupied as habitats. You can buy nothing scarcely and what is for sale is at a fabulous price. Such shoes as I used to wear cost $18 and $20 per pair and boots $25 and $30." Meanwhile, more than a few Confederate soldiers were going into battle barefoot.

The exorbitant prices would increase tenfold by the end of the war thanks to speculators who were not squeamish about turning privation into profit. Some filled warehouses with barrels of flour then held out until hunger and desperation pushed prices to "fabulous" levels. Before one major battle, speculators bought up every coffin in town, then jacked up prices when the shooting stopped and the burying began.

⸎

They must have made an imposing couple, Charles and Mary Morris. They were first cousins once removed, a common arrangement at a time when virtually everyone living within thirty miles was some sort of relation. Charles was tall and austere, solidly built, with gingery hair swept sideways over a broad forehead. A brisk broom of a moustache was trimmed precisely along the top of his upper lip. His eyes were ice-blue and piercing. He was, by all accounts, not a man to trifle with.

Mary was also solidly built, no great beauty. Her maiden name was Mary Minor Morris, so in marriage she acquired the clunkily alliterative moniker of Mary Minor Morris Morris. Her eyes were warmer than her husband's, but they saw through things—and people. She noticed, then she assessed, then she acted on those assessments. She was not one to back down or be pushed around. The woman had starch in her.

Like many southerners, this couple tried to secure their family's survival by developing an impromptu wartime commerce. Moving back and forth between Richmond and Taylor's Creek was a steady flow of goods that could be consumed, worn, or sold at a profit, including flour, butter, ice, calves, blackberries, shoulders of bacon, nails, socks, sorghum, and bales of cotton. Sometimes Charles carried the goods with him on his way to or from one of his frequent weekend furloughs, traveling by train to nearby Beaverdam or by packet boat to Cedar Point in Goochland County, the closest stop on the James River and Kanawha Canal. And sometimes the goods were transported by neighbors, relatives, or slaves. On one occasion, a trusted slave named Uncle Jeems was ferrying a load of supplies to Richmond on a horse-drawn cart when he was overtaken by a troop of Union soldiers, who confiscated the horse, the cart, and the cargo. Uncle

Jeems walked back to Taylor's Creek empty-handed. The cart and the supplies were lost, but the next day the horse, known as Old Fashion, showed up at the back gate of the house in Richmond where Charles was staying. As one of Charles's sons would say years later about the old mare: "She had more sense than many men."

The wartime letters between Charles and Mary were a torrent, a daily ritual, nearly a nutrient. Charles always opens with the stiff salutation "Dear Wife" and he could be peevish and self-absorbed, but there is also genuine love in these pages, both for his wife and their sons. His letter to Mary lamenting the dire conditions in Richmond lurches to a close: "Please send me two or three shoulders of bacon when you send meat. I don't care much for the fresh meat, also a bag of corn meal. Your vegetables are always acceptable. Excuse this rambling letter. I write always in a sort of confusion. Write to me at every opportunity. Kiss my boys for me. Love to all." He sounds like a man coming unhinged.

And with good reason. Though Charles was spared the horrors of combat, he was confronted almost daily with privation, suffering, and death. Waves of smallpox and diphtheria swept the city. Food became so scarce and prices so high in the months before John's birth that thousands of women took to the streets, smashing their way into stores and scooping up armfuls of food, clothing and, for good measure, pieces of jewelry. When Confederate president Jefferson Davis arrived on the scene to restore order, an enraged woman threw a loaf of bread at him. The hospitals turned into charnel houses after major battles, and it was in one of those fetid, overwhelmed hospitals that Charles watched a cousin die from wounds suffered at Gaines' Mill. "Poor Billy Morris died last Thursday morning at 7 o'clock," Charles reports to Mary. "I sat with him all Wednesday night. When I went into his room I found him entirely insensible and pulseless and cold. I did not expect he would live half an hour, but he continued to gasp until 7 o'clock Thursday. The poor boy was terribly reduced and looked so different from what he did when I saw him before. All his friends and family were around him and he took leave of them all before he fell into the insensibility preceding death. He was carried up to Louisa to be buried."

Charles paid an even ghastlier visit to a close family friend, Col. Lewis Minor Coleman, who'd been wounded at Fredericksburg. "I found poor Lewis much the same as when I was last there, certainly no better," Charles writes to Mary. "He is a great sufferer and can not be moved in the slightest. It gives him exquisite pain to move even his toe . . . The discharge from his thigh continues very large, at least 3 full cups per day. He can only sleep under the influence of morphine and then he talks and wanders all the time. I can't help hoping he may get well, but I greatly fear he never will." He never did. Lewis Coleman endured another year of agony before dying in the spring of 1864.

⁂

As wrenching as these encounters were, Charles's concern for his family's survival outweighed them. One of his chief fears was that Mary, alone in the remote farmhouse with three sickly boys, would be driven to despair by loneliness. Suicidal depression was not uncommon on the home front, so Charles constantly urged Mary to take the boys to Aspenwall to be with her parents and other relatives, and she regularly did so. But she still had to keep the farm running, which she did with the help of two overseers, named Hackett and Luck, and Charles's brother Edward, who lived nearby in a house called Clazemont. In the same letter reporting Billy Morris's death, Charles veers into a panic about money matters: "I do wish we could put the wheat to market. I wish you would say to Hackett that it must be delivered at once. I can wait no longer . . . We must have money in view of dire coming events and that is my only source of money."

But loneliness, illness, and money weren't the only worries. As Uncle Jeems had learned firsthand, Union troops were buzzing in the neighborhood. They had burned the depot and stores at Beaverdam on the Virginia Central Railroad, which linked Richmond to the fertile Shenandoah Valley, and Charles was surely terrified they would start burning Hanover County's houses, barns, and crops, as they had been doing so mercilessly in the Shenandoah. One weekend night when Charles was home on furlough, Confederate soldiers came to the house to tell the family that Yankees were nearby, moving on Richmond. Charles and Mary bundled the children and set out for her father's house in Goochland about two hours before the raiders passed through Taylor's Creek. Traveling by horseback and carriage, the family reached Aspenwall at sunrise.

On another occasion, when Charles was away in Richmond, several Black men knocked on the door to inform Mary that Yankees were at the overseers' house. She got the children dressed and hurried them to her brother-in-law's. A nurse named Tina carried John, a slave named Old Dick carried Jim, and Mary and Sylvanus walked the mile through moonlit fields and forests to Clazemont. The Yankees, if they were Yankees, were gone in the morning, and the unnerved family walked back home.

———

Lt. John Morris, John's uncle, was not so lucky. On the first day of the Battle of Gettysburg, his left leg was shorn off at the knee by a Union artillery shell, and he bled to death in agony two hours later. After the killing stopped on July 3, the job of dealing with 50,000 casualties began. It has been estimated that six million pounds of human and animal carcasses lay rotting in the sun, bloated, blackened, sizzling with maggots. John Morris was buried by comrades in an orchard on the battlefield. It's possible he was immortalized by Matthew Brady, who took hundreds of photographs of the blasted landscape, including rows of Confederate soldiers in shallow graves before they were covered with dirt. Was Lt. John Morris one of Brady's silent subjects?

It sometimes took three days or more for Charles's letters to travel from Richmond to Taylor's Creek. Troops, munitions, and supplies frequently moved by train or steamboat, and President Lincoln set up a telegraph office in the White House so he could receive news of battles as they unfolded. Yet the reality for most southerners, including Charles Morris, was that the initial reports of battles were slow to reach them and often wildly inaccurate. As Robert E. Lee's shattered army was limping back to the Potomac River—a seventeen-mile-long wagon train of misery the Union army could have annihilated with ease—Charles sent Mary this buoyant report on July 6: "The news from Gettysburg which you will see in the papers is regarded here as a victory. The city is full of rumors from Lee's army that the enemy have been heavily defeated and that we are in full march with the whole army on Baltimore. Gen. Stuart is all around it with his cavalry . . . The news from the South is also good."

No, it was not. On July 4, after a forty-eight-day siege, the starving Confederate soldiers and citizens of Vicksburg, Mississippi, surrendered to Gen. Ulysses S. Grant. The South had been cut in two. On successive days, the Confederacy suffered back-to-back blows from which it would never recover.

Five days later, after learning about the fall of Vicksburg via telegraph, Charles writes to Mary: "Yesterday was the bitterest and darkest day I have ever spent here. Early in the morning bad news commenced arriving. 1st a Baltimore paper of the 6th in which the complete rout and pursuit of our army under Gen. Lee was given with much circumstantiality and detail . . . Gettysburg seems to have been another Sharpsburg [Antietam] . . . We have lost 11000 killed and wounded and 4000 prisoners and have been compelled to fall back for want of ammunition to be nearer our base. Any loss such as this is equal to defeat for us . . . Only three days ago we were in the flood of success and now in so short a time on the very ebb of despondency."

Then, as he so often did, Charles abruptly cuts from war news to a deeply personal confession: "I feel sick whenever my thoughts turn to that place [Taylor's Creek] and its hopeless prospects. If I allowed myself to dwell on it I believe I should go melancholy mad."

Melancholy mad. A powerful alliteration, and the first hint that Charles was suffering from something darker than war-induced gloom. As the war drags on, his letters become sprinkled with mentions of "the winds of melancholy" and the "blue devils" that afflict him: "I do feel most dreadfully depressed and pray for consolation. I believe I am mad about the corn. I dream of it nightly and about starvation at home. I have never been so 'blue' in all my life."

Richmond in Ruins.

A WORLD REMADE

Eventually, perhaps inevitably, the "goods" moving back and forth between Taylor's Creek and Richmond came to include human beings. Desperate for cash and tormented by nightmares of starvation, Charles decided to try to hire out some of his young slaves in Richmond, possibly as maids or orderlies, a practice that had become so commonplace that there was a glut of available labor in the city. Late in the cataclysmic summer of 1863, Charles writes to Mary: "I can hire out some girls and boys, I want you to get them ready and I will bring down some with me and you can send the others. I propose to hire out all of the age of Tina, Catherine, John, Fleming and others even smaller. I don't like to sell them."

Why not? Was it because Charles was shrewd enough to know that it was a bad business move to forfeit a valuable, cradle-to-grave asset for a short-term gain? Or was it because Charles, out of something that might be called compassion, was averse to breaking up his slaves' families? The answer will never be known, but there is evidence that Charles was fighting his own internal war between two powerful forces: conscience and commerce. This inner war was such a fact of contemporary life that it had recently animated one of the most influential and enduring works of American literature.

Uncle Tom's Cabin, Harriet Beecher Stowe's runaway best-selling novel published on the eve of the Civil War, was a teeming gallery of broad-brush types, including the brutal slave owner Simon Legree, the stoic slave Uncle Tom, and the sadistic overseers Sambo and Quimbo. Much more subtly, Stowe painted Tom's owner, Arthur Shelby, as a decent man who feels genuine affection for Tom but reluctantly decides to sell him and another slave, Harry, to pay off debts. Upon learning of the plan, Harry's mother, Eliza, flees with her son. The novel brilliantly illustrated the harsh truth that in the slave owner's internal war between conscience and commerce, the winner would almost always be the dollar. Just about everyone read the book, which inflamed antislavery sentiment in the North and fanned secessionist leanings in the South. Harriet Beecher Stowe didn't start the Civil War, but she surely hastened its arrival.

Charles Morris may have been soldiering alongside Arthur Shelby, but that didn't compel him to free his slaves or speak out for abolition. His history wouldn't allow it—or even allow him to consider it. The slave trade had begun in Virginia more than a century before the paterfamilias, William Morris, built Taylor's Creek, and by the outbreak of the Civil War the family had owned slaves for nearly a century and a half. For White people in colonial and antebellum Virginia, slavery was an unquestioned fact of the entire social order, from the bottom rungs of society to the Founding Fathers. In his 2018 book, *The War Before the War*, the historian Andrew

Delbanco pointed out that most White people in the American colonies thought enslaving a Black person was as reasonable as saddling a horse or training a dog.

Patrick Henry, the most famous son of Hanover County, was both an abolitionist and a fiery promoter of rebellion against the British crown. He was also a slave owner. He readily confessed that he was "drawn along" to keep his slaves because he did not want to go through "the general Inconveniency of living here without them." The simple truth, as Delbanco has noted, was that Patrick Henry and people of like mind—including Charles Morris?—learned to live with their misgivings about slavery because it served their interests. It was convenient, it was profitable and, perhaps most crucial of all, it had always been so. "All other arguments on its behalf were bogus . . ." Delbanco writes, "and somewhere, in heart if not head, they knew it."

George Washington and Thomas Jefferson, to name just two of the Founding Fathers who owned slaves, both knew it. And yet both managed to reconcile their inner conflict. At the age of eleven, Washington inherited ten slaves from his father, and at the outbreak of the Revolutionary War he owned more than a hundred. He claimed he did so "very repugnantly to my own feelings" and kept them only because "imperious necessity compels." His repugnance may have been genuine, but it did not stop him from clinging tenaciously to his human property. While serving as president in the new national capital of Philadelphia, Washington placed advertisements in three newspapers offering a $10 reward for the return of a twenty-three-year-old fugitive slave named Ona Judge—"a light Mulatto girl, much freckled, with very black eyes and bushy hair"—who had slipped out of the president's mansion in the spring of 1796 and would eventually make her way to a new life as a free woman in New Hampshire. Judge was Martha Washington's personal maid and she "absconded," to use the president's language, because Martha Washington planned to give her to her granddaughter Eliza as a wedding gift, which would have meant returning to the Washingtons' plantation, Mount Vernon, in the slave state of Virginia. George Washington never caught Ona Judge, but he pursued her like a bloodhound for more than three years. His will stipulated that his slaves were to be freed after his death, in December 1799 (although not Ona Judge, who was owned by Martha Washington). The historian Annette Gordon-Reed, author of *The Hemingses of Monticello*, offers a plausible explanation for the disconnect between Washington's words and his actions: "It's saying, 'Whatever I might think about slavery in the abstract, I should be able to do what I want with my property.'"

By the time of Ona Judge's flight to freedom, Thomas Jefferson had spent years mastering the steps of this tricky dance. In 1769 he posted an advertisement in the *Virginia Gazette* offering a cash reward for the return of a fugitive "Mulatto" slave named Sandy, a shoemaker who had fled Monticello with his cobbler's tools and one of Jefferson's horses. Sandy, according to the advertisement, was "greatly addicted to drink, and when drunk is insolent and disorderly, and in his conversation he swears much, and in his behavior is artful and knavish." It's hard to grasp that the author of this peevish thumbnail sketch would soon pen lofty words about the equality of all men in the Declaration of Independence.

Sandy wasn't the only light-skinned slave at Monticello, of course. After his wife's death, Jefferson fathered six children with a slave named Sally Hemings, the focus of Gordon-Reed's decorated book. Meanwhile, twenty-nine miles to the north, Jefferson's neighbor James Madison was known to sit at the dinner table in his mansion, Montpelier, expounding on the evils of slavery—while being waited on by slaves.

Charles Morris left the expounding to others. In keeping with family tradition, he neither publicly denounced slavery nor embraced the windy rhetoric of its proponents who, quoting everyone from Aristotle to Saint Paul, claimed it was a blessing for African savages because it allowed them to escape the Dark Continent and taste the glorious fruits of Christian civilization. Charles lived in a lukewarm middle ground between these fevered extremes. He regarded slavery, almost blandly, as a business arrangement with benefits for both master and slave. Years after the war and emancipation, his eldest son Sylvanus would recall: "I frequently heard (my father) describe the relation between master and slave. He owned the land and the negroes, he supervised it and them, they cultivated the land, and thus a livelihood was made for him and his family, and for them and their families. He had the responsibility, they did the work." This matter-of-fact formulation indicates that Charles neither sugarcoated the institution nor flinched at the coldest fact at the heart of it: that human beings owned other human beings, and the owned were nothing more (or less) than the legal property of the owner. And Charles Morris, like George Washington and Thomas Jefferson before him, believed he should be able to do what he wanted to do with his property.

What he wanted to do in the summer of 1863 was turn his young slaves' labor into desperately needed cash. But his experiment with trying to hire them out did not start off well. Two weeks after the first boys and girls arrived in Richmond, he writes to Mary: "Our negroes are not yet hired and I fear they will eat their heads off before they are. Edith, Catherine, and Hugh Ella are still on hand." Remember that name: Catherine.

Two weeks later, the news is better. A couple of slaves have been hired at a new hospital: "I saw Isaac yesterday. He and Cornelius are well and I told them if they could get off I would take them up with me on Saturday (to Taylor's Creek). I am not sure they can leave. They are hired at Camp Jackson a new hospital near Hollywood (Cemetery) and have an easy time I reckon from what he tells me but says he is mighty lonesome."

This is revealing on two levels. First, Charles is sensitive to his young slaves' loneliness and homesickness, and he tries to make arrangements for them to spend a weekend with their families—hardly the actions of an uncaring taskmaster. Second, Isaac and Cornelius are employed in the new hospital strategically located next to Hollywood Cemetery, west of Richmond, where 18,000 Confederate dead would eventually be buried.

At Jackson, the wounded had a conveniently short journey from operating room to sick bed to grave.

In February, Charles reports that the last of his slaves have been hired out, but his relief is short-lived. The girls keep getting fired for various acts of insubordination, inspiring Charles to send Mary a curious plea: "These negro girls will run me distracted. They are out of hand again. Shall I sell them? I wish you would advise it. I can't stand them much longer. They are utterly worthless, and don't give satisfaction any where."

I wish you would advise it. Clearly, the thought of selling his slaves is still repellent to Charles, but now a new factor has joined the clash between conscience and commerce: the quest for peace of mind. It sounds as though he would be willing to offload these "worthless" girls at any price just to be rid of them, but he begs his wife to condone the distasteful—and imprudent—act because he doesn't want to shoulder the responsibility alone. It's possible to read this plea as equivocation, or weakness, or an inability to rise above one of slavery's most fundamental cruelties. Whatever the case, Charles is approaching the breaking point.

In April, he breaks. In a letter to Mary, he says, "I write you a hasty line by Billy who takes Catherine home because she is too bad to hire out. I wish you to tell Mr. Luck (the overseer) from me that I want him to take her and give her a good whipping for two things, one for being a rogue as she has shown herself and 2d for failing to behave herself in two places she was hired."

Just as he pleaded with Mary to condone the sale of the young slaves, Charles now delegates the distasteful act of punishing Catherine to unlucky Luck. Or did Luck relish such assignments? There is a sizable literature revealing that many white southerners—overseers, masters, even mistresses—derived pleasure from punishing slaves that bordered on the erotic. Another detail remains unknown: what constituted a "good whipping" at Taylor's Creek? Was it a flogging with the dreaded cat-o'-nine-tails, which left ropy scars? Or was it a whipping with a willow switch, the sort of corporal punishment commonly applied by parents to wayward children at that time? The answer is unknowable, but the fact is that Catherine, at Charles's orders, was whipped.

⸺

As spring blurred into the oppressively hot summer of 1864, the two armies were locked, like scorpions in a bottle, in a bloody rolling struggle to the death. Gen. Ulysses S. Grant was determined to seize Richmond and put an end to the war, and Gen. Robert E. Lee was just as determined to prevent that from happening. The preceding three years, bloody as they were, were a mere warm-up for an entirely new level of slaughter. Lee's hope, still alive from the previous summer, was to hold out until the fall election, when the war-weary northern electorate would surely vote out President Abraham Lincoln and a new president would sue for peace. But first Lee had to deal with Grant, a different breed of northern general, one who pushed his army southward with a merciless whip, unfazed by heavy losses, always advancing. From the Wilderness to Spotsylvania to Cold Harbor, the carnage continued until June, when the Union army crossed the James River and approached fortified Petersburg, the last obstacle standing between it and Richmond. The Army of the Potomac had lost 50,000 men in a month of savage fighting, half as many as it had lost in the three previous years, prompting First Lady Mary Lincoln to call Grant "a butcher" with "no regard for life."

The encroaching butchery had begun to affect Charles's body as well as his mind. "This very hot weather I stay indoors as it makes me very weak and languid," he writes to Mary. "I think I have fallen off a great deal, my clothes hang on me loosely . . . I suppose it must be continued anxiety of my mind that makes me so." He adds: "The rumors of raids and Yankees in every direction keeps us in such a panic that I hardly know what to do."

Mary, meanwhile, is anxious about their year-old son John. She writes to a cousin: "My darling little baby is very poorly, teething with a high fever and his mouth in such a fix he can't nurse." Then Mary reports that an aunt and her family have moved in with her because the Yankees ruined their farm, killing sixty hogs, taking three horses, cutting up the carpets for saddle blankets, stripping the house, knocking down the slave cabins, and stealing potatoes, salt, and peas. Four of the family's slaves ran away with the Yankees, but the rest brought the surviving livestock to Taylor's Creek. The place was beginning to resemble a refugee camp.

By then the siege of Petersburg had settled into a stalemate, a bearable state of affairs for the Confederacy, but the news from elsewhere was bad and about to get worse. Atlanta fell in early September, freeing Gen. William Tecumseh Sherman to march to the sea, then slash his way through the Carolinas to join forces with Grant. Virginia's Shenandoah Valley, the breadbasket of the Confederacy, was finally lost to Union Gen. Philip Sheridan, who set about turning the fertile farmland into scorched earth. Hundreds of Confederate soldiers were deserting every day, further thinning the gray thread around Petersburg.

Charles, meanwhile, offers this assessment of his home county: "Hanover is becoming entirely lawless, robbery and pillage are all the time going on." Concerned about Mary and the boys, and convinced that Richmond was safe—or at least safer than lawless Hanover County—Charles rented the second floor of a three-story apartment house on Grace Street not far from the quartermaster's office and the capitol. As snow and ice blanketed the countryside and fighting ground to a halt, the Morris family welcomed "much company and numbers of visitors," according to one account, and their flat became "the scene of much activity." It was also the scene of much illness. Sylvanus and Jim were revisited by whooping cough during that bitter winter, and John nearly died of pneumonia.

When the spring thaw came, Mary returned to Taylor's Creek with the boys, Grant resumed his efforts to strangle Lee at Petersburg, and Charles began to prepare for the inevitable—and its inevitable aftermath. He used four hundred of his shrinking Confederate dollars to buy an ounce of gold—"because they charge $250 for ½ ounce" and because gold would be the only thing sure to have value after the fall of the Confederacy and the collapse of its currency. He then gives Mary instructions for a top-secret mission: "I suggest to you and Cousin Sara while (Mary's brother) Walter is at home to get him in the most secret manner, without the knowledge of a single negro, to bury all the silver plate and valuables of that kind you have, securing them as well as you can. It may be all that will be left to us to live on and it is very essential it should be done at a quiet time and in a quiet way. If the enemy come a search will be made for such things and if found all will go. It makes me sick to hear how desolate some persons have been left, without food, or money. It is well to provide against contingencies."

While Mary was carrying out this clandestine mission, Charles received a belated promotion to the rank of major by his superior officer, Quarter-master Gen. Alexander Lawton, whom Charles scorned as "a martinet and strict, the usual military style." Though welcome, Charles's promotion could not postpone the inevitable. The news reached Jefferson Davis while he was attending Sunday services at St. Paul's Episcopal Church in Richmond on the morning of April 2. The color drained from Davis's face as he read the note from Lee: "My lines are broken in three places. Richmond must be evacuated this evening."

And so, as Lee's army retreated, Charles boarded the train carrying the Confederate government out of Richmond, headed for Danville. Richmond was already being put to the torch to ensure the Yankees would seize a tarnished prize. First to go were the remnants of the Confederate fleet docked in the James River, then, spectacularly, the nearby arsenals, with shells exploding in the sky and magazines igniting. It looked and sounded like a battle as the flames swallowed hundreds of buildings. The next day the city, like Atlanta months before, was in ruins as President Lincoln walked the streets, cheered by ecstatic Black people. The world's first modern war—the first to use the telegraph, the railroad, the camera, hot-air balloons, rifled gun barrels, repeating rifles, ironclads, mines, and entrenched defenses—was all but over.

Charles made it as far as Charlotte, North Carolina, where he was captured by victorious Yankees, informed of Lee's surrender, and made a prisoner of war. He was returned to Dover Mines in Goochland County, not far from his father-in-law's house, where John had been born two summers earlier. There, on May 13, after swearing "not to take part in hostilities against the Government of the United States," Maj. Charles Morris was paroled by the order of Maj. George W. Hindes of the 96th New York Volunteers and given permission to return to his home in Hanover County.

Charles arrived at Taylor's Creek with a few gold pieces hidden in the band of his hat, his capital for starting a new life in a world remade by war. On his three-hundred-mile journey home, all he saw was devastation and sorrow. It would have been impossible for him to know that the nation was on the brink of the Age of Astonishment.

Slaves in Hanover County, Virginia, during the Civil War.

LET IT BURN

When he came out of the woods and up the steep lane that leads to the front door of Taylor's Creek, Charles Morris was burning with two questions: How will my family survive? And what will become of the former slaves still living on my land?

The answer to the first question came with surprising ease. Hackett and Luck had overseen the spring planting, and the farm, unlike so many across the South, had been untouched by the war. The place was well stocked with implements, sheep, hogs, cattle, and work animals, and the crops would flourish that summer. Considering what he'd witnessed on his long journey home, Charles must have felt that he and his family had been blessed with incredible luck.

The answer to the second question proved thornier. Charles had dreamed of setting up a law practice in Richmond after the war, but the city's physical and economic ruin, coupled with the day-to-day challenges of reviving the farm operation, ruled out that option. By the time Charles returned home, some of the family's slaves had surely melted away, most likely drawn to Richmond, a magnet for Black people giddy with newfound freedom and eager to find well-paid jobs far from the scenes of their bondage. They were almost always disappointed. The Black population of the South's ten largest cities doubled in the five years after the war, and instead of finding good jobs, these new arrivals found glutted labor markets that shunted them into grunt work and filthy, crowded shantytowns. Occupying federal troops took to rounding up "vagrants" in these proto-ghettos and delivering them to plantation owners to work the fields.

The freed slaves who decided to stay on at Taylor's Creek appeared to fare better. While many southerners treated their former slaves harshly, Charles, as recounted by his son Sylvanus, took a relatively benign approach: "He called up his negroes and told them they were free, offered to let them parcels of land on long, easy leases, helped them get farming implements, and for some of them went security on the purchase of work animals." In addition to tending their leased plots, freedmen could work Charles's land under contract.

These actions did not go unnoticed. There is compelling evidence that Hanover County freedmen pushed for Charles to serve on the three-man Freedmen's Court, which was charged with adjudicating civil and criminal cases between Black and White citizens as well as between freedmen. Many of the disputes were over nonpayment of wages, since contracts with illiterate freedmen were usually oral and therefore easy to ignore. This judicial system was far from perfect, but for the first time, a Black man in Hanover County could have his day in court.

Even more striking than his largess and his pursuit of justice for freedmen was Charles's contribution to one of the central transformations of postwar Black life. Early in 1869 he donated an acre of land about a mile from the farmhouse to a former slave named Stephen Anderson, leader of a congregation of Black Baptists who set about erecting a crude weatherboard church on the property. No longer willing to sit in the back pews or the balconies of White churches listening to White preachers, freedmen yearned to establish churches of their own, an impulse that led to a revolution within the larger drama of Reconstruction. On the eve of the war, more than 40,000 Blacks worshiped in biracial Methodist churches in South Carolina. By the 1870s, all but 600 had left for Black churches.

During Reconstruction and beyond, Black churches like Montpelier's Bethany Baptist, which is still in operation today, would become much more than houses of worship. They were the glue of an emerging Black social order, offering political gatherings, picnics, forums for resolving disputes, and schools to augment those set up under the Freedmen's Bureau. More than 90 percent of the South's Black populace had been illiterate at the outbreak of the Civil War, and now young and old flocked to the nearest schools, hungry to learn, convinced that the ability to read and write and tot up figures, along with the right to vote, were the surest tools for digging their way out of centuries of poverty and invisibility.

It was natural that the men at the center of these self-contained universes—Black preachers like Stephen Anderson—would become the first foot soldiers in the Black political struggle, performing tasks that ranged from registering voters to running for elective office. In 1870, Hiram Rhodes Revels of Mississippi, a teacher and ordained minister in the African Methodist Episcopal Church, became the first Black man to serve in the US Senate. More than one hundred Black ministers would win legislative seats by the end of Reconstruction, and it's possible to draw a line from Bethany Baptist Church to Dexter Avenue Baptist Church and the emergence of Martin Luther King Jr. and other Black preachers a century later as the vanguard of the civil rights movement.

Charles's treatment of his former slaves and his gift of land to Bethany Baptist are not to suggest that kumbaya racial harmony was universal at Taylor's Creek. History and the nature of American slavery made that impossible. There were signs of festering resentment even among the former slaves who decided to stay on after the war. It began with thwarting Charles's clandestine plot to hide the family's precious silverware. As instructed, Mary had put all the silver in a chest and all the jewelry in a tin box, which she and her brother Walter took into the woods and buried. When Charles went to dig up this treasure after the war, he discovered that the chest was gone and someone had rifled through the tin box. The only things the thieves left behind were a sugar bowl and a soup ladle. Mary began to put two and two together. She remembered that when she and her brother were carrying the treasure into the woods, they'd passed a Black boy named Wilson, the son of slaves, who appeared to be minding cows but was, Mary realized in retrospect, paying close attention to what he was witnessing. Wilson had been a sickly baby, and Mary had ordered him brought to the house every morning to be fed. As soon as the war ended, Wilson's family was the first to leave, and it was reported later that they were living in Richmond and were known to have "a lot of pretty things." Mary's indignation over the betrayal must have been bitter and deep.

Now she embarked on a more treacherous mission. The family had moved to Williamsburg before the war when Charles was hired to teach law at William & Mary, and they had carried furniture with them, including heirlooms that had been in the family for generations. Shortly after the war, Mary went to Williamsburg with Charles's brother Sylvanus to fetch the furniture, but they were told that a former slave named Martha Morris had taken the furniture to a boarding house she was running in Norfolk. Now Mary was on fire. She and Sylvanus continued on to Norfolk and confronted Martha, a brazen thing to do in a city that had been under Yankee control for years and was now disinclined to welcome a former slave owner come to reclaim property from a former slave. But in the face of Mary's fury, Martha relinquished the furniture, and Mary had it shipped back to Taylor's Creek, where it's still in use today. Yes, the woman had starch in her.

There were other signs of ill will among the family's former slaves. Charles had built a kitchen on the back of the house, and one night, under suspicious circumstances, fire broke out there. The kitchen was gutted and the paint on the back of the house was scorched, but a lack of wind kept the fire from spreading. Charles had an inordinate fear of fire, and a suspicious one like this would have been enough to make anyone uneasy.

—◈—

As that fall's crops were being harvested, Charles hit on a new moneymaking scheme. He converted the dining room into a classroom and began teaching a few dozen sons of his neighbors and relatives, including teenagers who had fought in the war. Virginia did not yet have public schools, and children were educated, if they were educated at all, at such impromptu private academies. Though tuition and board were low and some of it was never paid, the school was a success for three years, and Charles later claimed he made more clear profit from it than he ever made before or since. John, now walking and talking, might have wandered into that makeshift schoolroom from time to time and become intoxicated by the sight of his father scribbling equations on a chalkboard, lecturing rows of attentive boys, drilling them on Latin and Greek verbs. The power of the man at the front of that snug little room was absolute, and to an impressionable, bookish boy it would have been absolutely seductive.

—◈—

Mary gave birth to a fourth son, Charles Ed, in the fall of 1866. On John's fifth birthday two summers later, June 23, 1868, a Wisconsin tinkerer patented an invention that would become central to John's life. The man was named Christopher Latham Sholes, and he called his rudimentary creation the typewriter.

It was an inelegant wooden box that resembled a miniature piano, right down to its two rows of keys made of ebony and ivory. The machine's numerals and letters, all capitals, were arranged this way:

$$3\ 5\ 7\ 9\ N\ O\ P\ Q\ R\ S\ T\ U\ V\ W\ X\ Y\ Z$$
$$2\ 4\ 6\ 8\ .\ A\ B\ C\ D\ E\ F\ G\ H\ I\ J\ K\ L\ M$$

I and O served as 1 and 0. Though crude, the basic principles were in place, including keys that struck an inked tape of tissue paper against a sheet of paper fastened to a cylindrical platen and a ratchet that moved the carriage by the width of a tooth every time a key was struck.

With his colleagues, Carlos Glidden and Samuel Soulé, Sholes worked feverishly to refine the machine. A thousand miles away, first in Boston and then in New York, a telegrapher named Thomas Alva Edison was working even more feverishly to produce his own earliest innovations, including a stock ticker, a fire alarm, a facsimile telegraph printer, and, the winner of his first patent, 1868's electrochemical vote recorder.

In an effort to satisfy the speed demands of telegraph operators, the trio of Wisconsin inventors eventually developed the QWERTY keyboard arrangement still in use on typewriters, laptops, and smart phones, with keys for both upper- and lower-case letters as well as assorted symbols. In 1874, they produced their first marketable machine, which was manufactured by the Remington Arms Company and priced at $125, a small fortune at the time. The typewriter was, in the words of the Smithsonian Museum, "one of the most complicated pieces of mechanical machinery ever to enter mass production and widespread use." Mark Twain was an early adopter.

His 1883 memoir, *Life on the Mississippi*, is believed to be the first book delivered to a publisher as a typescript rather than a manuscript—though his secretary did the typing, giving birth to the stubborn stigma that typing was "woman's work." By 1890, 100,000 Remington typewriters were in use, more commonly in offices and banks than in writers' garrets.

The typewriter, along with Edison's early inventions and the thousands of others that would soon pour out of laboratories and workshops around the world, had the cumulative effect of shrinking distances and speeding up life. The typewriter would become a vital tool in John Morris's working life and in the working lives of the next two generations of his family, up to and beyond the advent of the personal computer. I'm writing these words on a Royal manual typewriter built in 1940, toward the end of John's long, word-drenched life. The machine works as well today as it did the day it came off the assembly line in Hartford, Connecticut, eighty years ago. It's my lone cherished relic from the Age of Astonishment.

Charles Morris had been two weeks shy of his thirty-fifth birthday when the Civil War broke out, a college graduate and law professor with no military training—hardly the stuff of an officer or a foot soldier. But there were other factors besides age and lack of training that led to his assignment to the quartermaster's corps, far from the shooting and with frequent weekend furloughs. "That right there," my father said only half-jokingly, "showed him to be a man of superior intelligence." But smarts was not the whole story. Charles had volunteered for military service and, with the original one-year enlistments due to expire in the spring of 1862, the Confederate Congress, fearful of a looming troop shortage, passed the first conscription act in American history, a year ahead of President Abraham Lincoln's. The Confederate Congress's fear was understandable. After a year of brutal, inconclusive fighting, the giddy post-Sumter euphoria was long gone. Few volunteers were inclined to reenlist. The draft law required three years of military service by all White males between the ages of eighteen and thirty-five. The law was modified in the fall, granting an exemption to one White male per plantation with twenty or more slaves, the so-called Twenty-Slave Law, which was designed to secure the food supply and control the slave populace but sparked bitter grumbling among small farmers and foot soldiers that this had become a rich man's war and a poor man's fight. Though Charles, now thirty-six and the owner of more than twenty slaves, was free to leave the army and go home, he stayed at his post in Richmond. The only explanation was that he felt a sense of duty to a cause he believed in. Yet the fact remains that an office job with frequent weekend furloughs was, indeed, a light wartime assignment. What was behind it? Quite simply, his family's station in society. In a word: Class.

Class—the unspeakable taboo of America's fantasy life, the dogged driver of its factual life from the very beginning right down to today—had steered the family's fate long before the war. In a sense, class had always been in play, ever since William Morris arrived in Hanover County in the early eighteenth century and the family began acquiring slaves and amassing thousands of acres of land. Little is known about William Morris's life in Europe, but he is believed to have sailed from Glamorgan County in southern Wales, probably from Swansea or Cardiff. It's safe to assume that anyone who undertook the treacherous North Atlantic crossing to a volatile and violent New World was in less than solid circumstances, possibly in serious legal trouble or debt, at the very least hungry for a fresh start and willing to roll the dice. The gentleman, the prosperous merchant, the member of the landed gentry—he almost never traded the comfort and familiarity of the Old World for the harshness and uncertainty of the New.

Though William Morris and his immediate descendants were quick to prosper, there was nothing refined about them or the country they worked so vigorously to tame. Hanover County was a frontier, and these were raw, striving, barely literate men. In a memoir composed in the mid–nineteenth century, a cousin named John Blair Dabney wrote that William was "endowed with a full share of the resolute will and impatience of dictation which still remains a distinctive trait in the character of his descendants." William was "imperfectly educated," Dabney adds, but "versed in the transaction of business." The business was farming, particularly the culti-vation of tobacco, which was carted to one of the nearby landings on the Pamunkey River and loaded onto boats that carried it down to the York River and the harbor at Hampton Roads and then across the Atlantic to London, where it fetched a handsome price. Sot weed, as it was known, made William Morris and many of his descendants nearly rich, but it did not bring instantaneous refinement.

"Never have I known a family, whose lineaments either good, or bad, are stamped on more indelible characters," Dabney writes of his Morris cousins. William's only son, Sylvanus, is described as "a man of tempestuous and vindictive passions" with "an impulsive and ungovernable temperament." The following generations produced men who were "unduly disputatious and unyielding" or "prone to suspicion, distrustful of the professions, and a harsh judge of the motives of men." Some were gripped by "an inordinate love of money." One had a "blunt and almost rude manner." Another "a lofty self-reliance bordering on churlishness." Their nicknames revealed their rusticity: Creek Billy and Billy Beeswax.

They may have had rough edges, but the Morris men knew how to make money. They kept precise ledgers, down to the penny, of a lively commerce that included the buying and selling of hogsheads of tobacco, barrels of flour, bushels of wheat and corn, kegs of horseshoes, gallons of whisky, sides of beef. Their business dealings were marked by disputes—over the precise acreage of a plat of land, over the quality of a shipment of "old" bacon, over how much a worker was owed, and when. There were detailed notations on the costs of "drayage" and "cooperage" and "canal tolls." Bills of sale reveal that slaves changed hands for $500 to $750 apiece, and they were rented out for $14 a month. Rewards were paid to the captors of runaways. Over time, William's descendants settled in neighboring Louisa County and even bought land as far west as Kentucky. They built handsome homes called Grassdale, Hawkwood, Sylvania, and Green Springs, far grander than Taylor's Creek, emblems of expanding prosperity and prestige. Their correspondents included Hanover County natives Henry Clay and Patrick Henry, and they were never shy about letting their feelings, however unpleasant, be known. As Dabney put it: "It was a distinguishing trait in the whole Morris family, at least in its elder branch, that they abhorred all disguise & dissimulation—that they wore no mask over their opinions, & were too frank & open, too indifferent to the censure of the world, to conceal their feelings. . . . They had no spice of that politic hypocrisy, which consults appearances in every action, & by servile subserviency to public opinion in externals, contrives to hide its infirmities, & to win an undeserved popularity in the world."

These words, written more than a decade before John Morris's birth, predicted his character with uncanny precision and led me to twinned realizations: blood is destiny; and the key to John's character was that he, even more starkly than his forebears, was indifferent to censure and had no interest in winning the world's approval. I would come to see this defining trait as a virtue and a vice, John's blessing and his curse.

From the very beginning, the family's bad lineaments were on vivid, sometimes lurid, display. After William Morris's wife died, he took the scandalous step of marrying an indentured servant many years his junior, opening a bitter rift with his son, who, according to Dabney, became "highly incensed at this degradation of the family dignity." The marriage produced five daughters and it was, Dabney added, "at all times indiscreet, from the disparity of years and condition, but particularly objectionable at that period when the distinction of classes was much more clearly defined, & vigorously enforced than in our present state of society."

Why did William do it? Because, quite simply, he was indifferent to censure—from both his class and his family. So bitter was the rift between father and son that William disinherited Sylvanus and willed his thousands of acres and his forty slaves to his daughters and their children. The names of those slaves make for a haunting litany: Sillah, Fellishie, Canterberry, Sibba, Obie, Hamick, Jocko, and Tom. After parceling them out to everyone but his son, William drives home the snub: "I give and bequeath to my son Sylvanus Morris one brindle cow and calf at my home plantation, and two steers at Duckinghole plantation."

This detail in William Morris's will was a revelation to me. Since boyhood I have regarded slavery as an abomination, and the American strain as particularly virulent. Slaves in antebellum America had little hope of tasting freedom, and their bondage was passed on to all successive generations. The horrors of slavery have been well documented, but William Morris opened my eyes to one of its subtler evils. Slaves were personal property, yes, but until I read William's will I had failed to appreciate that chattel could be put to *any* use their owner desired. They could even be turned into the flesh-and-blood coinage of reward and punishment. To me—to *naïve* me?—this was a new level of dehumanization.

Ralph Ellison said we don't choose our relatives but we do choose our ancestors. Until I read William Morris's will, I had not fully understood why I was drawn to John Morris but not to his forebears. It's not only because John lived in remarkable times; it's also at least partly because John was born at the moment when slavery was abolished, and thus he was a member of the first generation of the family free of its moral stain. We don't choose the circumstances of our birth any more than we choose our relatives, but eventually we do choose what to believe about those circumstances. John would grow up to see slavery as evil, and he would refuse to join the White South's campaigns to romanticize the Lost Cause or subjugate and ostracize freed Negroes. He then went a step further to acknowledge something I also acknowledge: that being born into America's White middle class bestows privileges unknown to Sillah and Obie and Jocko and Tom—or to their descendants, including those alive today. And, going even further, John and I acknowledge that this privilege carries responsibility, which is very different from guilt. Like Edward Ball, another descendant of slave owners, who is quoted in this book's epigraph, John and I never felt guilt over the crimes of our ancestors. No one can be culpable for acts of people long dead. But, like Ball, I do feel accountable—responsible to try to understand the past, and explain it. That responsibility begets another: I cannot allow myself to ignore or forget the fact that the circumstances of my birth have given me privileges many people will never know.

So in taking up with a servant girl many years his junior, William Morris not only alienated his son and produced a will that opened my eyes; he also flouted eighteenth-century Virginia's clearly defined and rigorously enforced class distinctions. During the Revolutionary War, a British officer named Thomas Anbury traveled extensively through Virginia, which was still largely frontier, the roads often little more than rutted, haphazard tracks through fields and blue forests. While staying in Goochland County with cousins of Thomas Jefferson, not far from John Morris's birthplace, Anbury produced this sketch of Virginia's class hierarchy:

> There were, and still are, three degrees of ranks among the inhabitants, exclusive of negroes. . . . The first class consists of gentlemen of the best families and fortunes (who) for the most part have had liberal educations . . . The second class consists of such a strange mixture. . . . They are, however, hospitable, generous and friendly; but for want of a proper knowledge of the world, and a good education, as well as from their continual intercourse with their slaves, over whom they are accustomed to tyrannize, with all their good qualities they are rude, ferocious, and haughty, much attached to gaming and dissipation, particularly horse-racing and cock-fighting.
>
> The third class . . . are averse to labor, much addicted to liquor, and when intoxicated, extremely savage and revengeful.

For all their unruly passions and occasional flouting of these rigid class distinctions, the Morrises assumed a respectable station in colonial and post-Revolutionary society. They were members of a nascent rural gentry—Anbury's "first class"—that was self-contained and self-perpetuating, rarely touched by the wider world. Most of them were respectable and a few of them were interesting, as a cousin of mine noted, but none were important. The Morris who came closest to breaking out of this insular cocoon was Charles's father, known in the family as "Great Richard," an orator in league with Patrick Henry who attended Washington College (now Washington & Lee University), practiced law with considerable success, was a rapt spectator at Aaron Burr's trial for treason in Richmond, then ran for Congress in 1814 as a Federalist and staunch opponent of "Mr. Madison's War" of 1812. Richard lost the election but served on the commission that rewrote the state constitution in 1829, and he was elected to several terms as Hanover County's representative in the Virginia House of Delegates. A portrait of him now hanging at Taylor's Creek reveals a delicate, almost foppish man with side whiskers, forward-swept curls, and a hawkish nose. An imperious smile is beginning to dance on his shiny pink lips. It would surprise me if this grandee ever spent a day working with his hands.

With Great Richard, the Morrises began to look beyond the cloistered world of the Virginia gentleman farmer. They pursued higher education that would afford them entry to the more esteemed professions, as lawyers, doctors, academics, writers, businessmen, and journalists. W. J. Cash, one of the most astute students of the southern mind, noted that the Morris family's striving was part of a regional trend. A southerner like Great Richard, Cash wrote, "sent his sons to William & Mary and afterward to the English universities or the law schools of London. These sons brought home . . . more developed and subtle notions of class." Richard and his descendants didn't follow this blueprint precisely, but close enough. Richard's youngest son, Charles, got his bachelor's and law degrees from the University of Virginia, then toured Europe and taught law at William & Mary. Charles's father-in-law, Dr. John Morris, studied medicine in Edinburgh. Charles's son John, my grandfather, studied in Berlin, Freiburg, and Copenhagen. His son Charles spent a postgraduate year at Oxford, birthplace of his son, yet another John (Nelson) Morris, who grew up to be a professor and an acclaimed poet. Once Great Richard set the ball rolling, it refused to stop.

The first years of Reconstruction brought whiplash change to the nation, to the South, and to the Morris family. The war and the Thirteenth Amendment of 1865 had forever freed the slaves, but monumental questions still loomed. Would freedmen be granted the right to vote? Would former Confederates be barred from voting or holding elective office? And under what conditions would southern states be readmitted to the Union?

The answers were quick to arrive. The establishment of the Freedmen's Bureau in 1865 and the passage of the Civil Rights Act a year later initiated a flurry of new laws. In addition to reuniting Black families, the Freedmen's Bureau worked with northern societies committed to educating former slaves and giving them the tools to participate in a democracy. By 1869, some 3,000 schools with 150,000 pupils were reporting to the bureau—and those figures don't include the ubiquitous evening schools operated by churches, missionary societies, and literate Black individuals. One such school was established at Bethany Baptist Church. The Civil Rights Act codified the freedoms guaranteed by the Emancipation Proclamation and the Thirteenth Amendment, defining a citizen as any person born in the United States (except Indigenous people) and spelling out the rights they were to enjoy without regard to race, including the rights to make contracts and bring lawsuits. It prohibited states from denying any citizen equal protection under the law.

The Reconstruction Act of 1867 divided the South into five military districts, with Union Gen. John Schofield in charge of Virginia, the First

Military District. In 1868, while a new state constitution was being hammered out in Richmond, Schofield appointed a Michigan lawyer and former Union officer named Henry Horatio Wells as provisional governor. Wells advocated full civil and voting rights for freedmen, free public schools for all children, and the shifting of tax burdens from poor Virginians to wealthier landowners. His northern origins and Radical Republican views branded him a carpetbagger of the worst kind in the eyes of the Morris family and many of their White neighbors.

That year also brought the election of Ulysses S. Grant as president and passage of the Fourteenth Amendment, which the historian Eric Foner has called "the most important ever added to the Constitution." The first of its five clauses prohibited states from abridging equality before the law of any person born or naturalized in the United States. The second clause stopped short of bestowing universal suffrage and instead offered southern states a choice: enfranchise freedmen or forfeit seats in Congress. The third clause did not deny former Confederates the vote, but it barred from state and local office men who had sworn allegiance to the US Constitution and then aided the Confederacy. Though he had no political ambitions, Charles Morris was surely stung by this last rebuke.

As important as it was, the Fourteenth Amendment was "a fatal and total surrender" in the eyes of many Radical Republicans because it kept alive the right of states to limit voting based on race. It was also a bitter disappointment to Susan B. Anthony and her fellow advocates of women's suffrage because it injected the word "male" into the Constitution and failed to give women the vote. For that they would have to wait another half-century.

Amid this political upheaval, Charles came to a sobering realization: land could no longer be equated with wealth in the South because landowners no longer controlled the labor market. He was learning firsthand what it meant to be land rich and cash poor. Great Richard's turn away from farming and toward the law and politics may have been a luxury made possible by wealth and privilege, but for Charles and succeeding generations, such a turn was no luxury. It was their response to that most fundamental Darwinian mandate: adapt or die. And so when his old friend William LeRoy Broun alerted him to a vacant professorship in English and Belles Lettres at the University of Georgia, Charles eagerly applied. He got the job, and in January of 1869, after shuttering his school, he left alone on the three-day journey to Athens, a charming, drowsy college town perched on a hill sixty miles northeast of Atlanta. It was a momentous start to a momentous year.

"That year," Charles's eldest son Sylvanus would recall later, "Virginia made a successful effort to free herself from carpetbag, scalawag, and Negro rule." That effort was centered on one of the first major tests of Reconstruction. With a new state constitution ratified, it was time for all male Virginians—Black and White—to elect a governor. On a ticket with a Black physician named Joseph Harris as candidate for lieutenant governor, Wells ran against Gilbert Walker, who had the support of moderate Republicans and conservatives—and the Morris family. "The situation was explained to the Negroes at Taylor's Creek," Sylvanus wrote, "and all said: 'We is gwine do like Marster said.'" Slavery may have been dead, but the old honorifics of "Marster" and "Mistiss" lived on; Charles and Mary were about to learn that their control over their former slaves did not.

When the votes were tallied, Walker had soundly defeated Wells. "The evening of election day," Sylvanus continued, "Mother went down to the (Negro) quarters and asked how they had voted. Old Washington said they had all voted for Wells." What he surely meant was that they had all voted for Wells's Black running mate. Mary flew into a rage. "Mother then said: *Every one of you move off this place at once!*' When she returned to the house and told my grandmother, who was there, what she had done, the latter said: 'I wonder you were not afraid.' This was the first moment the thought of fear had entered Mother's mind."

If this is a fact, it's an astounding one. From the very beginning, from the day in 1619 when some two dozen enslaved Africans shuffled off a ship at Point Comfort, Virginia, fear was woven deeply into the fabric of American slavery. Slaves feared the lash and the shackle, torture, mutilation, family separation, and death, while Whites feared acts of insurrection, from "absconding" to arson fires to poisoned food, on up to terror of a full-blown slave revolt. Nearly half of the residents of Virginia were Black, and Taylor's Creek is a hundred miles from Southampton County, where in 1831 a slave named Nat Turner led an uprising in which fifty White people were killed before two hundred of the rebels were captured, beaten, and executed. The escaped slave and abolitionist Frederick Douglass applauded the sowing of fear in the slave owner. "We must make him feel that there is death in the air about him," Douglass wrote, "that there is death in the pot before him, that there is death all around him." Charles and Mary Morris surely grew up hearing stories about Nat Turner and the ship *Creole*, which was transporting more than one hundred slaves from Richmond to New Orleans when the slaves, according to widespread newspaper accounts, attacked one of the owners with clubs, spikes, and knives, stabbing him to death.

It took starch for Mary to order the former slaves to move off her property at once, but if it's true that this was the first time fear had entered her mind, she was either immensely brave or immensely obtuse. Maybe both. Whatever the case, her impetuous act worsened the already-dire labor shortage. She wrote at once to Charles, who got leave from the university and hurried home two weeks ahead of schedule. The day after he arrived, a steamy July afternoon when no one would have started a fire in any of the house's six fireplaces, flames in an upstairs room sent smoke gushing from a dormer window. In years past, such a calamity would have brought slaves running to help extinguish the flames, but on this day not one of the remaining freedmen emerged from their quarters. *We must make him feel that there is death in the air about him.* The message of this and the earlier kitchen fire was chillingly clear: Let it burn.

Promontory Summit, Utah, May 10, 1869.

"DONE!"

Two months before these events, on May 10, 1869, two locomotives were parked nose-to-nose on a stark stretch of Utah desert called Promontory Summit. Facing east was the Jupiter of the Central Pacific Railroad; a few yards away, facing west, was No. 119 of the Union Pacific. Standing on the tracks between them, with a silver maul in his soft hands, was a portly bearded robber baron named Leland Stanford, a former Sacramento shopkeeper and former governor of California who had used lavish federal subsidies to buy the land and lay the track from Sacramento to this historic spot. He was surrounded by a boisterous throng of politicians, dignitaries, businessmen, reporters, and photographers, plus a few of the Union Pacific's Irish laborers. Someone held a bottle of champagne aloft, the crowning touch on the nation's first orchestrated media event. As cameras clicked, Stanford raised the maul and dropped it on a ceremonial golden spike, sinking it into a pre-drilled hole in a laurel tie. The spike was wired to a telegraph line that sent a simple message jittering across the land and, via the undersea telegraphic cable, all the way to the United Kingdom: "DONE!" The transcontinental railroad was complete. It was now possible for people and goods to travel from the Atlantic to the Pacific on a patchwork of rails that had only one gap. The Missouri River would not be spanned for another three years, so passengers and cargo had to be ferried between Omaha, Nebraska, and Council Bluffs, Iowa.

This trifle failed to dampen the coast-to-coast rejoicing. Newspaper publisher and future presidential candidate Horace Greeley called the transcontinental railroad "the grandest and noblest enterprise of our age." A hundred guns were fired in New York's City Hall Park while, a few blocks down Broadway, bells pealed at Trinity Church. People poured into the streets of Philadelphia to the gonging of bells at Independence Hall, ebullience not seen since Lee's surrender at Appomattox. A seven-mile-long line of celebrants snaked through the streets of Chicago, and cannons boomed in San Francisco. The nation was, according to the New York *Sun*, "ablaze with unfeigned enthusiasm."

Lost in the euphoria were some inconvenient truths which would shape both the national narrative and the character of John Morris in the coming decades. The first of these truths is revealed by the photograph of that historic day at Promontory Summit—or, more precisely, by what is missing from that photograph. In keeping with the jingoistic spirit of the pre-packaged event, there are no foreigners in the picture, even though Stanford and his partners—known alternately as the Big Four and the Associates—employed more than 10,000 Chinese laborers to do the brutal, deadly work of blasting a path and laying track from Sacramento through the Sierra Nevada mountains to Utah. And they paid these "coolies" half of what they paid White workers. Also missing from the record of that day are these remarks Stanford had made at his inauguration as governor of California in 1862: "To my mind it is clear, that the settlement among us of an inferior race is to be discouraged by every legitimate means. Asia, with her numberless millions, sends to our shores the dregs of her population . . . It will afford me great pleasure to concur with the Legislature in any constitutional action, having for its object the repression of the immigration of the Asiatic races."

Stanford's dream would come true in 1882 with the passage of the Chinese Exclusion Act, which suspended Chinese immigration for ten years and made Chinese immigrants already in the country ineligible for naturalization. It was the first of many laws to restrict immigration, but it fit a pattern already established in California and much of the rest of the nation. Stanford had been swept west with the gold rush, but when the Opium Wars and famine led tens of thousands of Chinese to cross the Pacific and flood the California gold fields, violence flared between White miners and the Chinese newcomers. In response, the state in 1852 passed the Foreign Miners Tax—$3 a month on noncitizens—and two years later the US Supreme Court ruled that Chinese Americans, like African Americans and Native Americans, were forbidden from testifying in court, leaving them defenseless against mob violence.

But the disconnect between Stanford's rhetoric and his actions was just the beginning of the inconvenient truths about the first transcontinental railroad. It was not a grand and noble enterprise, as Horace Greeley claimed. It was an idea whose time had not yet come, and it was destined to be a business, political, and social failure, with consequences that would multiply as John Morris came of age. "Why were so many of these railroads built at a time when there was so little need of them?" asks the historian Richard White. "Their costs over the long term, and the short term, exceeded their benefits." He adds: "They lured settlers into places where they produced crops, cattle and minerals beyond what markets could profitably absorb and where their production yielded great environmental and social harm."

If they weren't built for sound economic reasons, why were the transcontinental railroads built? And more to the point, *how* were they built? The answer to the first question springs from the engine that drove White America's relentless push westward: hubris: the arrogance that compels one to take something because it's there and because one has the desire and the ability to take it, a desire so powerful that it must be made to seem ordained and therefore it must be given a name. That name was Manifest Destiny.

And how were these railroads built? The conventional answer is that they were a product of those most mythic of American virtues—rugged individualism, inventiveness, determination, fearlessness, and hard work. The writer Joan Didion, born and raised in Leland Stanford's adopted hometown of Sacramento, is a direct descendant of people who made the treacherous crossing before the railroad went through, a journey typically beset by mountain fever, cholera, hostile natives, murderous weather, and starvation that led, on occasion, to cannibalism. Didion offers this pungent synopsis of "the code of the West" that, according to her early education, guided her forebears during the crossing: "show spirit, kill the rattlesnake, keep moving." Didion's 2003 memoir, *Where I Was From*, is a clear-eyed reappraisal of this and other myths she was fed as a child. "A good deal about California does not, on its own preferred terms, add up," she writes. It is a state, and a state of mind, "where distrust of centralized governmental authority has historically passed for an ethic." Which brings Didion to the railroad. It was a quartet of Sacramento shopkeepers who built the railroad that linked California with the world markets and opened the state to extensive settlement, she notes, "but it was the citizens of the rest of the country who paid for it, through a federal cash subsidy (sixteen thousand dollars a mile in the valley and forty-eight thousand dollars a mile in the 'mountains,' which were contractually defined as beginning six miles east of Sacramento) plus a federal land grant, ten or twenty checker-boarded square-mile sections, for each mile of track laid."

In fact, the Sierra Nevada mountains begin their rise some *thirty* miles east of Sacramento, a bit of contractual chicanery that added about $750,000 of taxpayers' money to the Big Four's bottom line. And the laying of track wasn't even the greatest source of profits for the men who owned the Central Pacific and, later, the Southern Pacific. Their true wealth came from the acquisition of land and subsidies on the taxpayers' dime. All of which begins to explain how the expression "robber barons" came into the American vernacular.

Echoing White's contention that the transcontinental railroad made no economic sense, Didion continues: "Nor did the role of the government stop with the construction of the railroad: the citizens of the rest of the country would also, in time, subsidize the crops the railroad carried, make possible the irrigation of millions of acres of essentially arid land, underwrite the rhythms of planting and not planting, and create, finally, a vast agricultural mechanism in a kind of market vacuum, quite remote from the normal necessity of measuring supply against demand and cost against return." Among the crops the government, in its wisdom, subsidized with tax dollars in this water-starved state were water-guzzling alfalfa, cotton, and rice. Nor did the role of the government stop there. It went on to subsidize California's military installations and defense contractors, its aerospace industry, and the construction of a vast network of dams, irrigation systems, and aqueducts—"the massive rearrangement of the water," in Didion's phrase. In addition to benefiting "big ag," this rearrangement benefited corporate and real estate interests and made possible such unsustainable California totems as Los Angeles's emerald lawns, swimming pools, and chronic water shortages. If Leland Stanford's railroad was the beginning of misguided governmental profligacy, Ronald Reagan's cockamamie "Star Wars" defense system was its logical, possibly inevitable, conclusion.

Didion concludes: "(T)he idea of depending on the government of course ran counter to the preferred self-image of most Californians." Of course it did. And of course it would be possible to substitute *Americans* for *Californians* in that sentence without sacrificing its hard kernel of truth.

That truth exposed the lie that John Morris would spend his life trying to ignore, resist, and outwit. It was the fantasy that America was a land full of self-made visionaries chasing limitless opportunity, and all a man—a White man—had to do was roll up his sleeves and go get his share. In reality, the fix was in from the beginning of the post–Civil War era, which is to say from the beginning of the Age of Astonishment. And it was the Leland Stanfords who grasped this fact and took advantage of it copiously, shamelessly, and repeatedly. If rolling up the sleeves meant knowing how to pay bribes and bestow favors in the halls of Congress and various state capitols, it also entailed signing on, playing ball, joining some hierarchy—a club, a lobbying organization, a political party, a corporation, even a monopoly. It required conformity, and it produced a loose national class of true believers, a club stocked with joiners, go-getters, and back-slappers. It was a club John Morris would steadfastly refuse to join.

As that momentous year—and decade—came to an end, it was apparent that Virginia's effort to rid herself of carpetbag, scalawag, and Black rule was not the complete success Sylvanus Morris had claimed. Not yet, anyway. Gov. Gilbert Walker may have been more moderate than Henry Horatio Wells and therefore more palatable to Charles and Mary, but he was from Pennsylvania, which branded him a card-carrying carpetbagger. Scalawags, those southerners who had resisted secession, assumed positions of political power. And twenty-seven of the 180 new members of the Virginia General Assembly were Black. "Negro rule" would peak in 1881, when Black "Readjusters" swept control of both houses of the General

Assembly. In 1888, John Mercer Langston became Virginia's first Black Congressman—and, as it turned out, the last for more than a century. Sylvanus's claim may have been premature, but eventually it would come to pass. Though no one knew it at the end of the 1860s, Reconstruction had reached the middle of its tumultuous life, and it was already dying.

University of Georgia in the late 18th century.

THE ONSET OF RUIN

The family traveled south for three days and two nights. Imagine such a journey at such a time. They were leaving the Upland South, heading down through the Carolinas, destined for the doorway to the Deep South: Georgia. For four young boys who had never traveled farther than Richmond, this must have been thrilling at first, but with each passing mile the air got hotter and the world grew shabbier. The South's railroads had been ravaged during the war, both by advancing Yankees and retreating Confederates, and while most of the tracks had been repaired, they were a patchwork of intrastate lines, which meant hours of sitting in dusty depots during transfers within states and at state borders. The condition of the tracks did not allow trains to reach full speed, and it's not hard to imagine the August heat pouring through the cars' windows, the sullen conductors, the flies and mosquitoes, the cushioned seats only slightly better than wooden ones because of their frayed and grimy upholstery. Everything was dirty and the food was always bad.

It's possible, even probable, that the family had companions on this trip. Faced with the prospect of setting up house in a strange town, Mary would have wanted a woman who could double as maid and cook, and Charles would have wanted a man to serve as gardener, waiter, and overseer of the household. Mary might have offered the job to Tina, the former slave who had carried infant John through the woods to safety the night of the Yankee raid, and Charles almost surely would have turned to Uncle Jeems, who had gotten waylaid by Yankees on his way to Richmond during the war and had served for years as waiter and butler, a "house Negro." Sylvanus would later say of him: "No more elegant and aristocratic attendant ever lived." Uncle Jeems once uttered a line that has come to serve as a caricature. One day before the war, cousins from two fine old Virginia families, the Nelsons and the Pages, had come calling at Taylor's Creek. As they approached the front door, Uncle Jeems had whispered to Mary, "Now, Mistiss, these are our quality."

It would have been natural for Tina and Uncle Jeems to travel with the family. Though Reconstruction had begun erecting new barriers between the races, the Morris children, like most southerners, had grown up in inti-mate contact with Black people, who were always nearby in the house and in the fields, cooking, washing, harvesting, shoeing horses, going to church, sometimes playing, sometimes serving as wet nurses. Slavery, for all its hor-rors, had produced the opposite of segregation: a physical closeness that bred a complex and visceral web of emotions between the races, ranging from bitter loathing to genuine affection, from deep hostility to undying loyalty. While proximity must not be correlated with equality, the freeing of the slaves seems to have intensified these emotions rather than erasing them. Tina and Uncle

Jeems may have been free now, but they had chosen to stay on at Taylor's Creek and now they chose to travel with the family.

The towns they passed through—Danville, Greensboro, Salisbury, Charlotte—surely brought Charles bitter memories of his journey home after the surrender. Now those towns looked even drearier, with buildings missing windows and porches, the streets pocked or unpaved, jobless people lolling in the heat amid blowing scraps of garbage, and packs of bony, menacing dogs. Gazing at the blurry scenery, John and his brothers must have felt their initial giddiness shading toward dread.

At the end of the second day, the family crossed into Georgia at Augusta and spent the night at Berzelia, a depot town on the Georgia Railroad. On the final leg of their journey the next day, the boys got a shock: the earth here was *orange*, gullied from erosion, and the fields were carpeted with plump snowballs of cotton. Men, Black and White, dragged long sacks along the rows, stooping, moving at a crawl through the scorching heat. Every man wore a hat. There were no women or children in the fields. Many of the forests had been mowed down—it looked like a tornado had just roared through—and few had been replanted. The land was being bled dry, and even at the age of six, John might have sensed that he was witnessing the onset of ruin.

They passed through a place called Saw Dust, where men fed pine logs into the teeth of a shrieking silver disc, then on through meager little hamlets called Harlem and Camak and Norwood, each announced by a cotton gin or a general store, always the same cluster of drab buildings, always the same heavy heat.

In Union Point they had to change trains one last time, and maybe they had time to enjoy a leisurely lunch on the broad porch of the town's most imposing building, the Terrace Hotel. John's glass of iced tea would not stop sweating. They ate pork chops and mashed potatoes, collard greens and steaming biscuits, the best food they had tasted since leaving home.

Their train pulled into Athens depot just as the great orange blob of the sun began melting into the trees. They were met at the station by Charles's old friend and sponsor from Virginia, William LeRoy Broun, now the professor of Natural Philosophy and Astronomy at the University of Georgia, and his wife, Sallie. After porters loaded the family's belongings onto the Gann & Reaves four-horse bus, the party was ferried across the Oconee River and started to climb the hill toward the town and the sinking sun. There was a foundry and a textile mill on the river's western bank, and to the boys' amazement they were soon passing a gallery of stores and shops selling groceries, hardware, and dry goods. The tree-lined sidewalks and dirt streets were not yet bustling with returning students, but compared to the places they had passed through, this hilltop village of 4,000 souls must have seemed like paradise.

The college campus came into view on their left, and they glimpsed the cool green quadrangle shaded by ancient trees. There was some sort of ceremony taking place near the arch that led onto the campus. A crowd had gathered around a gleaming new fire truck with *Pioneer Hook and Ladder Company* painted on its side while one man tooted a fife, a second banged a bass drum, a third rattled a kettle drum. As the bus passed, a woman raised a bottle of champagne and smashed it against the fire truck's front fender, startling the four dray horses and drawing a roar from the crowd. At the corner the bus turned left and descended a hill to a frame house with a spacious front porch that looked across Lumpkin Street to the campus: the Morris family's new home.

The South was beginning a long backward slide into poverty and illiteracy, but the rest of the nation was booming. While northern and European capitalists shied from investing in the politically and socially unstable South, the second Industrial Revolution was revving up elsewhere, especially in the cities of the Northeast, New England, and the Midwest. In a curious paradox, the Morris family was part of the momentous changes that were beginning to remake American life, yet apart from them. They had landed on a tiny island of cultivation in the midst of a vast backwater, far removed from the strivings and upheavals of the age, and yet their move from Taylor's Creek to a growing town placed them in the vanguard of the movement that would soon transform the United States from a rural nation into an urban one. Over the next forty years, the percentage of the population living in cities and towns would double thanks to the mass migration of Americans from farms to the thriving centers of manufacturing and finance, coupled with an influx of immigrants to the cities of the Eastern Seaboard and the West Coast. By 1920, the majority of Americans would live in cities, and the population of Athens would quadruple. The galloping national economy outside the South led to the building of new factories, new railroads, new urban infrastructure—and to stunning new levels of wealth and poverty, opulence and squalor, corruption and chicanery. It was, in the words of the historian Sean Wilentz, an age of "extravagance, mismanagement and predatory flimflam." Mark Twain would soon come up with a far pithier moniker. As President Ulysses S. Grant's first term passed its midpoint, the nation became a vast hothouse where scams and scandals flourished like mad orchids. In New York City, the construction of the so-called Tweed Courthouse, named in honor of the shamelessly corrupt boss of the shamelessly corrupt Tammany Hall machine, was budgeted at $250,000 but wound up costing fifty times that—some $13 million—after an unknowable number of pockets had been lavishly lined with taxpayers' money. Such acts of pillage would soon become irresistible fodder for the satirist in Mark Twain.

Meanwhile, the Union Pacific of transcontinental railroad lore had been using the Crédit Mobilier, a construction and finance company, to inflate construction costs and funnel stocks at below-market prices to influential politicians, from Vice President Schuyler Colfax to the Speaker of the

House and a sizable platoon of senators and congressmen, including future president James Garfield. The *New York Sun* proclaimed the Crédit Mobilier "the King of Frauds," which may have been overblown considering the stiffness of the competition. After a congressional investigation, a total of two congressmen were censured, no one else was punished, and no money was recovered. Corruption wasn't a blot on the age; it was the oxygen of the age.

The webs of corruption spread across the continent. An organized network of internal revenue agents—strung from Chicago to Indianapolis, Milwaukee, St. Louis, and New Orleans—developed a particularly ingenious scheme. Instead of taxing whiskey, they issued revenue stamps in exchange for bribes, pocketed 60 percent of the money, and kicked 40 percent back to government officials. Whiskey that was supposedly being taxed at $2 a gallon was selling for $1.25. Among the beneficiaries of the scam were revenue agents, politicians, and lovers of cheap whiskey. The loser was the US Treasury, which was plundered of millions of dollars. The scandals came in so many flavors it was hard to keep track of them: the Indian Ring, the Gold Ring, the New York Custom House Ring, the Gold Star Postal Route Ring, the Sanborn Contract, and the Safe Burglary Conspiracy, an operation so exquisitely amateurish that it can be seen as a dry run for the bungled Watergate break-in a century later.

The South may have been lagging economically, but it was quick to get in on the fun. Like the rest of the country, the region was on a railroad-building binge and, as the Crédit Mobilier scandal had shown, where there is a state-supported railroad there is most likely some form of predatory flimflam. In Virginia, a trio of robber barons—Collis P. Huntington of the Central Pacific, Tom Scott, and William Mahone—used bribes and favors to extract $26 million in subsidies from compliant state legislators. In Georgia, the state legislature had come, in the words of historian Peter S. McGuire, "completely under the sway of the governor's friend and financial agent, Hannibal I. Kimball, who was interested in many schemes but chiefly in the construction of railroads on the proceeds of State-endorsed bonds."

A Dixie incarnation of Leland Stanford, if you will. One of Kimball's pet projects was the Brunswick and Albany Railroad, which McGuire dubbed "the Union Pacific of Georgia." Taking a page from the Crédit Mobilier's playbook, a purchasing agent with the Dickensian name of Foster Blodgett set up false accounts for goods that were never delivered, doubled the price of goods that were delivered, then split the take with cronies. Their single most inspired scam was paying themselves $30,000 for train cars that never arrived. It wasn't the Tweed Courthouse, but it wasn't too shabby. To top it off, $1,650 was spent on "liquor, cigars, etc." to entertain the committee charged with investigating the scheme. The committee's report found no evidence of wrongdoing.

Charles Morris had accepted the position as professor of Belles Lettres and Rhetoric at Georgia for several reasons. First was the disappearance of his captive labor force at Taylor's Creek after the abolition of slavery, which led to a decline in land values just as Virginia and many other states, hungry for funds to subsidize their railroad giveaways and other ambitious projects, were forced to raise taxes on those less-valuable lands. This created a wicked bind for landowners like Charles, a bind made worse by the ongoing battle over Reconstruction, which continued to scare away outside investment as it moved toward an unknowable conclusion.

Given his predicament, the offer of the professorship at Georgia must have felt like an answered prayer to Charles, not least because it came with an annual salary of $2,000 paid out of an appropriation by the state legislature. It was not enough to make the family rich, but as long as Taylor's Creek broke close to even, the salary and the many amenities of Athens, home to the nation's oldest state-supported university, lifted the family out of a life of isolation and uncertainty into a life that must have felt secure and positively cosmopolitan. Campus life offered a ready social network of faculty members and their wives, easy access to lectures, libraries, concerts, and theatrical productions, and the boys were set loose on the ball fields, gymnasiums, parks, and backstreets of this picturesque old town. Two years earlier, on his thousand-mile walk from Kentucky to Florida's Gulf Coast, the naturalist John Muir had passed through Athens, which he described as "magnificent" and "aristocratic," adding that "it is the most beautiful town I have seen on the journey so far, and the only one in the South that I would want to revisit."

Surely Charles and Mary were pleased by the rise in the family's fortunes, and just as surely they were surprised to realize they had, unwittingly, landed on the front lines of the ongoing battle over Reconstruction. White Democrats who styled themselves "Redeemers" were leading a campaign to thwart or dismantle the central pillars of Reconstruction, from Black suffrage and civil rights to labor contracts, tax-supported schools for all children, the Freedmen's Bureau, and that dependable bogeyman, the gimlet-eyed carpetbagger come down from the North to profit from the misery of a devastated society. Corruption, extravagance, and free-spending state governments further galvanized the opposition to Reconstruction. Oppressive taxes became the battle cry of the Redeemers, but their ultimate goal was, quite simply, to turn back the clock and reassert White supremacy. Nowhere in the Reconstruction era was this yearning to return to a lost status quo more forcefully expressed than in the state the Morris family now called home.

Even as the Fifteenth Amendment was being ratified, the Georgia state legislature was falling into Democratic hands, and the governorship followed a year later. These Redeemers promptly instituted a poll tax along with new residency and registration requirements, which had the immediate effect of sharply curtailing the Black vote in direct defiance of the spirit, if not the letter, of the Fifteenth Amendment. When such ploys failed to achieve their desired ends, the Redeemers were happy to turn to that reliable old American remedy: violence.

The former Confederate general Nathan Bedford Forrest had become the first Grand Wizard of a loosely organized group of White supremacists who called themselves the Ku Klux Klan. Forrest claimed to have had twenty-nine horses shot out from under him and to have killed thirty Yankees during the Civil War, which left him, as he put it, "a horse ahead." The eminent historian Shelby Foote regarded Forrest as one of the two geniuses produced by the Civil War—Abraham Lincoln was the other—and in his postwar career Forrest channeled his genius for killing into a genius for organizing. He made several trips from Tennessee to Atlanta to promote the Klan, making it clear that the only qualifications for membership were a good horse, a good gun, and a desire to wipe away Reconstruction by muzzling its White supporters and Black beneficiaries. In Georgia, Forrest spoke to willing ears. By the time Democrats took control of the legislature, there was an extensive statewide network of KKK cells, and Georgia voters sent the Klan's Grand Titan to Congress.

The campaign of terror spread across the state. Republican organizer George Ashburn was murdered in Columbus in the spring of 1868, and by the end of the year the Freedmen's Bureau reported more than 300 cases of murder or assault with intent to kill freedmen across the state. Whippings and beatings were common. Black churches and schools were torched. Armed White men patrolled polling places, with the desired result of Blacks staying away.

While the Georgia Klan might have been the shock troop in the war against Reconstruction, it was hardly fighting alone. As like-minded organizations such as the White Brotherhood and the Knights of the White Camellia thrived across the South, the violence rose to a lurid pitch. Jack Dupree, a prominent Black Republican in Mississippi, was beaten, his throat was slit, and he was disemboweled—while his wife and their newborn twins looked on. The Klan burned the offices of the pro-Union *Rutherford Star* newspaper in North Carolina. In Laurensville, South Carolina, an altercation led to White mobs chasing 150 freedmen from their homes and murdering thirteen of them. In Georgia, meanwhile, Klansmen murdered three members of the state legislature whom they'd identified as pro-Union scalawags, then murdered a freedman named Washington Eager because he was "too big a man," as his brother put it. "He can write and read and put it down himself." Educational achievement and financial success, no less than the will to vote, could be a death sentence for a Black man.

Based on his treatment of his former slaves at Taylor's Creek—and his new position at a respected university—Charles would have taken a dim view of these horrors. Knowing what I do now about two encounters John would have with armed terrorists many years after these events, I'm inclined to believe John was steeled for those later encounters by something he witnessed in Athens as a boy, something unforgettable. Imagine it with me. The family had been in town for a year now, and the 1870 elections were just weeks away. John and his brothers Sylvanus and Jim might have been playing marbles on the front porch of the house on Lumpkin Street one sultry late-summer evening while their father sat nearby, reading the newspaper in the failing light. Gretchen had put the baby, Charles Ed, to bed, and she was in her room upstairs, resting. She was pregnant again. The campus across the street was backlit by the day's last rosy sunlight, and cicadas twanged high in the trees. The boys heard it before they saw it— the low moaning of some angry beast, but no, it was a hum coming from the throats of many men, growing louder, followed by the neighing of horses and finally the first spurts of fire. The men were carrying torches, and as they came up the hill and into full view, the boys turned toward them and Charles lowered his newspaper. A gasp might have escaped: "What in the . . . ?" John and his brothers were transfixed. The horses were draped with sugar-white sheets, and all the men, those riding and those walking, carried rifles and wore flowing white gowns and white hoods with cut-out eye holes and sharp points at the peaks. The men were humming and singing, sending up an occasional hurrah as the torches and rifles were lifted into the air. One man carried a cross. And then, as suddenly as they had appeared, they evaporated into the gloom, and the four spectators on the porch all had the same thought: they had just seen a parade of ghosts.

Sylvanus, the oldest of the boys, would have been first to speak. "Who were those men, Daddy?"

Charles's reply would come back to John fifty years later, when he passed his father's words down to his eldest daughter, and again sixty years later, when he passed his father's words down to his youngest son in Berlin, where the terrorists wore brown shirts instead of white sheets: "Those are terrible men, and I don't want any of you to ever have anything to do with such trash, you hear me?"

The boys nodded, too numb to speak.

Charles's message to his sons was clear, but his facts were murky. The men in the white sheets and pointy white hoods were not, as Charles and many others supposed, from the lower classes. To the contrary, the men who joined this first incarnation of the Ku Klux Klan were often respectable citizens. In 1868, Abram Colby, an illiterate freed slave, was elected to the Georgia House of Representatives as a Radical Republican from Greene County, a dozen miles south of Athens. The county voted for Ulysses S. Grant in that year's presidential election, infuriating local Democrats. Merchants offered Colby $5,000 to switch to the Democratic party or $2,500 to resign his seat. He refused. Two nights later, Klansmen burst into his home, dragged him into the woods, and whipped him savagely for three hours with sticks and leather straps, leaving him for dead. The beating crippled Colby and ended his political career, but he managed to testify before the joint US House and Senate committee investigating racial violence in the South. Asked to describe his attackers, Colby said, "Some are first-class men in our town. One is a lawyer, one a doctor, and some are farmers." This proved to be a precedent, not an anomaly. The second incarnation of the Klan, fifty years after this one, would also draw from the middle and upper classes.

Congress responded to the spreading violence by enacting a series of Enforcement Acts, including the sweeping Ku Klux Klan Act of 1871, which represented an immense escalation of federal power in local affairs. If states failed to stop conspiracies or denied citizens equal protection under the laws, the cases could now be prosecuted by federal attorneys and even lead to military intervention. It was a significant shift in the balance of state and federal authority, but Democrats, unimpressed, offered rationalizations for the Klan's activities or denied that the organization even existed. They dismissed reports of violence, such as Colby's testimony, as propaganda emanating from a Republican "slander mill." Congress followed up with the Civil Rights Act of 1875, which provided equal treatment in public accommodations and public transportation and prohibited exclusion from jury service based on race. It was the last piece of civil rights legislation to pass in John's long lifetime.

An Early Edition of Mark Twain's The Gilded Age.

THE LIFE OF THE MIND IN THE SOUTH

harles now belonged to the faculty of the oldest state university in the nation, nearly a century old when he arrived. But just how progressive and academically rigorous was the University of Georgia? The answer matters because the school would come to play a central, even dominant, role in John's life. Maybe the best way to approach the question is by looking at the level of educational and intellectual achievement across the South.

While the South had more colleges, and a higher percentage of the population enrolled in those schools, than the North did at the outbreak of the Civil War, the social critic W. J. Cash offers this withering assessment of higher education in the South in those years: "The majority of the colleges were no more than academies. And of the whole number of them perhaps the University of Virginia alone was worthy to be named in the same breath with half a dozen Yankee universities and colleges, and as time went on, even it tended to sink into a hotbed of obscurantism and a sort of fashionable club, propagating dueling, drinking, and gambling." Cash pointedly omits the College of William & Mary (founded in 1693), the University of Georgia (1785), and the University of North Carolina (1789) as worthy of comparison with the best northern universities.

To support his claim, Cash turns to the Pulitzer Prize–winning autobiography *The Education of Henry Adams*, specifically a sketch Adams drew of his roommate at Harvard in the years leading up to the Civil War. This roommate was, in Cash's estimation, "the typical flower of the Old South at its highest and best." He was a member of a First Family of Virginia. His nickname was Rooney, and he was the second son of Robert E. Lee.

"Tall, largely built, handsome, genial, with liberal Virginian openness towards all he liked," Adams wrote of his roommate, "he also had the Virginian habit of command and took leadership as his natural habit. No one cared to contest it. None of the New Englanders wanted command. For a year, at least, Lee was the most popular and prominent young man in his class, but then seemed slowly to drop into the background. The habit of command was not enough, and the Virginian had little else. He was simple beyond analysis; so simple that even the simple New England student could not realize him. No one knew enough to know how ignorant he was; how childlike; how helpless before the relative complexity of a school. As an animal the Southerner seemed to have every advantage, but even as an animal he steadily lost ground."

Now Adams drives home the dagger: "Strictly, the Southerner had no mind; he had temperament. He was not a scholar; he had no intellectual training; he could not analyze an idea, and he could not even conceive of admitting two; but in life one could get along very well without ideas, if one had only the social instinct."

Adams adds a coda that looks to both the past and the future and, in doing so, reveals he was in a predicament remarkably similar to that shared by Rooney Lee and John Morris: "Roony (sic) Lee had changed little from the Virginian of a century before; but Adams himself was a good deal nearer to the type of his great-grandfather (President John Adams) than that of a railway superintendent. He was little more fit than the Virginians to deal with a future America which showed no fancy for the past." Then Adams freely, even proudly, admitted that he "found himself fifty years behind his time."

Here is the challenge that would shape John Morris: his drive to refute Henry Adams's portrait of the southerner as a person of childlike simplicity untouched by intellectual training and incapable of rigorous scholarship. John Morris would decide at an early age to go in the opposite direction, but in making this choice he would come to understand that he was going doubly against the grain. First, he was living in a nation that was rapidly expanding and industrializing, where men were amassing unfathomable fortunes and the view was becoming widespread that property, wealth, and status were the only things worth attaining. It was a world, in Adams's phrase, that looked only to the future and showed no fancy with the past. Second, John was growing up in a region where temperament, character, and action were more prized than education, cultivation, and reflection. It was a sun-drenched, outdoorsy, social—and deeply anti-intellectual—world, so resistant to change that it was clawing to restore the social order extinguished by the war. A world, in Cash's words, "in which horses, dogs, guns, not books, and ideas and art, were normal and absorbing interests." In this world, Cash concludes, "the pursuit of knowledge, the writing of books, the painting of pictures, the life of the mind, seemed an anemic and despicable business, fit only for eunuchs." Nevertheless, John would embrace such a life, even if it meant he would wind up stranded fifty years behind his time.

Another way to assess the University of Georgia is to look at the man who was chancellor when the Morris family arrived in Athens. Andrew

Lipscomb had been ordained a Methodist minister at the age of nineteen, and before his arrival in Athens in 1860 he had earned a reputation as something of a progressive. For starters, he believed higher education should be available to women, hardly a universal view at the time—the University of Georgia would not admit its first female students until 1918—and this belief had led Lipscomb to accept the presidency of the newly formed Tuskegee Female College in Alabama in 1856. With his waterfall of white hair and a lush bush of whiskers tumbling from his chin, Lipscomb looked like an Old Testament prophet, and indeed he was a voluble orator and tireless promoter of the university, traveling the state to preach the gospel of higher education, lobby the legislature, and raise funds, all while tending to his administrative duties and delivering an occasional lecture to students on Shakespeare, Milton, or Raphael. He had rebuilt the school after it was shuttered during the war, and now he was busily promoting programs in such utilitarian subjects as civil engineering, agriculture, commerce, and modern languages, as well as elective courses then gaining favor at Harvard. He tried to push the university to move beyond the outmoded classical education men like Charles Morris had received and instead offer an education more suited to the rapidly modernizing world. "The remnants of the old monastic scheme of education yet exists," Lipscomb told the Board of Trustees a few weeks before the Morris family arrived on campus, "a scheme that denies the name of an educated gentleman to one who happens to prefer the Modern Languages or the Physical Sciences to the Ancient Classics, a scheme that sets up an aristocracy of pretensions to culture."

Here Lipscomb hit a nerve. Generations of cultivated southerners had proudly pointed to the region's intellectual and cultural achievements: the abundance of colleges and universities, the flourishing Shakespeare societies and Dickens clubs, the fact that Charleston had a public library before Boston. They pointed to men like Charles Morris, who had traveled widely in Europe, could quote Tacitus in the original, and had both taught law and argued cases before judge and jury. But such achievements and such men did not, in Cash's view, mean that there was "profound and esoteric sympathy with the humanities in the South." Rather, they meant that "the great body of men in the land remained continuously under the influence of the simple man's almost superstitious awe for the classics."

Lipscomb's desire to get rid of this "aristocracy of pretensions to culture" and "superstitious awe for the classics" hardly qualified him as a radical reformer. This was Georgia, one of the most conservative states in the most conservative region of the country, where radicals were unwelcome and where all questions returned, sooner or later, to the abiding obsession with race. And so Lipscomb had delivered a speech shortly after his appointment as chancellor in 1860—three weeks after Abraham Lincoln's election as president—a speech that can be seen as his way of reassuring his employers that he possessed the essential credential for his new job. Lipscomb traveled to the state capital in Milledgeville to address the legislature, delivering a rambling, gassy oration full of biblical references that would have been more at home in a church pulpit than a state capitol. As his speech was winding down, Lipscomb finally got to the point. He avowed that Providence had charged "the Anglo-Saxon race" with "the advancement of the African race," adding, "I urge that Slavery in these states, is doing a vast humanizing work. . . . On the one hand, I think then that Slavery has proved an immense benefit to the negro, while on the other hand, it has enriched and exalted our country, and at the same time, promoted beyond computation the peace and prosperity of the world." Five months later the bloodbath began. By the time it ended, as many as a million Americans were dead and the South lay in ruins. So much for slavery's power to promote peace and prosperity. And so much for Andrew Lipscomb's progressive bona fides.

The year 1870 was noteworthy for more than the passage of the Fifteenth Amendment and the emergence of the Ku Klux Klan. It was the year John D. Rockefeller and Henry Flagler formed Standard Oil. Charles Dickens died that summer, and Robert E. Lee followed him in the fall—two deaths which unleashed very different shades of grief. The death of Dickens inspired adulation on both sides of the Atlantic. "Sorrow," the *New York Times* reported, "is universal." Not so with Lee. While Virginia Gov. Gilbert Walker described Lee as "a noble example of the sublime principles and teachings of the Christian religion," Frederick Douglass offered a tart dissent: "We can scarcely take up a newspaper . . . that is not filled with nauseating flatteries. It would seem that the soldier who kills the most men in battle, even in a bad cause, is the greatest Christian, entitled to the highest place in heaven."

The fall elections of 1870, held shortly after John and his father and brothers witnessed the ghostly parade of Klansmen, dealt a fatal blow to Lipscomb's ambitions to modernize and expand the university. Though Lipscomb had offered numerous administrative and teaching jobs to former Confederate officers—not only Charles Morris and William LeRoy Broun but also the former vice president of the Confederacy, Alexander Stephens, and Robert E. Lee's eldest son, Custis Lee—the Redeemers who swept to power in the new state capital at Atlanta were deeply suspicious of the university. Reactionary, anti-intellectual, and averse to taxing the public for services of any kind, including education, they viewed the university as little more than a drinking club and finishing school for the sons of privilege. The charges were not groundless. Then, as now, Georgia students were known as ardent drinkers. At that time, when few children attended school after the age of twelve and a staggering 50 percent of teenage boys were in the labor force, a college education was available only to the elite. Thanks to the state's lack of secondary education, many of the students admitted to the agricultural college were "almost wholly illiterate," according to Lipscomb's successor, and many admitted to the liberal arts college were not "vastly better." In the absence of reliable state appropriations, the university had to scuffle, staying afloat with the help of federal land-grant funds under the

Morrill Act, which was designed to promote agricultural and mechanical education.

Lipscomb held on gamely for a few more years. After his retirement in 1874, the university would be led for the rest of the century by a string of bland traditionalists, not unlike the mediocrities who occupied the White House in those years. These traditionalists rejected modernizing the school based on the university models of Harvard, Virginia, Great Britain, and Europe. They were content to let the nation's oldest state-supported "university" sink into the status of a sleepy second-rate liberal arts college with an ag school attached. Not much more, in Cash's apt phrase, than an academy.

Mark Twain enjoyed a stroke of magical timing in 1873 when he published his rollicking satire of that era's synthetic wave of prosperity, much of it built on the extravagance, mismanagement, and predatory flimflam of railroad corporations. The title of Twain's novel, written in collaboration with Charles Dudley Warner, was *The Gilded Age*, which entered the vernacular and is still in use today to describe the gaudy final quarter of the nineteenth century.

Twain's railroad speculators in *The Gilded Age* are "men who wear big diamond breastpins, flourish their knives at table, and use bad grammar, and cheat." The president of the Columbus Slackwater Navigation Company offers a brief tutorial on Gilded Age politics: "A Congressional appropriation costs money," he explains, noting that payoffs must be made to a small army of committee members and lobbyists as well as "a high moral Congressman or Senator here and there—the high moral ones cost more, because they give tone to the measure. Then a lot of small-fry country members who won't vote for anything whatever without pay."

What made *The Gilded Age*'s timing so magical was that within weeks of its publication, the age's gilding turned, overnight, to tin. On

September 18, 1873, the banking bedrock Jay Cooke & Co., unable to market millions of dollars in bonds of the Northern Pacific Railroad, closed the doors of its New York office. Depositors rushed other banks to withdraw their money. Banks and brokerages collapsed, the New York Stock Exchange suspended trading temporarily for the first time in its history, and layoffs began to sweep the nation. The Panic of 1873 launched a depression that would last six years and by 1876 more than half of the railroad companies were in receivership and some 10,000 businesses had gone bankrupt. As labor unrest spread from railroads to factories to mines to farms, the nation fractured along class lines. Violence was inevitable.

But the suffering was not universal. During and after the depression of the 1870s, the wealthy built rococo palaces on Fifth Avenue and at Newport, Asheville, and Palm Beach, while immigrants were packed so tightly into fetid airless tenements on the Lower East Side of Manhattan that it became one of the most densely populated and disease-ridden places on the planet. With unemployment soaring and wages falling, the rich kept getting richer. John D. Rockefeller consolidated his control of the oil industry, Andrew Carnegie laid the foundation for his empire by building his first steel mill, Cornelius Vanderbilt's New York Central remained a rare profitable railroad, and J. P. Morgan solidified his position as the nation's premier financier. These robber barons succeeded by "investing against the trend," as one historian put it. For the fortunate few, bad times can be the best of times.

It's possible *The Gilded Age* was the first "grown-up" novel John Morris read. He was ten years old when it came out, a bookish boy poised to move beyond his McGuffey Readers and the juvenilia available at Scudder's School for Boys. Maybe I imagine John reading Twain's new novel because I, too, was introduced to literature at the age of ten. This introduction took place at the newly formed Great Books Club, which met after the final bell at my parochial school in suburban Detroit. I was the lone boy in the club, which would seem to indicate that the Old South was not the only place in America where the life of the mind was viewed as an anemic and despicable business, fit only for eunuchs—and girls. Yet, after years of following the predictable adventures of the Hardy Boys, I found myself transported to new places by Stephen Crane's *Red Badge of Courage* and Kipling's *The Jungle Book*, by Malory's *Le Morte d'Arthur* and, to leaven the loaf, some Arthur Conan Doyle. This was the birth of my love for reading, which is to say it was my birth as a writer. The novelist Donna Tartt recently recalled that she was given a copy of one of her all-time favorite novels, Charles Portis's *True Grit*, when she was ten years old. Maybe that's the age when children begin to want to understand how people work, the age when readers, and writers, are ready to be born.

The Gilded Age would have been a revelation to an impressionable ten-year-old boy, his gateway into mysterious and messy worlds where good and evil are not always drawn in black and white, where decent people often act badly out of dark motives, including self-interest, lust for power, and raw greed. Yet John was keen enough to understand that Twain's book was meant to be *funny*, and that evil could be made to look deliciously ridiculous. The Honorable Patrique Oreille (O-re*lay*), for instance, posed as "a wealthy Frenchman from Cork," while in truth he was nothing but an Irish peasant named Patrick O'Reilly. One of his many sidelines was selling shingle nails to the builders of the "Weed" Courthouse—for the handsome sum of $3,000 a keg. It amazed John that men could hatch such brazen schemes, and it delighted him that they could get away with it. Most of all, the novel awakened him to the writer's power to bring imaginary worlds to life on the page. He had glimpsed an alluring new side of life, and he wanted more, much more. It may have been a life fit only for eunuchs in the South, but it was the life John would soon choose to pursue with pit-bull singleness of purpose: the life of the mind.

Statue of Booker Washington at Tuskegee.

A BRIEF MOMENT IN THE SUN

John's was a charmed boyhood in those early Athens years. Mary finally had the daughter she'd always wanted—Mary Louisa Bolling Morris, whom everyone called Louise—and on summer mornings John and his three brothers were turned loose to join the other town boys playing the latest craze, a new game called baseball. Sylvanus, now a teenager and something of a dandy, showed more interest in chasing girls at church socials than in chasing fly balls on the diamond, but John and Jim became avid players. Surprisingly, it was the baby, Charles Ed, just entering school, who showed true promise. His right arm was a cannon, able to throw the ball not only at blazing speed but with startling accuracy right past much bigger boys. It was a skill that would soon make him a local legend.

When the Morris boys were given use of a corner plot near their Lumpkin Street home, they decided to become gentlemen farmers, cultivating a cotton patch that netted the tidy annual sum of $15 and made a small contribution to the miles of yarn, gingham, and denim spun in the Athens Manufacturing Company, on the bank of the Oconee River, the oldest cotton mill south of the Potomac. The boys were also allowed to roam the woods that surrounded the imposing granite mansion of Gov. Wilson Lumpkin, on the southern edge of town. In that wilderness they spent the endless summer days fishing, gigging frogs, and hunting rabbits and birds. Nearby was the state's Agricultural College, where they attended county fairs and horse races. Walking back to town, the boys had to pass over Tanyard Creek and the grimy tanneries owned by Irishmen named Kirkpatrick and Doyle, which were guarded by snarling chained dogs and always given a wide berth.

Up in town there were more urbane amusements. Their parents regularly took them to Deupree Hall, where they saw shows starring the Berger Family of Swiss Bell Ringers and the popular mimic and singer Sol Smith Russell, who was billed, with apologies to Mark Twain, as "America's Greatest Humorist." There were also light operas, which John loved, especially Gilbert and Sullivan's *The Mikado*. A nearby lot had been turned into a croquet field, a popular gathering spot, and just around the corner was the block of Jackson Street known as Cat Alley, a reliable source of entertainment. Every evening at dusk, a restaurant owner named Joe Keno would come out on the street with a bucket of food scraps, let out a shrill whistle, and wait for downtown's squad of rat-killing cats to converge for their evening meal. Joe had served as cook in the local Troup Artillery during the war, and he loved to regale the town's boys with stories about the horrors and gallantry he had witnessed at Gettysburg, the Wilderness, Petersburg, and, saddest of all, the surrender at Appomattox. After closing his restaurant for the day, Joe picked up a lantern and a walking stick and, accompanied by his three-legged dog, assumed his role as downtown's night watchman. Whenever the ice wagon passed, pulled by an ancient mule named Doofunny, John always nodded to the deaf Black boy at the reins, Isaiah Stroud, who always nodded back and tipped his hat. The boys were the same age and nearly neighbors, but they lived in different worlds. John found it hard to imagine being unable to hear or speak and yet working as hard as Isaiah worked. And as slowly as Doofunny shuffled along the unpaved streets, it was equally hard to imagine that the blocks of ice on the wagon didn't turn to puddles by the time Isaiah delivered them to his customers' doors. Isaiah had attended Knox School, the thriving school built by the Freedmen's Bureau west of downtown, but like so many southern boys dropped out soon after he learned to read and write. His family depended on his income from driving the ice wagon.

John's Athens boyhood may have been charmed, unlike Isaiah Stroud's, but it wasn't destined to last. The depression that descended after the Panic of 1873 was especially cruel in the South. Cotton prices plummeted by nearly half in five years, and tobacco, sugar, and rice prices also fell sharply. Sources of credit dried up. The economic downturn depleted tax revenues, which led the tight-fisted Georgia legislature to trim its already paltry contributions to education and other services. Enrollment at the university declined along with state appropriations—a college education was suddenly an unaffordable luxury even for many of the elite—while the nationwide wave of railroad failures had a cascading effect among the producers of iron, steel, timber, and coal that fed the nation's sputtering industrial machine. Richmond's Tredegar Iron Works, a rare manufacturing success story in the postwar South, declared bankruptcy. As the crisis deepened, a new phenomenon darkened the land: mass unemployment.

Despite wide disparities in class, the South had been relatively free of class antagonisms, at least among White people. Here, of course, antagonisms were based almost entirely on race. But elsewhere in the country, wage cuts and layoffs led to violence along class lines—militant bloody strikes by railroad workers, miners, and textile mill hands. After their bitter strike was crushed, twenty Pennsylvania coal miners known as the Molly Maguires were tried and convicted of murder, then hanged. Their employer served as judge, jury, and executioner. One local official lamented that the episode deepened the "antagonism between rich and poor." The antagonism was felt everywhere but the South.

The unrest and economic hardship led to a massive repudiation of the Republican party in the midterm elections of 1874. Overnight, Republicans in the House of Representatives went from a 70 percent majority to a 37 percent minority. In addition to corruption, the second Grant administration was now saddled with economic failure, which had its own cascading effect on the struggle over Reconstruction. Support in the North for the exhausting fight to secure rights for freedmen began giving way to calls for reform. With Redeemers now in control of much of the South, Reconstruction was suddenly under attack from its northern allies as well as its southern enemies.

By now the Morris family was living in what had once been the chancellor's home, an elegant two-story Greek Revival house with a portico jutting onto the campus quad. The family lived on the ground floor, and the second floor was occupied by students, which meant the noises of undergraduate life were a more-or-less constant family companion. Mary gave birth to a second daughter in that house in the summer of 1874, her last child, Susan Rose Pleasants Morris, whom everyone called Susie.

This was also the year Andrew Lipscomb retired as chancellor and Charles's friend and patron, William LeRoy Broun, stepped down as president of the College of Agricultural and Mechanical Arts. There was vague talk in the Morris family about an "upstir" at the university that year, which may have stemmed from Broun daring to suggest that the Board of Trustees had been guilty of misappropriating funds when it distributed federal land-scrip money to the state's branch colleges instead of keeping it in Athens. The trustees could not have been pleased by the insinuation, but it's unknown if they forced Broun out or if he quit on principle. In any event, Charles was dismayed by his friend's departure. He was even more dismayed by Lipscomb's successor as chancellor, an ordained Baptist minister, lawyer, and former president of Mercer College named Henry Holcombe Tucker, who sported a white beard even more luxuriously biblical than Lipscomb's, yet another reminder that the Gilded Age was also the golden age of facial hair. Tucker had no use for progressive ideas, and he soon took steps to get rid of elective courses and revert to the lockstep classical system with its emphasis on grammar, logic, rhetoric, and ancient languages. To this end, Tucker separated the professorships of Latin and Greek, which Lipscomb had combined so more emphasis could be placed on modern languages. Charles was named professor of Greek, which he viewed as a step backward. Worse, Tucker was a strict disciplinarian, determined to shore up what he saw as the lax morals of the student body. Why, Lipscomb had done away with the mandatory 6:00 A.M. prayer hour! When Tucker made the announcement that he opposed allowing students and faculty to borrow books from the library, Charles might have had an unpleasant flashback to his wartime service under that insufferable martinet Alexander Lawton. All this—coupled with declining enrollment, lack of state support, rumors of looming faculty pay cuts, and the departure of his dear friend Broun—convinced Charles that the university was headed in the wrong direction. He wanted out. His ticket arrived in the form of a job offer as professor of Latin and Greek at Randolph-Macon College in Ashland, Virginia, fifteen miles east of Taylor's Creek and fifteen miles north of Richmond. The family could go home again.

Sylvanus, now enrolled at the university, opted to stay in Athens—after graduation he planned to study law—but the rest of the family packed up and retraced the journey through towns and countryside that looked even sorrier than they had six years earlier. Through the train's windows John would have seen dozens, perhaps hundreds, of badly dressed men, Black and White, walking along the dirt roads, their shoulders slumped, their heads down. He might have asked his father where the men were going, and Charles would have explained that they were out of work—"unemployed" was the strange word he used—and walking from town to town looking for jobs that didn't exist. "Those poor men," Charles said, "are what's known as tramps."

"Tramps?" Another unfamiliar word. "Does that mean they're bad men?"

"No, just very, very unlucky. Not like us."

A little over a year after he uttered those words, Charles was beginning to suspect he'd misspoken. Gazing out his office window at the campus on a drizzly fall morning, he couldn't shake the feeling that his luck was turning. One of the reasons he had agreed to take the job here at Randolph-Macon was that knowledgeable friends had assured him the college, unlike the University of Georgia, was on solid financial footing. And indeed, when Charles had dug through the minutes of the Randolph-Macon Board of Trustees' annual meeting from 1874, he had been reassured to learn the college was $50,000 in the black. In their annual report, the trustees couldn't hide their relief: "This exhibit of the finances was particularly favorable and gratifying when it is remembered that the country in the past year has passed through one of the severest financial panics ever known."

Just then a pack of students hurried past the window, holding books over their heads against the drizzle. Among the boys was Charles's second son, Jim, now a freshman at the college and beginning to exhibit an interest in religious studies. He thought he might want to become a preacher, maybe a missionary. Jim was still brown as a berry from the enchanted summer the family had spent at Taylor's Creek. Sylvanus had come up from Georgia, and every morning Louise, now a certified tomboy, would join her brothers for the long days of swimming in the pond, playing baseball, and riding the old nags through the woods. Whenever the children went hunting, Louise always brought home more rabbits than any of the boys. While Mary doted on little Susie, Charles made the rounds in the neighborhood, catching up with relatives and old friends, sometimes venturing into Richmond. It felt good to be in familiar surroundings again. Charles made a major addition to the house that summer, outfitting the windows and doors with a new invention called screens, fine metal mesh that produced an immediate improvement: no more mosquitoes whining in the night, no more flies buzzing in from the barnyard to crawl across the dining room table and light upon the slices of ham and piles of biscuits. Everyone in the family was delighted with the new comfort, though they were unaware that it also carried health benefits. The germ theory of disease was still a decade away.

Charles was feeling expansive that summer, and I imagine him itching to travel to the Centennial International Exposition in Philadelphia and see what kinds of progress had been made in the quarter-century since he'd visited the Great Exhibition at the Crystal Palace in London. Mary wouldn't have wanted to leave the baby, but maybe Charles pestered her until she finally agreed to accompany him—provided they were away from home for just a few days.

It was their first trip to the North, their first visit to an actual American city—Richmond being little more than an overgrown town. It was also to be their introduction to the underbelly of the Industrial Revolution. As their train approached Philadelphia from the south on a scorching July afternoon, a conductor passed through their car, closing all the windows. When Charles and Mary objected that they preferred a breeze, the conductor said, "Trust me, folks, I'm doing you a favor."

Even with the windows closed, a deathly stench began leaking into the car. People held handkerchiefs to their noses. They were passing through a gray valley where entire city blocks were smoking mountains of manure, where blood ran in the gutters. As they approached a river, they could see men loading barges with the carcasses of horses, cows, dogs, and cats. The chimneys of fat-boiling factories emitted ribbons of ochre smoke. Bloody hides were draped on wires, curing in the sun. One building on the riverbank had a sign on its roof that said SCHUYLKILL DAIRY, and Charles remembered reading a magazine article about the "swill milk" produced in such establishments and sold to the poor, a rancid bluish substance squeezed from cows that were packed into stables and fed the hot alcoholic mash from nearby distilleries. The milk was doctored with plaster of paris, starch, eggs, and molasses until it resembled actual milk, and it was believed that thousands of children died every year from drinking it. After they crossed the river, the conductor returned and opened all the windows. As he passed Charles and Mary, who were speechless, he gave them an I-told-you-so nod.

Though not without its charms, the heart of Philadelphia struck them as a dirty, chaotic oven. They were both instantly homesick. Some ten million people would flock to the city over the course of that sweltering summer to gape at the wonders then pouring out of workshops and laboratories and factories across the land. The 700-ton, forty-foot-tall Corliss steam engine, a terrifying behemoth, drew the largest crowds, but Charles was more intrigued by less grandiose achievements. He and Mary floated above the grounds on an elevated monorail. They were transported vertically to an observation platform nearly two hundred feet from the ground in a contraption called an elevator. It amazed Charles to think the day was coming when people would no longer have to climb stairs. Many of the visitors, including the famously shaggy poet Walt Whitman, toured the grounds in wheeled chairs pushed by porters. Charles and Mary marveled at linoleum floor coverings, typewriters, canned food, dried yeast, and, most spectacular of all, a device called a telephone that made it possible for a person to talk to another person who was a mile or more away. It was, all of it, nothing short of a miracle.

On their last day in town, Mary insisted they visit the Women's Pavilion. She was disappointed by its displays on cooking, laundering, and ironing, but later perked up when five women strode up to the stage behind Independence Hall after a man finished reciting the Declaration of Independence. A woman handed a document to one of the bewildered officials, whose face, Mary noticed, turned white when he realized what he was holding in his hand. Then the woman announced she was going to read the document outside. Intrigued, Mary followed the women around to the front steps of the hall, where one of them was reading the Declaration of the Rights of the Women of the United States. One of those rights, which Mary wholly supported, was the right for women to vote. When the woman finished her recitation, Mary joined in the lusty applause.

On the train that afternoon, as they were passing back through the industrial hell, I imagine Charles saying to Mary, "Surely you're not serious about believing women should be allowed to vote."

Mary's eyes would have blazed. "I could not possibly be more serious. Your former slaves can vote and your wife cannot—where is the justice in that?"

Charles was surprised to realize he'd stepped on a hornet's nest. He was relieved when Mary hid behind the newspaper he'd bought at the station in Philadelphia. *Terrible Battle With Indians*, he read on the front page. *Gen. Custer, 15 Officers and every man of Five Companies Slain.* That made no sense. Custer was a dashing, yellow-haired Yankee war hero. Charles picked up his book, written by one of his Dabney cousins, a new biography that made Stonewall Jackson out to be a religious zealot. When the train reached farmland, the conductor reopened the windows. Soon the stench was gone, and Charles, who was being reminded just how unwise it was to make his wife angry, was lost in his book.

Now the centennial summer was over. Sylvanus returned to Athens, where he had begun studying law. John and Charles Ed would be following their brother Jim to college soon enough. The thought of these mounting expenses gave Charles the uneasy feeling that his luck was turning. On his desk was a letter he had received that morning from James Duncan, the president of the college, announcing that due to the worsening national economy and declining enrollment, the trustees had no choice but to withhold half of all professors' pay during the fall semester. Duncan offered hope that the situation would improve by the end of the year, but Charles had his doubts. Workers were walking off their jobs in New England textile mills even as the price of cotton continued to plummet, and the army of unemployed tramps walking from town to town continued to grow. No, the economy was not going to improve any time soon. This led Charles to consider ways he could cover this temporary—*hopefully* temporary—cut in pay. Since the income from the farm could not make up for the shortfall, he kept coming back to two distasteful options: sell off some of the land at Taylor's Creek, or sell the timber in the big woods behind the house, towering first-growth pine and cedar and spruce trees that were coveted by shipbuilders in Norfolk. Charles would rather sacrifice a tooth or a toe than sell that valuable timber or a chunk of his land, but looking out at the drizzly morning, he realized he might not have a choice.

———∞———

As the presidential election approached that fall, it was apparent to Charles and everyone in his circle that Reconstruction would soon run its course. This dismayed none of them. Virginia had joined the ranks of the "redeemed" southern states, and though Charles had no desire to enter politics, he was surely pleased that efforts to ban former Confederates like himself from holding elected office had largely come to nothing. The Ku Klux Klan had been silenced for the time being, another development that pleased Charles, but violence against Republicans and freedmen remained an unfortunate fixture of every election season across the South. When violence flared in Mississippi and the governor appealed for federal troops, President Grant replied: "The whole public are tired out with these annual autumnal outbreaks in the South." Americans, he added, "are ready now to condemn any interference on the part of the Government."

It was widely assumed that the end of federal intervention would be the end of Reconstruction, but the besieged Grant had not misread popular sentiment. Rampant corruption, extravagance, and the high taxes that paid for them were fueling a national reform movement that pushed to dismantle monopolies, political machines, and civil service patronage. With the depression and the wave of scandals dragging on, the Republican party's decade-long pursuit of equality for all citizens was giving way to the less lofty, more pragmatic pursuit of fiscal responsibility—and prosperity. If that meant freedmen would have to fend for themselves and White southerners would have to be trusted to treat them decently, well, so be it. "Reconstruction seems to be a more morally disastrous process than rebellion," *The Nation* wrote, adding that it had "totally failed."

The Republican party's presidential nominee that year was the spectacularly mediocre governor of Ohio, Rutherford B. Hayes, whose chief qualification for higher office was that he appeared to be one of the few elected officials in the land who had not bellied up to the public trough. The Democrats nominated the governor of New York, Samuel Tilden, who was favored to win if only because of the Republicans' horrific record under Grant. Voter turnout was unprecedented in American history despite the vicious suppression of Negro voters in the South, and though Tilden won the popular vote, the Electoral College was deadlocked and the counts in four states—South Carolina, Florida, Louisiana, and Oregon—were contested. A bipartisan electoral commission made up of members of Congress and the Supreme Court voted 8–7 to award the presidency to Hayes. But there were conditions. After receiving assurances from southern Democrats that they would recognize the political and civil equality of freedmen, Hayes agreed not to use federal troops in the South to enforce civil rights: the so-called Compromise of 1877. His outraged opponents, claiming the election had been stolen, took to calling the new president Rutherfraud B. Hayes.

Within two months of his inauguration, Hayes ordered federal troops protecting the South Carolina and Louisiana statehouses to return to their barracks. Meanwhile workers on the Baltimore & Ohio railroad walked off their jobs to protest wage cuts, and soon miners and steel workers went on sympathy strikes. Chicago and St. Louis were paralyzed. Pittsburgh rail yards were torched. The Great Strike of 1877 was as close as the nation has ever come to class warfare.

As cities seethed and burned, Black southerners began to grasp an appalling new reality. One freedman from Louisiana put it this way: "The whole South, every state in the South had got into the hands of the very men that held us as slaves." W. E. B. Du Bois offered this pithy epitaph for the remarkable but ephemeral gains of Reconstruction: "The slave went free; stood a brief moment in the sun; then moved back again toward slavery." The North may have won the war, but the White South had, without question, won the peace.

Karl Benz in his Motorwagen, the first automobile.

THE MUSIC OF THE FUTURE

Reconstruction did not vanish overnight, as many people seem to believe, and it was not a failure more disastrous than the bloodbath that birthed it, as *The Nation* had claimed. Nor did the Compromise of 1877 fling the door open to that hell-maker named Jim Crow. He would arrive later. Reconstruction lived on for decades, though with ever-diminishing force, and for all its missteps and failures it brought fundamental changes—improvements—to southern society that are still alive today.

Chief among them were the obvious things—freedmen's rising literacy rates and their right to vote, the linked ascendancy of the Black church and Black political awareness, and the first glimmers of a Black middle class. Racial integration, though somewhat curtailed during the height of Reconstruction, remained the norm. Practices that would eventually be made illegal were still common, including the mingling of the races on railroads and streetcars and in restaurants, bars, theaters, parks, and other public places. Blacks still served on police forces and juries, and they continued to vote and win elective office at the local, state, and national levels. To address violence and intimidation, Congress passed the Civil Rights Act of 1875, which stated that all persons were entitled to "the full and equal enjoyment" of public conveyances, inns, theaters, and other places of public amusement. Though it prohibited exclusion from jury service based on race, the act did not prevent segregation in schools. "From 1870 to 1900, there was no generally accepted code of racial mores," the historian Charles E. Wynes wrote. "At no time was it the general demand of the white populace that the Negro be disenfranchised and white supremacy be made the law of the land." This lack of a codified policy of exclusion and separation, Wynes added, "led many Negroes to keep trying for acceptance, just as it led some white people to accept them."

There is abundant firsthand testimony to support these claims. In 1885, a Black newspaperman named T. McCants Stewart set out from Boston to visit his home state of South Carolina. "On leaving Washington, DC, I put a chip on my shoulder and inwardly dared any man to knock it off," Stewart wrote in a series of dispatches to the *New York Freeman*. But on a crowded train in Virginia, Stewart got his first of many surprises: the conductor did not order him to vacate his seat so a White passenger could sit down. At the station in Petersburg, Stewart walked into the restaurant "bold as a lion" and took a seat at a table with White people—and was served without incident. As he traveled farther south, White people struck up casual conversations with him. In Charleston he watched a Black policeman arrest a White man, a potentially incendiary confrontation that was handled with impressive "coolness." Stewart was surprised to be able to report: "I think the whites of the South are really less afraid to have contact with colored people than the whites of the North. . . . I feel about as safe here as in Providence, R.I." After a few weeks, he stopped sending his dispatches for a reason every writer can appreciate: "nothing spicy or exciting to write."

Another credible firsthand account comes from Thomas Wentworth Higginson, a Bostonian whose disdain for White southerners' racial attitudes had a prodigious pedigree. A staunch abolitionist, Higginson was one of the Secret Six who had provided financial aid to John Brown before his doomed raid on the federal arsenal at Harpers Ferry—and the only one of the six to openly acknowledge his support after Brown's capture. During the war Higginson had commanded a troop of former South Carolina slaves who fought for the Union and now, in 1878, he returned to the South to try to divine the intentions of White people in the wake of the Compromise of 1877. His findings, published in the July 1878 issue of *The Atlantic Monthly*, were a mix of clear-eyed reportage and wildly uneven prophecies. As for race relations, Higginson found "a condition of outward peace and no conspicuous outrages." He knew men in the North who believed White southerners were planning to use "home rule" to re-enslave the freedmen, but after traveling through Virginia, South Carolina, and Florida, Higginson concluded that such suspicions were groundless: "I can only say that I thoroughly disbelieve it. . . . It is utterly inconceivable that such a plan, if formed, should not show itself in some personal ill usage of the blacks, in the withdrawal of privileges, in legislation endangering their rights. I can assert that, carrying with me the eyes of a tolerably suspicious abolitionist, I saw none of these indications." Higginson's tolerably suspicious eyes failed to see the indications he was looking for simply because they had not yet made themselves visible, which led him to the understandable mistake of believing they didn't exist. The truth was that these impulses were lying dormant, waiting to be roused.

However, Higginson proved prescient when he tried to imagine how freedmen might respond if White people tried to rob them of their hard-won civil rights: "If any abuses exist, the remedy is not to be found in federal interference, except in case of actual insurrection, but in the voting power of the blacks, so far as they have the strength or skill to assert it; and where that fails, in their power of locomotion. They must leave those counties or States which ill-use them for others that treat them better." Without realizing it, Higginson had foreseen how Jim Crow laws would ignite the Great Migration—four decades before it began.

What Higginson had witnessed was the lull before the gathering storm. When and where and with how much fury the storm would break were still unknown, but there was a sense that the South was now on its own and numerous camps were competing to harness the diffuse passions of southerners, Black and White. In this overheated atmosphere, Charles Morris took the cool middle ground, as he had earlier on the question of slavery.

On one extreme were the radicals, the Populist forerunners to the People's Party, who sought to unite freedmen and lower-class Whites against their common oppressor: the White elites who owned the land, controlled the capital, and kept sharecroppers and tenants locked in a cycle of perpetual debt. At the same time liberals promoted equal rights and protections for all citizens regardless of race or class, including equal opportunity in employment, justice, voting, and education. The radicals and liberals would produce some colorful candidates and eloquent spokesmen, but their views were too extreme to catch fire at that time. Joining them on the fringe were the rabid White fanatics who were not placated by home rule, who itched to strip Blacks of all rights and privileges won since the war. Nothing would do but to humiliate, ostracize, and terrorize all freedmen until the White race was once again supreme. These hellhounds were on leashes for now, but how long before the leash snapped?

Between these factions stood conservatives like Charles Morris. He may not have believed that Black people and White people could ever be true equals, but he believed that Black people should enjoy equal rights and opportunities, and he was appalled by calls for the total degradation of the Black populace. He was inclined to judge people less by the color of their skin than by their class, meaning their education, comportment, and manners. He valued what W. E. B. Du Bois called "an unmistakable air of good breeding." A Charleston newspaper neatly captured this inclination: "It is a great deal pleasanter to travel with respectable and well-behaved colored people than with unmannerly and ruffianly white men." There is a distinct whiff of upper-class paternalism in such sentiments, an undeniable smugness, which a South Carolina editor explained this way: "The old slave owner . . . feels no social fear of Negro equality. He feels no desire to maltreat or browbeat and spit upon the colored man. He feels no opposition to the education and elevation of the black man in the scale of civilized life." The reason he felt no opposition was because he did not feel threatened; he was secure in his station, and this gave him the latitude to be magnanimous, a luxury not known to lower-class Whites, whose abiding fear was that they would be surpassed by Black citizens and left on the bottom rung of the social ladder. Freedmen were keenly aware of both the protections and the threats presented by the various classes within White society. After witnessing a debate in the integrated Virginia Assembly, the educational reformer J. L. M. Curry wrote, "A Negro member said that he and his race relied for the protection of their rights & liberties, not on the 'poor white trash,' but on the 'well-raised' gentlemen." To the dismay of Charles and his fellow conservatives, the baying of the poor Whites would drive and dominate the coming storm.

John Morris was now sixteen years old, nearly six feet tall and still growing, a long-limbed, sandy-haired young man with his father's high forehead, solid build, and inquisitive eyes. His interests ranged broadly from academics to politics to athletics. In addition to baseball he had taken up golf, a social game ideally suited to the South's open spaces, mild climate, and love of camaraderie and the outdoors. And in addition to his mastery of the expected subjects—Latin, Greek, French, English, mathematics, philosophy, chemistry, and metaphysics—John had become an avid reader of newspapers, a student of current events not only in Virginia but in the rest of the nation and the wider world. This was the beginning of explosive growth in communications, led by newspapers, which were benefiting from new technology that lowered the costs of paper and printing. Newspaper circulation would increase more than fivefold by the end of the century.

When John matriculated as a freshman at Randolph-Macon College in the fall of 1879, the grinding depression had finally run its course, but he was aware of the mark it had left on the family. In order to finance John's and Jim's undergraduate tuition and Sylvanus's law school costs, Charles had been forced to do the two things he dreaded most: sell off a piece of land and a sizable swath of timber in the big woods. Given what his father had sacrificed to make a college education possible for his sons, John could not allow himself to fail. He had always been a diligent student, and in addition to his regular coursework he had taught himself German and was now beginning to read works of literature in the original.

That autumn was a season of breakthroughs. The first came in the small hours of October 22, 1879. Maybe John stayed up late that night reading by the flickering glow of a kerosene lamp. Maybe he was reading Goethe's *Faust* in German for the first time, experiencing that giddy moment when the student of a foreign language makes the break from mentally translating words and steps into the mind of the native speaker, suddenly able to sail along with the music of the prose. There is no need to speculate about what was taking place three hundred miles to the north in the quiet hamlet of Menlo Park, New Jersey, midway between New York and Philadelphia, where a team of inventors was about to make history. This was the dawn of the golden age of the independent American inventor, a surge of innovation that would blaze for the next half-century. There were tens of thousands of Americans inventing at this level, in spaces that ranged from well-equipped laboratories to homemade workshops in garages and basements.and barns. They pursued their inventions without the backing of large corporations—that would come later, when the fabulous economic potential of their work became apparent. Sometimes they were backed by independent investors, sometimes they worked day jobs, and sometimes they used the proceeds from their proliferating patents to finance their tinkering. Christopher Latham Sholes, the inventor of the typewriter, was a charter member of this vast informal club. Its members tended to be from small towns and rural areas and were rarely educated beyond high school, but from an early age they all exhibited a voracious curiosity about mechanical and electrical devices. They were young, usually in their teens and twenties, and they chafed at the meddling of their financial backers, if they had any, often choosing to assemble a team and work in isolation, free of organizational straitjackets. Above all, they wanted the freedom to choose which problems they would try to solve, in the formulation of the technology historian Thomas P. Hughes, who likened them to another breed of iconoclast: "In their withdrawal, the inventors were like avant-garde artists resorting to the atelier or the alternative life-style of a historic Montmartre, Schwabing, or Greenwich Village." Nikola Tesla, a fiercely independent member of the club whose pioneering work on electrical and magnetic force fields would win him the label of eccentric genius, sang the virtues of solitude to a *New York Times* reporter: "The mind is sharper and keener in seclusion and uninterrupted solitude. Originality thrives in seclusion free of outside influences beating upon us to cripple the creative mind. Be alone—that is the secret of invention: be alone, that is when ideas are born." John Morris would come to treat Tesla's words as gospel.

At his remote Menlo Park compound, known as the invention factory, Thomas Alva Edison was secluded but hardly alone. He had assembled a team of chemists, model builders, glassblowers, and highly skilled machinists to work uninterrupted at turning his tsunami of ideas into physical, usable—and salable—inventions. The compound was outfitted with a steam engine, library, drafting room, machine shop, and chemical laboratory—a setup few universities could match. In the decade since his first patent, for the electrochemical vote recorder, Edison and his team had pumped out a steady river of inventions, including an electric pen (precursor to A. B. Dick's mimeograph); an improvement on Bell's telephone; a machine that was able to record and reproduce sounds, alternately known as "the talking machine," "the recording phone," and now by Edison's preferred name, the "phonograph," whose awestruck earliest audiences included President Rutherford B. Hayes; and, perhaps most spectacular of all, the quadruplex telegraph, which allowed four signals to bypass one another along a single wire, bringing a revolution in telegraphy.

Impressive achievements, to be sure, but as the night of October 21, 1879 bled into the early hours of October 22—all-night work shifts were not unusual in the invention factory—Edison's team was on the verge of the breakthrough that would make his name. Dozens of inventors had produced electric light bulbs, but they all had fatal flaws. They weren't bright enough, the vacuums admitted oxygen, the filaments burned out after a short period of time, their copper or platinum components were too costly, the glass inside the bulb grew cloudy. Edison learned from these failed attempts and put the lessons to use, a method that illustrates the historian Jared Diamond's dictum that "technology develops cumulatively, rather than in isolated heroic acts."

The method paid off that night when a carbonized cotton-thread filament incandesced for fourteen and a half hours before burning out. In his logbook, an ecstatic Edison wrote the one word that said it all: "Eureka."

John would have been immediately aware of Edison's breakthrough—it made headlines around the world—but it had no immediate effect on John's life or anyone else's. That's because the first practical incandescent light bulb, like most inventions, was not the child of necessity. More often than not, demand comes after an act of invention, and in this case there was also the lack of a system to deliver electricity to a network of outlets that could power a virtually unlimited number of incandescent lamps and other yet-to-be-invented appliances and machines. Though Edison would soon jump into this delivery challenge, electric light would remain a luxury available only to the wealthy until the turn of the century.

Edison, the consummate showman, realized he needed to give the world an immediate taste of what was to come. So he strung fifty-nine of his bulbs around the property at Menlo Park on New Year's Eve, a dazzling Festival of Light that drew throngs of curiosity seekers and newspaper reporters like moths to witness this miracle. The Wizard of Menlo Park was able to turn night into day.

On that very New Year's Eve night, in the city of Mannheim, Germany, an engineer named Karl Benz was about to have a breakthrough of his own. Benz, like Edison, had been working cumulatively with—and against—other inventors racing to perfect an internal combustion engine. Three years earlier, fellow German Nikolaus Otto, working off a design by the Belgian Étienne Lenoir, had developed a four-stroke engine, but it didn't generate enough "horsepower," to use James Watts's century-old coinage, to be useful in transportation. On that New Year's Eve in 1879, Benz tried to fire up his own gasoline-fueled, two-stroke engine, but it kept sputtering and dying. Crestfallen, he went to the house to join his wife for supper. Bertha Benz was bankrolling her husband's experiments with her dowry and after the meal, in an effort to cheer Karl up—and protect her investment—she offered a suggestion: "Let's go over to the shop and try our luck once more."

Back in the shop, Benz recalled later, "My heart was pounding. I turned the crank. The engine started to go 'putt-putt-putt,' and the music of the future sounded with regular rhythm. We both listened to it run for a full hour. The longer it played its note, the more sorrow and anxiety it conjured away from my heart."

Like Edison's light bulb, Benz's engine could not immediately be put to its intended use of powering some sort of vehicle. Dozens of ancillary inventions were still needed, including a mechanism to turn the front wheel or wheels, a transmission and drive shaft to translate the engine's power into the turning of wheels, plus brakes, gears, bearings, ignition, cooling systems, and pneumatic tires. It wasn't until the summer of 1886 that Benz would patent the first motor vehicle, a three-wheeler with two seats perched high over a four-stroke engine. It was, as the historian Vaclav Smil wrote, "an invention that made him eventually famous as the 'inventor' of the automobile. Quotation marks are imperative because the motor car is one of the least appropriate artifacts to have its commercial introduction ascribed to a single inventor." Then, reluctantly, Smil made a concession: "But Benz was surely right about the music of the future."

Benz drove his creation, dubbed the Benz Patent Motorwagen, in public for the first time that summer, putt-putt-putting along Mannheim's Ringstrasse at the breathtaking speed of eight miles per hour, nearly three times as fast as a man can walk. As a mode of transportation, the horse was doomed.

John spent countless hours in the college library poring over the dozens of out-of-town newspapers arrayed neatly on bamboo rods like sheets on a laundry line. Every day freshly printed sheets awaited him. He loved everything about newspapers: the way their tidy columns let him travel the world, their illustrations and pictures and maps, even their smell, the bosky pulp, and the oily ink that blackened his fingers and gave him the satisfying sense that his hours in the library represented honest labor. In addition to feeding his curiosity about the world, newspapers gave him ammunition for the family's lively dinner-table discussions of current affairs, which ranged from the Indian Wars in the West to the latest medical breakthroughs to the recent unification of small states and duchies that had birthed the German Empire.

John had heard his parents' stories about the marvels they'd witnessed at the Centennial Exhibition in Philadelphia, including the machine that carried them vertically for hundreds of feet. Now, in the college library, he was reading stories in the New York and Philadelphia and Chicago papers about buildings growing taller and taller thanks to Elisha Otis's elevator, which made it possible for developers to offset soaring urban land values by building upward into the sky. John's occasional trips by train to Washington and Richmond, two sleepy, low-rise towns, made it hard to imagine that the major cities were now sprouting buildings six, seven, even eight stories tall. He must have been stunned by the announcement that the newspaper publisher Joseph Pulitzer was planning to build the tallest structure on the planet to house his *New York World*—a tower *fifteen* stories tall.

The Germans Karl Benz and Otto von Bismarck weren't the only Europeans making news in the American papers. John was surely aware of the work of the celebrated French biologist and chemist Louis Pasteur, whose study of fermentation had revealed that certain organisms grow only in the absence of air. In 1863, the year of John's birth, Pasteur had coined the term "anaerobic" to differentiate these organisms. These observations led Pasteur to see the link between fermentation and putrefaction—namely that both were caused by the activity of microscopic organisms. This germ theory overturned a belief, widespread since Aristotle, that living creatures can arise from other living creatures but also from lifeless matter through a process called spontaneous generation. The "miasmas" in the noxious air generated by swamps and rotting matter were believed to be the cause of such diseases as bubonic plague and cholera. Pasteur was able to demonstrate that all life comes from living matter—and only from living matter. His findings found a ready audience in a Scottish surgeon named Joseph Lister, who had noticed while treating bone fractures that infection was more likely to occur if the bone punctured the skin and came in contact with air. Since the year of President Lincoln's assassination, Lister had been urging doctors to treat wounds with carbolic acid, an "antiseptic," during surgery and also to sterilize their instruments and hands. Such practices were found to greatly reduce infections, post-operative amputations, and deaths. More recently, a German country doctor named Robert Koch had isolated the rod-shaped bacterium that causes anthrax. In a brilliant three-day demonstration in 1876, Koch was able to prove for the first time that a disease had a microbial origin. John found these discoveries thrilling. Wisdom that had gone unquestioned for thousands of years had been proven wrong.

So when President James Garfield was shot in the back while preparing to board a train in Washington in the summer of 1881, John was shocked to read that a dozen doctors probed the wound with unsterilized hands and instruments, desperately trying to locate the bullet even though the wound did not appear to be life-threatening. Andrew Jackson, one newspaper article pointed out, had served eight years as president with at least one bullet lodged somewhere in his body. Garfield was taken to the White House, which was infested with rats and humming with mosquitoes from nearby swamps. Doctors summoned Alexander Graham Bell, who tried to locate the bullet inside Garfield with a primitive metal detector. He failed. After a second attempt produced dubious results, the president's lead surgeon, Dr. Willard Bliss, who had treated President Lincoln on his death bed, declared emphatically that the bullet was lodged precisely where he had predicted: about five inches below the navel. Determined to locate and remove the bullet, Bliss performed a series of surgeries without benefit of sterilization or antiseptics. Like many in the medical establishment on both sides of the Atlantic, Bliss ridiculed Lister's proclamations. As one American skeptic put it: "In order to successfully practice Mr. Lister's Antiseptic Method, it is necessary that we should believe, or act as if we believed, the atmosphere is loaded with germs." Such attitudes helped explain why hospitals were glorified charnel houses, their filthy operating rooms serving as incubators of deadly infections known as "hospital gangrene" or even more mistily as "hospitalism."

Bliss worked all summer at killing the president. The patient was injected with morphine, which made him vomit. His doctors switched to champagne, which made him even sicker. There were more surgical probings. Garfield suffered horribly. As infections bloomed, his body filled with pus, and abscesses had to be drained. The president's weight plunged from 210 to 130 pounds. To lessen his agony, fans were blown over ice in the stuffy vermin-infested sickroom, a crude precursor to air conditioning. Finally Garfield was transported to the New Jersey shore to rejoin his wife, Lucretia, who was recuperating from malaria contracted in Washington. On September 9, 1881, his withered body awash with infections, James Garfield died after just 189 days as president. Dr. Willard Bliss now had the rare distinction of completing the handiwork of two presidential assassins.

John, like most Americans, was riveted by this disaster and the ensuing trial of Garfield's assassin, a failed evangelist named Charles Guiteau who had come to Washington seeking an office in the Garfield administration—possibly minister to Austria, possibly even general consul in Paris—though he had no qualifications for such diplomatic posts. When his entreaties were met with silence, Guiteau set out to kill the president.

At his trial, a clearly unhinged Guiteau entered a plea of not guilty by virtue of temporary insanity. The trial was a sensation. A leading alienist testified as an expert witness. Guiteau cursed the judge and his lawyers. From the witness stand he recited rambling epic poems and smiled and waved at reporters and spectators, including the ubiquitous Henry Adams. And then Guiteau made a startling claim: "The doctors killed Garfield. I just shot him." John had to admit that the man, crazy as he was, had a point.

The jury disagreed. Guiteau was executed by hanging the summer before John's senior year of college. The yearlong drama was an eye-opener. John had never been inclined to question authority, but now, for the first time, he understood that wise men can be fools, even quacks. Since it is indeed possible, even likely, that the emperor is stark naked, received wisdom should never be blindly accepted. This, for John, was the birth of doubt. This was the birth of an iconoclast, of a questioner. Of a misfit.

For reasons unknown, Charles had accepted an offer to return to the University of Georgia as an English teacher. Maybe he was tired of the petty politics at the deeply conservative Methodist college. Maybe he yearned for the relatively cosmopolitan atmospheres of Athens and Atlanta. Maybe now that his old nemesis, Henry Holcombe Tucker, was no longer chancellor, Charles imagined campus life would be more to his liking. Whatever his reasons, he and Mary returned to Athens that fall with Charles Ed and the girls, leaving John behind at Randolph-Macon.

As John's senior year drew to a close, his preparations for final exams were besieged by distractions. I picture him in the college library trying to memorize a passage from Virgil's *Georgics*, or maybe Xenophon's *Cryopaedia*—and suddenly, as though pulled by a string, he finds himself drifting over to the newspaper racks to get the latest news about the latest marvel. There were so many! In the town of Roselle, New Jersey, eight miles from his invention factory, Thomas Edison had built a steam generator, strung overhead wires, and powered enough of his light bulbs to illuminate the town's streets, stores, railroad depot, and even the Presbyterian church. Every month seemed to bring forth new magazines devoted to every imaginable topic, from the niche to the general, from satirical *Judge* to domestic *Ladies' Home Journal* to *Life* itself. This could have been when John had his first encounter with a flush toilet, a porcelain bowl rimmed with a wooden seat and equipped with a pull chain that sent a gush of water cascading from a tank to carry away waste. This could also have been when he bought his first "fountain" pen, a device patented by Lewis Waterman that allowed him to draw ink into a reservoir inside the pen: no more dipping pen nibs into bottles of ink, a major improvement. He read about a new form of entertainment called vaudeville that was flourishing in the cities, the mongrel spawn of minstrelsy, burlesque, and medicine shows, a blur of song-and-dance acts, acrobats, trained animals, jugglers, ventriloquists, pugilists, strongmen, and female impersonators. It was enough to make him dizzy.

John became particularly enthralled by a marvel that was already being called the Eighth Wonder of the World, though it had not yet been built. When complete, the New York and Brooklyn Bridge was going to be the longest suspension bridge in the world—made of cut stone and steel, not iron—the creation of a German immigrant named John Augustus Roebling. Before construction began, Roebling was taking compass readings on a jetty when a boat smashed his right foot, crushing his toes. After two toes were amputated without benefit of anesthesia or antiseptics, Roebling underwent hydrotherapy treatments, which called for repeatedly pouring unsterilized well water over the wound. Within a month he developed tetanus and died in agony—a death every bit as preventable as James Garfield's. After Roebling's son Washington took over, men kept dying. They fell into the river from great heights. They were crushed by falling blocks of granite, by falling derricks. Workers called sandhogs, who toiled in airtight under-water chambers digging out the river bottom where the bridge's two towers were to be planted, contracted "caisson disease," which could twist a man's legs like braided hair and cause shrieking headaches, convulsions, paralysis, and death. Washington Roebling contracted the disease, also known as the bends, and was forced to supervise construction while recuperating in an apartment in Brooklyn, gazing through field glasses, growing addicted to morphine, scribbling instructions on scraps of paper that his wife Emily, an accomplished engineer, relayed to the crews. A compressed-air blast ruined one caisson. Fire destroyed another. Tons of shoddy steel cables had to be removed and replaced. What amazed John more than the technical wizardry of the bridge was the determination of the men—and the woman—who built it. Nothing could stop them. Men were willing to risk their lives for a couple of dollars a day to make this marvel a reality. It was brutal and ghastly, such an act of will, and it struck John as a pure expression of America. Yet when he saw the newspaper pictures of the opening ceremony on May 24, he had to admit the bridge's cables glinting in the sunlight looked as lovely and elegant as the strings of a harp.

Despite this array of distractions, John managed to pass his final exams and earn his Master of Arts degree. What next? An ambitious young college graduate would have been lured by the seductions of the accelerating, urbanizing world, would have made his way to Washington or Philadelphia or New York to pursue a career in politics or business, maybe journalism or teaching. John, the misfit, went in the opposite direction. He accepted a position as principal of a public school in Smithfield, Virginia, a sleepy backwater near the mouth of the James River, less than a hundred miles from where he was born and raised. It was a place lost in time, known for its hams and for pretending that the Civil War and Reconstruction had never happened and the faraway Industrial Revolution never would. It was deep in the heart of nowhere. Moving there was John's first step in a decade of fruitless drifting.

The first electric streetlights in New York City.

THE GREATEST ADVENTURE

By the time John got settled into his job in sleepy Smithfield, Thomas Edison was immersed in what he called "the greatest adventure" of his career—inventing, fabricating, and installing an urban illumination system that would power hundreds, thousands, then tens of thousands of his incandescent bulbs and serve as nothing less than the template for electrifying the planet. Even by Edison's standards, he had entered a phase of white-hot, nearly manic activity, filing for more than three hundred patents from 1880 to 1883, a flurry never equaled by him or any other inventor.

The challenges of creating an illumination system ranged from miniscule to monstrous. With a new factory gearing up to produce half a million of his light bulbs a year, Edison set out to find a substance that was more durable and reliable than the carbonized cotton-thread filament that had glowed so promisingly in the early morning hours of October 22, 1879. The quest was typical of how the invention factory functioned. Edison and his trusted lieutenant Charles Batchelor spent weeks cutting, planing, and carbonizing a smorgasbord of fibrous substances, including pomegranate peel, eucalyptus bark, jute boiled in maple syrup, milkweed, palm fronds, flax, hemp, cork, even asphalt, banknote paper, and macaroni. After more than six thousand failed experiments, the idea of bamboo came to Edison. He sliced the edge off a fan blade made of cheap Calcutta bamboo, but it went out after burning for just an hour. When Edison learned there are more than a thousand species of bamboo in the world, he spent $100,000 of his own money, a fortune, to dispatch half a dozen freelance explorers to South America, the Caribbean, and Asia in pursuit of the ideal strain. Eventually he would settle on *yawata madake* bamboo, giants that grow in a forest between Osaka and Kyoto in Japan. Carbonized cotton-fiber filaments burned for an unsatisfactory forty hours; the Japanese bamboo burned for thousands of hours. Problem solved.

Others took its place. Edison had won approval to illuminate a square mile of Lower Manhattan, the first of twenty-six projected electric districts in New York City. The streets of the financial district in those days lived in perpetual dusk thanks to the tangle of sun-blotting overhead telegraph and telephone wires. To avoid compounding a problem that was largely the result of his own inventions, Edison was determined to bury his electrical wires beneath the streets, a tricky bit of engineering coupled with brute pick-and-shovel work already accomplished by the gas companies Edison intended to put out of business. This would require not only digging miles of trenches through heavily trafficked streets and sidewalks during the warm months but also developing insulation that would keep the electric current inside the conduits and keep water out while protecting the wires against the gnawing teeth of rats. In a quest that echoed the hunt for the perfect filament fiber, the crew experimented with dozens of wrappings. All admitted water, which caused short circuits. Finally, after much trial and error, a successful recipe was achieved: asphalt boiled in a puree of linseed oil and paraffin, topped with a dash of beeswax. Ribbons of muslin were dipped in the broth, then triple-wrapped around the wires. There were no leaks, no short circuits. Another problem solved.

While the stone towers of Washington Roebling's bridge were rising out of the East River nearby, Edison was feverishly designing a complex web of underground mains, feeders, and branch lines that would radiate from a central generating station, along with a host of generators, sockets, fixtures, and meters. He bought two side-by-side buildings on Pearl Street and set about constructing the beating heart of his illuminating system. One of the buildings was soon filled with a terrifying jumble of six jumbo dynamos powered by boilers fired by coal that rose from the basement on conveyors. The monster was so heavy it would have caused the building to collapse, so Edison had his team construct an indoor cast-iron bridge strong enough to support a locomotive. The third floor was filled with voltage regulators, the fourth with a thousand pulsing lamps to monitor loads throughout the system. It was glorious, and terrifying.

The setbacks kept coming. The city would not allow the laying of feeders and mains beneath the busy streets during business hours, so trenches had to be dug at night. Designs had to be tweaked and re-tweaked to minimize the use of costly copper cables. There were delays on the delivery of parts. And since this was the glittering peak of the Gilded Age in a city dominated by the Tammany Hall machine, platoons of bureaucrats, inspectors, and aldermen had to be constantly lubricated with unmarked envelopes of cash. Some parts of the project forged ahead while others lagged. Subscribers had electrical wires sticking out of their wall sockets long before the first volt of electricity was generated. Investors grumbled. There were rumors of imminent failure. It appeared the Wizard of Menlo Park was human after all.

A young man as intellectually hungry as John must have felt starved in a backwater like Smithfield, with no theaters or museums, no college library, no racks of fresh newspapers awaiting his perusal every morning. I imagine him feeding his hunger with regular trips to the nearest cities—downriver to Norfolk, upriver to Williamsburg and Richmond, maybe an occasional train trip to Washington to buy newspapers and books, to visit libraries and the new Arts and Industries Building at the Smithsonian.

The newspapers were then covering a remarkable news story coming out of Tennessee. It involved a Black schoolteacher named Ida B. Wells who set out on the ten-mile trip from Memphis to Woodstock on the Chesapeake, Ohio & Southwestern Railroad, a routine ride that went terribly wrong. Wells, who was born into slavery in Mississippi the year before John's birth, was the only Black person in the rear car of the three-car train, the first-class car. "Rougher people ride in the front car than in the rear car," she would say later. When the conductor, William Murry, came to collect tickets, he refused to accept Wells's ticket and told her the rear car was reserved for White passengers. He ordered her to move to the next car, where she could see a racially mixed crowd of men smoking and talking loudly. At least one of the White men was flamboyantly drunk. That Charleston newspaper editor had predicted Wells's thoughts: *It is a great deal pleasanter to travel with respectable and well-behaved colored people than with unmannerly and ruffianly White men.* Wells had purchased a first-class ticket for thirty cents, and she refused to leave her seat. When the train reached its first stop, the town of Frayser, Murry tried to remove her forcibly. Wells resisted, clung to her seat, scratched Murry, and bit his hand. The left sleeve of her dress was nearly torn off in the scuffle. Bleeding freely, Murry summoned two more men, and together they carried Wells out of the car. The White passengers applauded, compounding her humiliation.

Indignant, Wells stopped on the platform between the cars, again refusing to enter the forward car. Instead she stepped onto the station platform and, still clutching her ticket, watched the train pull away. After hitching a ride home on a wagon, she filed a lawsuit against the railroad. Good for her, John thought.

The trial got extensive press coverage—a twenty-one-year-old colored woman suing the mighty Chesapeake and Ohio! Hanging over the proceeding was a decision a year earlier by the US Supreme Court that overturned the Civil Rights Act of 1875. In a landmark decision that bundled five civil rights cases into one, the court held, in an 8-to-1 vote, that the Thirteenth Amendment merely abolished slavery and the Fourteenth Amendment granted Congress the right to regulate racial discrimination by states but not by individuals or corporations, including railroads. Two years before that, the Tennessee General Assembly had passed a law requiring railroads to make available separate first-class cars or areas in first-class cars "which all colored passengers who shall pay first-class rates of fare may have the privilege to enter."

Wells's train had no formally designated "white" and "colored" cars. Instead, as Murry explained during the trial, it was understood that the rear car was reserved for White ladies and their traveling companions, and the middle car was for both races. A Black minister named T. H. Clowers testified about the behavior of the passengers in the mixed car: "They were smoking, talking and drinking, very rough. It was no fit place for a lady. There were no white ladies."

Murry testified that he always tried, with mixed success, to send smokers to the train's first car, which was equipped with baggage racks and passenger seats. Why the informal separation of the races? Murry replied, "This rule was made because that division of passengers was found to be most pleasant for the large majority of people who traveled. (As) it tended to avoid unpleasant association and antagonism of race, we had these cars for that train—two passenger coaches which were alike in every respect, built, equipped and furnished alike."

Here, in embryo, was the doctrine of separate but equal.

Now came the climax of the trial: Wells won her lawsuit and was awarded the staggering sum of $500. As one headline writer put it: "Darky Damsel Obtains Verdict for Damages Against the Chesapeake & Ohio Railroad." In his ruling, Judge James O. Pierce cited an 1867 Pennsylvania law that allowed railroads to separate Black and White passengers "provided each class has comfortable, safe and convenient accommodations, not inferior in any of these respects to those enjoyed by the other." So in Pierce's reading of the law, the Chesapeake & Ohio erred not in removing a Black passenger from a White car, but in providing inferior—smoky, boisterous, "rough," *unequal*—accommodations for the Black holder of a first-class ticket. Though no one realized it at the time, Jim Crow now had his foot in the door. This was not the last John was to hear from him or his sworn enemy Ida B. Wells.

⸺

The rumors of the imminent failure of Thomas Edison's New York City illuminating system proved to be overblown. Somewhat. On a Monday afternoon in the fall of 1882, Edison had his first small success when he powered up a single dynamo at Pearl Street and sent a current skittering underground to a third of the customers scattered across the district. This was done quietly, with none of Edison's usual fanfare, possibly because he was afraid the system would fail, and if it did, he wanted to keep it quiet. But the system failed to fail. As dusk gave way to night, reporters and editors in the newsroom at the *New York Times* on Park Row noticed something was different. Instead of the jumpy glare of gas lamps they had become accustomed to, the room swam in the warm and steady glow of Edison's electric lights. Commuters walking down Fulton Street for the ferry ride to Brooklyn passed through discs of the same pleasant glow. Much as Karl Benz's motorwagen would soon doom the horse as a means of transportation, Thomas Edison's illuminating system had just signed the death warrant for gaslight.

Within a year of this modest, barely noticed debut, there were more than a hundred power plants in private homes and industrial enterprises scattered across the globe, all of them powered by Edison dynamos and burning Edison lights. J. P. Morgan's mansion on Madison Avenue had its own thrumming power plant, to the annoyance of his horses and his neighbors, and so did a remote sawmill in Russia and a steamer in a Glasgow shipyard, along with the municipalities of Sunbury and Shamokin in Pennsylvania and Brockton, Lawrence, and Lowell in Massachusetts. These municipal systems were fed by overhead wires, which were unsightly but much cheaper and easier to install than the lines buried beneath the downtown streets of New York City. American towns were about to get brighter, and uglier. By the middle of John's year in Smithfield, there were more than 12,000 lights burning in the Pearl Street district and more than 64,000 nationwide. Electric light would remain a luxury for years to come, but Edison was on his way.

He wasn't working alone. An impressive roster of inventors and scientists—Tesla, Sperry, Fessenden, Marconi, De Forest, Benz, and Pasteur, to name a few—were making advances in arc lighting, turbines, magnetic fields, wireless communications, combustion engines, and the sources and treatments of infectious diseases. The quickening pace of their inventions and discoveries, led by Edison's electric light, inspired a wave of newspaper and magazine articles that claimed a seismic shift was taking place in the average American's attitudes toward advanced technology. Initial misgivings were turning into something very different. "The wizardry of scientific technology was now a source, not of distrust, but rather, of hope," wrote Robert Friedel and Paul Israel in their history of Edison's electric light. "This attitude toward the powers of science and technology was one of the nineteenth century's most important legacies." In a small but telling sign of this shift, people were ignoring the skeptical medical establishment and eagerly buying a disinfectant mouthwash named after Joseph Lister. Edison's lights were glowing in more and more homes and stores and factories. Corporations were jockeying for exclusive rights to the latest inventions—and the profits that came with them. Thomas Edison was far more famous—and respected—than President Chester A. Arthur. While John had begun to question the purveyors of conventional wisdom in medicine and other fields, the skeptic in him cautioned against climbing aboard this technology-worshiping bandwagon just yet. Misfits rarely rush to join the herd.

Even for a young man as rudderless as John, one year in Smithfield was enough. As he celebrated his twenty-first birthday that summer, he decided it was time to get serious. He would follow his father and brother Sylvanus into the study of law. Aside from his fascination with Guiteau's sensational murder trial and Ida B. Wells's ill-fated lawsuit, John was not known to have exhibited any great passion for legal matters. But law school would get him out of Smithfield, it would feed his itch to learn, and it would add polish to his educational credentials. There's reason to doubt that John saw a law degree as a meal ticket, but there was little doubt about which law school he should attend. He packed his bags and headed back to Athens.

When he arrived, he found the town had changed visibly in his decade-long absence. The population had risen by half to more than 6,000. There was now rudimentary telephone service, some of the downtown streets had been paved, and tracks were being laid for trolleys that would be drawn by teams of Texas mules. The freedmen's Knox School had been expanded and renamed Knox Institute, and the White female teachers sent from the North by the American Missionary Association had been replaced by

Black teachers, which seemed to placate the town's many White residents who bristled at any whiff of the carpetbag or forced integration. There were other signs of an emerging Black middle class, including two new schools for Black children—the Methodist School and Jeruel Academy—plus several new Black churches. The town now had a Black postmaster, one of only a few in the state, as well as a Black newspaper called the Athens *Blade*. These developments would have pleased John, who, like his father, believed freedmen should enjoy the same rights and opportunities as White people. Did he wonder what had become of deaf Isaiah Stroud and his ice wagon?

An imposing new four-story classroom building called Moore College, topped by a Mansard roof, had risen on the campus, flanked by a platter of barbered grass where students and faculty played the increasingly popular games of football and baseball. A crude tennis court, the first John had ever seen, took up the patchy lawn in front of Charles and Mary's house on the campus—a net strung between two pine posts with squiggly lime lines. But overall the university was still little more than a glorified academy wedded to the classical system, with a faculty that possessed, in one historian's tepid estimation, a "relatively high" level of skills in their chosen disciplines. The new chancellor, Patrick Hues Mell, was a pious Baptist minister who spent much of his energy trying to rehabilitate the university's image as a breeder of iniquity, which he blamed on the university's unpoliced dormitories. As Mell wrote: "In such dormitories, organized vice would entrench itself and hold high carnival. Drunkenness and gambling and licentiousness would there fix their permanent headquarters." It's unlikely John was impressed by the preachings of this seventy-year-old mossback. The library was understaffed and understocked, the faculty was underpaid, the buildings were drafty and unkempt, the unpaved pathways turned to viscous red soup after a heavy rain—and all the chancellor cared about was stamping out vice and burnishing the university's reputation with the church crowd.

Two of the more conspicuous changes that greeted John were personal. His eldest brother Sylvanus had opened a successful law practice in town in 1877, and he had just been elected to the faculty of the Lumpkin Law School and appointed city solicitor. During John's absence, Sylvanus had become something of a man about town, a gregarious, nattily dressed bachelor who loved to take long leisurely walks through the town, pausing to converse with fellow strollers, stopping to visit at the homes of longtime friends. He was working up to an avocation as a writer, a walking gatherer of random insights and historical tidbits, a connoisseur of the streets, a creature of leisure that the French poet Charles Baudelaire had recently dubbed a *flâneur*.

The other big change was the status of John's father. At a time when the life expectancy for White males was about fifty years, Charles had reached the advanced age of sixty. His hair and moustache had gone to silver, and he was now an imposing figure known alternately as "the Major," a nod to his Civil War service, and "the old Roman," a nod to his classical training. When John sat in on his father's English classes, he noticed the undergraduates were every bit as attentive as the young boys and teenagers had been in Charles's dining-room school at Taylor's Creek after the war. But John's trained eye picked up something lost on these undergraduates. As they filed into the classroom, Charles would settle behind his desk and slip his right hand into his jacket pocket. John knew what was in there—a rubber pouch filled with shredded tobacco called "moss." Charles rolled the tobacco into a pea-sized pellet, then passed his hand across his face like a magician, slipping the unseen pellet into his mouth and working it between cheek and gum, where it would slowly dissolve while he delivered the day's lesson. John knew the pleasurable hum infusing his father's nerves. He, too, had started chewing tobacco.

Charles put his students through three years of rigorous writing assignments, a sort of compositional boot camp, before introducing them to literature during their senior year via *Kames's Elements of Criticism*, a staple in American and British colleges at the time, a book John knew well from his own undergraduate years at Randolph-Macon. Henry Home, known as Lord Kames, was a lawyer, judge, and member of the Scottish Enlightenment, which had flourished in Edinburgh in the second half of the eighteenth century, a dazzling constellation of thinkers that included poet Robert Burns, economist Adam Smith, philosophers Thomas Reid and Francis Hutcheson, and Thomas Boswell, writer of travel stories and a biography of the great English lexicographer Samuel Johnson. John would have been aware of the speculation that Reid's and Hutcheson's ideas on life and liberty had seeped into the inkwell Thomas Jefferson dipped into while writing the Declaration of Independence. Much more intriguing to John was the pairing of Johnson and Boswell—the writer of a magisterial dictionary who claimed he was nothing but a "harmless drudge" yet had lived a life so intellectually and socially vivid that it inspired a biography that was itself a work of high art.

Charles's incessant writing drills led some of his students to grumble that their professor must have been in cahoots with the manufacturers of pencils and paper. But stern as he was in the classroom, the Major had a softer side. He loved to hunt and had become an avid, nearly rabid sports fan who could frequently be seen beside the tennis court in front of his house, down on one knee, giving pointers and encouragement to the few boys who owned rackets, trying to plant a seed of refinement in the uneven grass and red clay. He was also a fixture in the bleachers at the school's first baseball and football games, sitting with the students, shouting encouragement to the players and mercilessly riding the umpires and referees, sometimes jumping to his feet after a questionable call and bellowing, "Take him out! He's rotten!"

There was an ulterior motive for some of these displays of passion. The university's first organized athletic team was its baseball nine, and the Major was partial to the battery, which consisted of his youngest son, flame-throwing Charles Ed as pitcher and John as catcher, while Jim played the infield. Charles Ed, dissatisfied with merely being able to throw the ball hard and with accuracy, had figured out that if he placed his middle finger on the top seam of the ball and his thumb on the bottom seam, then snapped his wrist when he released the pitch, the ball dove sharply just before it reached the batter, producing a flurry of strikeouts. Charles Ed is believed to be the first southern player to throw this pitch, which became known as a drop-shoot, or curveball. While Charles Ed was becoming a legend, his catcher was not so lucky. Playing with a crude mitt and no mask, John usually caught his brother's offerings on the first bounce. But drop-shoots had a way of taking erratic hops, and John's unprotected nose was broken more than once.

When the day's classes and sporting events were over and the sun was low in the sky, Charles draped his gray Confederate cape over his shoulders and took long walks with his devoted setter, Niblo, one hand clutching a walking stick while the other held the hand of his youngest daughter, Susie. Charles had become a character bordering on caricature, what one student called, with unfeigned reverence, "a Southern gentleman of the old regime."

The Watts Building in Birmingham during the funeral of local madam Louise Wooster.

THAT MOST UN-AMERICAN THING

After earning his law degree, John spent a pleasant summer in Charlottesville, Virginia, attending lectures at the university, reading, loafing, burying himself in a library that shamed the one in Athens. This may have been when he first imagined the joy of spending days, weeks, years lost in a first-rate research library. At the end of that idyllic summer, John took the most mystifying misstep of them all. For reasons unlikely ever to be known, he decided to move to that brawling Gehenna called Birmingham, Alabama, and hang out a shingle: *John Morris, Esq., Attorney at Law.*

Located at the tail end of the Appalachian Mountains, Birmingham was then a raw and raucous boomtown, a city blessed—and cursed—by its proximity to vast deposits of the three elements needed to make steel and iron: coal, limestone, and iron ore. Drawn by these three treasures as well as a cheap native labor force—both Black and White—entrepreneurs were erecting mills and furnaces in the city, gouging mines and quarries into the surrounding hills, and transforming Birmingham, during the 1880s, from a sleepy village into a blazing rival of Chattanooga and Pittsburgh. Some men were getting rich and building palaces while others were packed into teeming slums. The mills roared round the clock, their chimneys belching smoke that cloaked the town in a perpetual fog.

While John tried to get acclimated to this alien world, he got wind of two competing ideas he viewed with distrust that would harden into disdain. One school of thought urged southerners to retreat into a gauzy idealized past, to a world where the White people were chivalrous and the Black people were content and the Civil War was a noble effort to preserve a way of life built on the benign institution of slavery. The other school of thought urged southerners to forget their disastrous feudal past and march boldly into a modern, industrialized future, which is precisely what the citizens of Birmingham were so enthusiastically doing when John arrived in town.

The appeals from these two opposed camps had one thing in common: both were in keeping with the spirit of the Gilded Age—or, as some would have it, "the Guilded Age"—a time when Americans were becoming eager joiners, willingly adopting the latest philosophy and technology, enthusiastically pursuing a proliferating array of professions—in accounting, academia, insurance, finance and management, to name a few. In the four decades beginning in 1870, the number of all professionals increased fourfold to more than a million. These professionals then joined organizations spawned by their jobs, devoured new periodicals such as *Journal of Accountancy*, *American Engineer*, and *Industrial Management*, attended national meetings, underwent specialized training, and strove to meet the standards set by new accrediting associations. For good measure, after having joined fraternities in college, they now eagerly signed on as members of the local social club's lodge, temple, conclave, castle, or hive, which ranged from the fake serious to the seriously silly, from the Ancient Arabic Order of Nobles of the Mystic Shrine all the way down to the Independent Order of Gophers and the Concatenated Order of Hoo-Hoo.

The gauzy view of the South's past came to be known as the Lost Cause, or the Moonlight and Magnolia School. Among its early champions were Jefferson Davis, the former president of the Confederacy, Jubal Early, a former Confederate general, and Thomas Nelson Page, a Hanover County native and a cousin of John's by marriage. One day, while perusing *The Century* magazine hoping to find a new story by Mark Twain or Henry James, John might have stumbled on Page's latest short story, "Marse Chan: A Tale of Old Virginia." Set in 1872, the story tells of a chance encounter between an aristocratic White Virginian and a former slave named Sam, who cross paths in a neighborhood of once-grand but now-derelict old mansions. With little prodding, Sam launches into a tale, told in dialect, about the bad blood between the two most prominent local families, that of his master, Channing, the "Marse Chan" of the story's title, and the family of the master's lifelong sweetheart, Anne Chamberlain. The feud led to an inconclusive duel between Marse Chan and Colonel Chamberlain that drove the lovers apart—until they finally reconciled, only to have their reunion cut short by Marse Chan's heroic death fighting to repel the Yankee invaders. By putting the defense of slavery in the mouth of a former slave, Page gives this soapy melodrama undeniable punch. Here's how Sam remembers slave times: "Dem was good ole times, marster—de bes' Sam uver see! Dey wuz, in fac'! Niggers didn' had nothin' '*t all* to do—jes' hed to 'ten' to de feedin' an' cleanin' de hosses, an' doin' what de marster tell 'em to do."

John wasn't buying this bill of goods—the benign and chivalrous slave owners, the happy "darkies," the noble-but-doomed defense of a refined way of life. He knew better. He had grown up hearing stories about runaways and whippings and suspicious fires at Taylor's Creek, about slaves stealing the family's furniture and silverware, about the many slaves who had melted away the moment they learned they were free. Yes, Aunt Dinah and Uncle Jeems and a few others had remained loyal right up to their deaths, but they were the exceptions, not the norm that Page and other purveyors of the Lost Cause were peddling. Slavery was an abomination in John's eyes, and no amount of sugarcoating could hide the fact that the enslaved had almost unanimously loathed their bondage and rejoiced when it came, almost miraculously, to an end.

Meanwhile, John's law practice was attracting few clients, mostly men arrested on drunk and disorderly charges or for disputes involving gambling and guns. As my father summed it up, "He hung out a shingle but found he didn't know anybody, and he just didn't get any clients. He was not a self-promoter."

Though little is known about John's years in Birmingham—other than the virtually preordained failure of his law practice—I believe it's possible to pinpoint this as the moment when he slipped forever out of sync with the spirit of his times. Americans had always been go-getters, but now, as the pace of life quickened and the nation became more urban and industrial, they were becoming joiners, back-slappers, and, worst of all in John's eyes, boosters and self-promoters. One of the gravest offenders on this last charge was an Athens native named Henry W. Grady, the publisher of the Atlanta *Constitution* and an enthusiastic booster of a modern, industrial New South. Grady was a renowned orator, and John was surely familiar with the popular collections of Grady's speeches that were circulating, especially the one he delivered at Delmonico's restaurant in New York City in 1886 in which he unveiled his vision of the New South to a crowd of potential investors that included J. P. Morgan. While John would have approved of Grady's call for more and better schools, including a new state technical college in Georgia, he would have been put off by Grady's hyperbole and outright lies. As Grady told his credulous New York audience, "The relations of the Southern people with the negro are close and cordial." To that whopper he added, almost truculently, "The South has nothing for which to apologize."

Grady reserved his hottest zeal for promoting investment in southern industries. Inspired by his oratory, ensuing generations of leaders from Atlanta to the smallest hamlet would come to see a factory as the Holy Grail, their lone hope for deliverance from backwardness, exhaustion, and defeat. Grady preached that it was time for the South to stop sending its cotton to New England textile mills, stop sending its timber to Grand Rapids furniture factories—and start bringing the textile mills to the cotton fields, start building furniture factories and paper mills beside the pine forests, cigarette factories beside the tobacco fields, and steel mills on the seams of coal and iron ore. Grady approached a state of rapture when he pointed out that the South had produced 212,000 tons of iron in 1880, and just six years later it was producing *four times* as much. "Birmingham alone will produce more iron in 1889 than the entire South produced in 1887," he crowed, adding that it was time for the South to get busy exploiting its other abundant resources, its timber, granite, marble, phosphate, the many crops it could—must!—grow in addition to cotton and tobacco, sugar and rice. Looking out his office window at the bustling streets of downtown Birmingham, John could see Grady's hoped-for future already arriving just as surely as Thomas Nelson Page's yearned-for past was forever gone, and good riddance. A misfit like John must have felt trapped between two worlds, unwilling to go back to an imaginary past and equally unwilling to step into a mad mechanized future. This was a moment of revelation. He was beginning to understand that he was falling hopelessly—willingly, *happily*—out of sync with the spirit of his times. He was also beginning to believe it might be possible to live a rich life in such limbo: a life of the mind.

A year after Grady's breakout speech in New York, he gave a speech to a more skeptical White audience in Dallas in which he finally addressed the unavoidable question, the question of race. The New South, he assured his

Texas audience, would be built on an unshakable foundation: the continuing supremacy of White people at the expense of Blacks, who Grady painted with broad strokes as "simple, credulous, impulsive, easily led and too often easily bought." He told his audience that equal power was "a thing not to be considered" for one simple reason: "The white race is the superior race." As John could see, Grady's "New" South was not so new, after all.

John's law practice must have enjoyed at least some modest success because he moved his office into the new Watts Building, at the corner of Third Avenue and 20th Street, shortly after it opened in 1888. This was a prestigious address, an ornate four-story Second Empire–style commercial building equipped with electric lights, gas heat, and flush toilets. Maybe John bought one of the new electric fans to stir the sluggish summertime air in his office. The building's roster of tenants showed just how much Birmingham had diversified in a few short years. Doctors, lawyers, dentists, and insurance salesmen had offices in the building, along with music teachers, photographers, architects, and artists. There was a funeral parlor on the ground floor that contributed to a colorful bit of local lore. An iconic photograph shows a dozen horse-drawn carriages parked outside the Watts Building. Curiously, there are no people in any of the carriages because, according to legend, a funeral was in progress on the ground floor for Louise Wooster, one of the most prominent madams in Birmingham's thriving red light district, and local grandees wanted to show their respect without showing their faces.

John was a sociable young man, and he would have gotten to know some of his neighbors in the Watts Building. It's easy to imagine the owner of the photography studio down the hall passing John's open office door one day and, seeing that John didn't seem to be busy—John rarely seemed to be busy—popping into the office to slump in the visitor's chair and unload a burden. "I'm doomed!" I imagine him crying. Intrigued, John would have put down the book or newspaper he was reading and asked the distraught photographer what he meant. "I spend my days lugging around a hundred pounds of equipment," he replied, "a camera the size of a soap box, the heavy tripod, lenses, a darkroom tent with chemicals. And now this amateur named Eastman—a *bank clerk* at that—he comes out with this little handheld box camera that you feed with a roll of film made of this new stuff called celluloid. They even develop the film for you! Now any idiot with twenty-five bucks who doesn't know the first thing about chemistry or photography can become an artist. I'm finished!"

Such a dramatic diatribe would have amused John, but he had to admit the man had a point. The proliferating inventions—new kinds of cameras, paints, papers, pens, typewriters—were democratizing creativity. The number of patents had been doubling every year since the war, and technology was now making it possible for anyone to claim to be an artist.

On the ground floor of the Watts Building, there was a tobacconist's shop where John bought his chewing tobacco and newspapers and absorbed the local gossip. Here he might have overheard men debating the outcome of the recent presidential election, one man opining that the new president, Benjamin Harrison, may have been a damn Republican but at least he favored keeping the tariffs in place, which could only be good news for the local iron industry. Or maybe the men speculated about how much tickets would cost to the execution of Richard Hawes, the local man who had become the talk of the town when he murdered his wife and two daughters, drowning them in East Lake so he could run off with a woman from Mississippi. On a lighter note, the smokers in the crowd might have debated the merits of hand-rolled versus machine-made cigarettes, for up in Durham, North Carolina, an enterprising tycoon named Buck Duke had gotten rid of his immigrant Jewish workers, who could roll four cigarettes a minute by hand, and replaced them with machines that could roll hundreds per minute. This news surely delighted Henry W. Grady. His vision was becoming reality. Factories across the South were now spitting out everything from steel to textiles to soft drinks to cigarettes.

But John would have been aware that Grady's vision of the South's future was nearly as illusory as Thomas Nelson Page's fantastical portrait of its past. The industrializing South was playing a game of catch-up with the rest of the country—and not playing it very well. Illiteracy rates were falling nationwide but in the South, despite the strides of freedmen, they were still the nation's highest thanks to the refusal of tightfisted state legislatures to build public schools. The South's infant mortality rates were also the nation's highest. Cotton was still king, though it fetched lower and lower prices, and the White sharecroppers who fled farms and flocked to the new textile mills—including women and children as young as six—earned about half what their northern counterparts earned. The work force's low skill levels produced low-quality goods, notably in Birmingham, where cheap native labor turned inferior coal and inferior iron ore into cheap pig iron, which was used primarily in piping for new gas and water lines. The high-quality steel and iron were coming out of mills in the North and Midwest. When he looked down from his office window at the smoke-hazed streets of Birmingham, when he let his imagination roam across the South to all the ugly new red-brick mills, to the shabby worker housing huddled beside them, to the towns and cities growing like haphazard weeds with their smokestacks and traffic and tangles of overhead wires, John could see that Henry Grady had made a Faustian bargain.

Meanwhile, Louis Pasteur and other scientists, mostly in France and Germany, were making discoveries at a rate so striking it could fairly be called a revolution. Every day, it seemed to John, he read a newspaper article about the discovery of another microorganism that caused an infectious disease. The discoveries were coming in a torrent, and suddenly scientists understood the sources of typhoid, leprosy, malaria, tuberculosis, cholera, diphtheria, and tetanus. Soon gangrene, plague, botulism, and dysentery would be added to the list. This work proceeded on parallel tracks. While Robert Koch and other Germans focused on isolating pathogens, Pasteur and other Frenchmen concentrated on preventing and treating them through vaccines. This was the birth of a new branch of science called immunology.

John's interest in Germany's language, literature, and history would have made him take particular note of the work of the German scientists. Led by Koch, they were making great strides at obtaining pure cultures of microorganisms, a crucial step in finding a cure for any contagious disease. Koch experimented with nutrient media to grow organisms while other scientists figured out ways to fix and stain them, which made it possible to track their avenues of attack. At first Koch used gelatin as a medium, then switched to agar-agar. Others tried staining the organisms with carmine and fuchsin before settling on methyl violet. After overcoming initial resistance, Joseph Lister's antiseptic surgery methods were gaining wide acceptance, and he had developed an atomizer that infused operating rooms with a disinfecting mist of carbolic acid, covering the wound, the surgeons, and their clothing and instruments, leading to a sharp decline in deaths from hospital gangrene. Amazing, John thought. These men were almost like chefs experimenting with ingredients until they perfected a recipe, only their dishes—their vaccines and devices and procedures—were changing the course of human history. In John's quarter-century of life, medical practices had vaulted from the Middle Ages to the threshold of the modern world.

⁂

And how was life in Birmingham for John? Living alone in some boarding house, taking his meals with a revolving cast of strangers, listening to the nighttime booms from the nearby switchyards, and finding himself unable to get in step with the city's mad rush to get rich as quickly as possible? Was he lonely, or content to be alone? Did he have a girlfriend—or was he a regular at Louise Wooster's place? Impossible to know the answers, but there's solid evidence he felt no love for the place. After a visit to Virginia, he confessed to a cousin in Charlottesville, "Birmingham always makes me weary—I am always glad to get away and sorry when I have to come back." By the summer of 1890, he was finally ready to admit he was not cut out for the lawyer hustle. It was time for another change. He closed his law office in the Watts Building and, surely feeling like that most un-American thing—a failure—he boarded a Louisville & Nashville passenger train headed for Atlanta. He had accepted a job as an instructor of English and Latin at Moreland Park Military Academy, where he intended to find out if he shared his father's passion and gift for teaching.

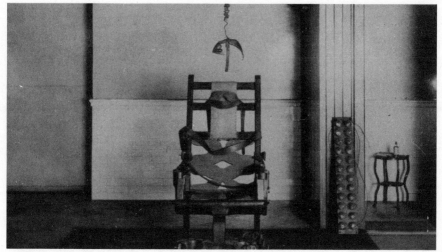

The first electric chair.

FAR WORSE THAN HANGING

On the train ride to Atlanta, John's dark mood would have been turned to deepest black by a story in all the newspapers. Months earlier, John had read enthusiastic articles praising the New York State Legislature for decreeing that criminals would no longer be executed by the barbaric method of hanging but would now be dispatched by the thoroughly modern method of sending thousands of volts of electricity coursing through their bodies. One headline stuck in John's mind: "Surer Than Rope" was the *New York Times*'s sanguine assessment of the electric chair being assembled inside the penitentiary at Sing Sing.

For the past two years, correspondents had been sending dispatches from the front lines of the so-called war of the currents, which pitted Thomas Edison and his favored direct current (DC) against George Westinghouse's alternating current (AC). It was a war that brought out all the best and worst impulses of the Gilded Age—ambition, greed, inventiveness, chicanery—and it was fought with take-no-prisoners ruthlessness because the stakes were so high: untold millions of dollars in electrification contracts with city governments across the country. The problem for Edison was that AC was more powerful and cheaper than DC, partly because it required fewer costly copper wires, and it was eating into a market Edison had created and treated as a virtual monopoly. Now Edison counterattacked, claiming that the high voltages required by AC, with its hundreds of sawing reversals per second, made it a threat to human life. He based the claim on animal tests he had conducted in his laboratory, and though he had opposed capital punishment in the past, he testified before the New York State Legislature that, yes, electricity could effect the quick and painless execution of humans—provided the electricity came from an AC current driven by a Westinghouse generator. Edison's claim may have been baldly self-serving, but it was soon backed by gruesome evidence that created a public panic. (Not until the 1970s would it be conclusively proven that alternating current is two-and-a-half to three times more lethal than direct current.)

At noon on an October day in 1888, a Western Union lineman named John Feeks scrambled up a power pole in his metal-cleated boots at the intersection of Centre and Chambers Streets in downtown Manhattan. The pole supported more than 250 wires, and Feeks's job that day was to cut away dead telegraph wires, a routine job since those wires, when live, were fed by low pressure that was not life-threatening. Feeks grabbed a dead wire in his bare right hand, unaware that it had crossed with an AC lighting wire several blocks away. A high-voltage charge surged from the AC wire into the dead telegraph wire, quickly traveled to the corner of

Centre and Chambers, then entered Feeks's right hand and exited through his left foot. Feeks stiffened, his right arm quivered.

As the lunch-hour crowd looked up from the sidewalk, Feeks's throat came to rest on the live wire. Flames jumped from his right hand and left foot. His body began smoking. Spectators screamed as blood poured from Feeks's right hand and throat, drizzling red rain on the horrified scattering crowd. The lineman was already dead. It was quick, but was it painless?

Two months later, a clerk in an Eighth Avenue dry goods store was getting ready to close for the day. As he picked up a metal display case from the sidewalk and carried it into the store, it touched a low-hanging, high-voltage arc lamp. The shopkeeper was dead when he hit the sidewalk.

Edison used these deaths by alternating current as ammunition in his war against Westinghouse, who was spending $100,000 of his own money—the same amount Edison had spent on finding the perfect bamboo for his filaments—paying lawyers to argue before the US Supreme Court that execution with electricity would be cruel and unusual punishment, in violation of the Eighth Amendment. Hanging, the lawyers seemed to imply, was less cruel and more usual. The Supreme Court took a pass and left the question to the states. Edison, meanwhile, was doing his best to keep people terrified that they could die simply from pressing an electric door buzzer or picking up a telephone whose wire had touched an AC line in one of the rats' nests of overhead wires that were becoming fixtures even in small towns. Burying the wires, he said, would merely turn metal manhole covers into instruments of death. In an essay titled "The Dangers of Electric Lighting" in the prestigious *North American Review*, Edison promoted "rigid rules" restricting electrical pressure—700 volts for DC, 200 for AC. "My personal desire," he concluded, "would be to prohibit the use of alternating currents. They are as unnecessary as they are dangerous."

After the state supreme court lifted an injunction, New York City ordered the removal of all AC wires above and beneath city streets. Edison had won the battle of New York, but the war of the currents was far from over.

Now, as John's train approached Atlanta, he saw that the *New York Times* was singing a different tune about the electric chair. Under the headline "Far Worse Than Hanging," there was a detailed report on the nation's first execution by electricity. William Kemmler, an illiterate drunkard from Buffalo, had been convicted of murdering his girlfriend, Tillie Ziegler, with a hatchet. In the predawn hours of August 6, Kemmler was led from his cell into a room in the basement of the state prison in Auburn, New York, where seventeen witnesses and a strange contraption awaited. It was an oaken chair outfitted with wires, metal plates, leather straps, and a metal skullcap. A throng of more than five hundred had gathered in the darkness outside, pressing against the stone prison's gates, climbing into trees and onto rooftops. There were about one hundred reporters in the crowd ready to dash across the street to the makeshift telegraph office to send dispatches around the world about the outcome of this historic experiment.

Kemmler remained calm as he was strapped into the chair, as the skullcap was placed on his shaved pate and electrodes were attached to his spine through holes cut in his clothing. When the day's first beams of sunshine slanted through a window and lit up Kemmler's face, he said a few words to the effect that he believed he was on his way to a better place. Then the warden, Charles Durston, said, "Goodbye, William," the signal for the executioner to pull the lever.

A forty-five-horsepower Westinghouse generator began sending 1,300 volts of alternating current through the wires into William Kemmler's body, which immediately went stiff as bronze. His eyes did not move. Spots bloomed on his skin, which turned an ashen color. The only part of his body that moved was his right index finger, which curled up so tightly that the nail penetrated the flesh of his palm, sending a trickle of blood onto the arm of the electric chair.

After seventeen seconds, Dr. Edward Charles Spitzka shook his head and said, "He is dead." The generator was switched off. The silence in the room gave way to a collective sigh from the witnesses. As men stood, groaning, moving for the exits, someone shouted, "Great God! He's alive!" A second man cried, "Turn on the current!" One of the reporters in the room said, "For God's sake, kill him and have it over." The reporter promptly crumpled to the floor in a dead faint.

Kemmler was now slumped in the chair, unconscious but breathing raggedly, still very much alive. Warden Durston had started to remove the skullcap but now refastened it. Dr. Spitzka barked an order: "Have the current turned on again—quick, no delay!" Durston sprang to the doorway and rang a bell twice. The executioner turned the generator back on.

Kemmler's slack body stiffened again. As the capillaries under his skin ruptured, he began to sweat blood. The flesh under the skullcap and around the electrodes on Kemmler's spine began to singe. The room filled with the stench of burning human flesh.

Some witnesses rushed from the room, slipping in their own vomit as they fled. Others sat bolted to their chairs. Finally, after about four minutes, Dr. Spitzka signaled for the current to be shut off. Now Kemmler's lifeless body was slumped in the chair. The witnesses who remained in the death chamber were as still and silent as stones. "Their minds were too busy to enable them to talk," according to the *New York Times*. "They all seemed to act as though they felt that they had taken part in a scene that would be told to the world as a public shame, as a legal crime."

John left the train feeling shaken and unclean, as though he, too, had just been witness to an appalling legal crime.

John might have taken one of the city's new electric trolleys from the train station to his new lodgings east of downtown. He ignored the passing scenery, unable to put down his newspaper. Many people were already calling for an end to executions by electricity, but Thomas Edison was not one of them. Approached by a reporter at his home in New Jersey, Edison said, "I have glanced over an account of Kemmler's death, and it was not pleasant reading." He went on: "One mistake, in my opinion, was in leaving everything to the doctors. With their great knowledge of nerves and nerve centers, they said the cap should be placed on top of the head and the shock given so as to affect the spinal column. Now, thirty or forty men have been killed by an electric current through their hands. Many of them died instantly. It is the water in the body that conducts the electricity. In the top of the head there is little water, and the current of electricity strikes the hard skull. In the hand there is a great deal of water, and the flesh is soft; here it is the best place to receive the shock. The better way is to place the hands in jars of water in which there is a little potash to eliminate all grease from the hands, and let the current be turned on there."

Jars of water. Potash. Grease. Current. As John stepped down off the trolley, he was convinced the Wizard of Menlo Park had turned into a monster.

The war of the currents had many fronts—legal, ethical, political, and, of course, financial. John might have been consoled that, amid all the battling for riches, there was a side skirmish that had nothing to do with money. It was etymological—that is, it involved the study of the origins of words, a field that had begun to fascinate John.

There was much lively debate in the newspapers over what to call this new method of executing human beings. Edison offered the somewhat clunky "ampermort," "dynamort," and "electromort." Someone suggested the slicker and more evocative "electricide." Someone else suggested the tongue twister "electrohanabia." One of Edison's lawyers posited that searchers for the *mot juste* should follow the lead of the French, who had adopted the family surname of Dr. Joseph-Ignace Guillotin to name the device that he promoted as more humane than beheading criminals by sword or ax. Taking the bait provided by Edison's lawyer, one headline writer came up with an eponymous coinage that must have delighted Edison: "Kemmler Westinghoused." In the end, the world would settle on the new locution "electrocution."

If this wordplay consoled John, the consolation would have been small compared to his horror over William Kemmler's death and Edison's heartless pronouncements. The accounts of the botched execution hardened John's inchoate misgivings about capital punishment into an iron question with only one answer: If it's wrong to murder a human being, how can it possibly be right to murder a murderer? As he took up his teaching duties in Atlanta, John realized there was now one more thing separating him from his money- and vengeance-hungry countrymen. That realization led to another. He told himself, with grim satisfaction, that he had been right not to jump on the bandwagon with the worshippers of technology. Progress was already beginning to reveal its dark side, and John had no doubt it was going to reveal much darker things in the years to come.

———

In moving from Birmingham to Atlanta, John traded one boomtown for another. Atlanta's population had doubled in the past ten years to 65,000, and it was now the largest city in Georgia, twice the size of Birmingham and growing even faster. It soon became apparent to John that Atlanta's brand of boosterism was even brassier than Birmingham's, with Henry W. Grady bloviating from his editorial pulpit at the *Constitution* and other civic boosters boasting that their city was too busy figuring out new ways to make money to be bothered with the petty racial nastiness that was swallowing other less progressive cities and towns across the South. Of course it wasn't true,

John could see, but he wouldn't have known it from reading the newspapers or attending a meeting of one of the dozens of civic clubs. And there was no denying that the Atlanta air was crackling with energy. Grady's dream, the Georgia Institute of Technology, was now reality. The city was also home to three Black colleges and a vibrant Black middle class. Typographers, machinists, and blacksmiths were organizing into labor unions. The place may not have been too busy to hate, but it was indeed busy.

It struck John that the citizens of Atlanta could make money out of absolutely anything, including sugar, water, cotton, wood, coal, empty land, even air. A new local soft drink called Coca-Cola was minting fortunes every day. While the Equitable Building was rising eight stories into the sky above downtown, real estate speculators, boosted by the city's new electric trolley system, were building residential developments farther and farther from the city center. One of the more ambitious developers had hired Frederick Law Olmsted of Central Park fame to lay out a new development called Druid Hills. It was the first time John heard the word "suburb."

There is no surviving record of John's year at Morehead Military Academy. What is known is that A. F. Moreland sold the land to the school's founder on the condition that girls be allowed to attend. Moreland's two daughters and two other girls were admitted, a "highly unusual" arrangement at that time, according to a local historian—one that delighted John because he believed that everyone was entitled to an education, regardless of gender, race, or age. If he got nothing else from his year at Morehead Military Academy, he got the satisfaction of taking part in a noble experiment. As a bonus, he learned that he did indeed share his father's passion and gift for teaching.

Now, after a decade of drift, John's life finally began to come into focus. Some money must have come his way—possibly a grant, possibly a small inheritance like the one that had financed Charles's grand tour of Europe in 1851—for John now arranged to spend a year studying at the University of Berlin. Such European sojourns were becoming fashionable for American intellectuals, academics, and artists, both accomplished and aspiring. John, squarely in the latter camp as his thirtieth birthday approached, knew only that he wanted to bury himself in a library that would put the one in Charlottesville to shame, wanted to perfect his already fluent German by attending lectures in history, economics, linguistics, and the emerging disciplines of political science and sociology.

Birmingham had taught John he was not cut out for the striving that consumed his countrymen, and his year in Atlanta had taught him he was fit for teaching. Now he needed to find out what he was meant to teach and, even more important, what he was meant to study. With his youth slipping away, it was time to get serious about pursuing a life of the mind.

Berlin in the 1890s.

EPIPHANIES IN BERLIN

After his purgatory years in Smithfield, Birmingham, and Atlanta, John must have felt like he had landed in heaven when he stepped off the train at the palatial Lehrter Bahnhof in Berlin. The train had carried him from Hanover at speeds in excess of fifty miles per hour, the fastest he had ever traveled, a blurry, thrilling experience.

German universities were considered the best in the world, and one in Berlin—then known as Friedrich-Wilhelms-Universität, later Humboldt Universität zu Berlin, but always simply the University of Berlin to John—was hands down the best of the best. Students from Europe and America flocked there, drawn as much by the city's pulsating life as by the university's vast research resources and progressive curriculum, its decorated faculty and guest lecturers and, above all, its system that combined research with teaching, the freedom to harvest new knowledge and disseminate it without the straitjacket of antiquated classical systems. Among the many Americans in the city that year were teams of university administrators sent to analyze various European university systems. They would conclude that Friedrich-Wilhelms's research-with-teaching model was the one to export to America. So in a sense John was present at the birth of the modern American university and its publish-or-perish mandate.

No less than the university's lecture halls and libraries, the coffee houses and beer halls in the academic quarter were vital to John's education. There, fueled by cigarettes, strong coffee, and stronger beer, students and teachers engaged in lively discussions about their chosen fields of study, about European politics, horse races, the latest lecture or theater opening, new inventions, and medical breakthroughs. Nietzsche was the rage. Marx was passé. There were socialists, communists, anarchists, and various hybrids from across the political spectrum, from arch-conservative mandarins to fire-breathing revolutionaries. The German socialists would have been a surprise to John. Unlike their American counterparts, they didn't push for the nationalization of industries and resources, and they rejected the American pursuit of a bogus and counterproductive individualism— the every-man-for-himself ethos John had seen on such lurid display in Birmingham and Atlanta. Instead, professors and students alike stressed that human beings were social animals, and they celebrated the institutions and traditions that shaped human society. They believed social welfare was the responsibility not of the individual but of society at large, which led to a curious conundrum. As chancellor, Otto von Bismarck had despised socialism—and its political mouthpiece, the Social Democratic party—so in a pre-emptive strike he had passed the socialistic Health Insurance Law, the *Krankenversicherungsgesetz*, the world's first mandatory health insurance plan. It was a huge success, with more than four million people already enrolled, and it had recently been expanded to include accident and disability insurance as well as pensions. John's socialist friends grumbled that the Iron Chancellor, of all people, had beaten them at their own game. Then they ordered another 7-pfennig beer and lit another cigarette. The air in Berlin's cafes and beer halls was even smokier than the air in Birmingham—and far more stimulating. Germans didn't grow morose or quarrelsome like Americans when they got drunk; Germans *sang* when they got drunk.

The city's streets were also part of John's awakening. Berlin's population had swelled to more than a million in the two decades since unification, and it was well on its way to becoming the most modern city in Europe. Yet it was still a city of extremes. Alongside the bohemian excess John enjoyed in the university quarter, there was evidence of strict military discipline—weekly parades on Unter den Linden, sometimes featuring Kaiser Wilhelm II himself, with even the fire brigades marching in rank and playing martial music. There was a strong police presence and a standing military of half a million men—while the US Army numbered just twenty-eight thousand. Along with the freedom and social experimentation, there were open expressions of distaste for Catholics and Jews. One of the most celebrated professors, the economist Adolf Wagner, was a candidate for the anti-Semitic, right-wing Christian Socialist Party. There were slums and luxurious homes, including the Kaiser's palace with massive statues on its roof, and the city was dotted with equestrian statues, ornate post offices, museums, and theaters. The center of the city looked like it had been built six months ago, its ruler-straight boulevards paved with asphalt, lit by dazzling lamps, and punctuated with newsstands and tall cylinders known as *Litfassäulen* that were plastered with posters and notices, magnets for crowds of kibitzers. The city's electric trolley system had been the first in the world, and a sophisticated underground sewer system pumped storm water and human waste to irrigation fields on the outskirts of the city. Magazine articles proclaimed that such infrastructure improvements, along

with laws promoting street cleaning and the prompt removal of animal carcasses, were doing as much as the new scientific breakthroughs to improve
public health. As the city expanded, enormous new factories were rising
on the outskirts, their corporate names blazing in the night sky: Siemens
& Halske, A.E.G., Borsig.

John might have encountered old timers who told him, with a mix of pride
and nostalgia, how much the city had changed in a few short years. They
missed the old days when there wasn't so much noise and bustle, but they had
to admit that some things had improved. Why, twenty years ago, they said,
human and animal waste ran so thick in the gutters that it was possible to
identify a Berliner by the smell of his clothes. No more. The city was now one
of the cleanest and most orderly in the world.

And so *alive*. Europe's first viaduct rail line—trains in the sky!—linked
the city's east and west ends. Ten thousand people had thronged to see
Buffalo Bill's Wild West show when it came to Berlin, which didn't surprise John given his familiarity with Karl May's popular books and his
understanding of the German fascination with the American West. John
fell in love with Schubert's symphonies, with Wagner's gargantuan operas.
The bright streets were crowded into the night with well-dressed couples,
the women's skirts brushing the pavements and their hats rising high atop
their heads, the men sporting elaborately sculpted facial hair—moustaches,
sideburns, mutton chops—along with canes, gloves, and silk ties. These
handsome couples might have been on their way to see the latest operetta at
the Apollo Theater, or to bask in the electric lights in Café Bauer, or simply
out on the town to see and be seen. Yes, John was learning, the Germans
were social animals.

Unlike some of his more dissolute fellow students, John didn't let the city's
seductions keep him out of the university's classrooms, lecture halls, and

libraries. In the baroque palace at Unter den Linden 6, in its dozens of lecture halls equipped with electric lights and central heat, he drank in the latest scholarship in economics, history, political science, and linguistics. It was this last discipline that would fire his imagination and give his life a sense of direction and purpose.

His major discovery was philology, also known as comparative linguistics, which was producing a rich body of scholarship, much of it emanating from Germany. It was a loose, wide-open field with room for studies of etymology, phonetics, alphabets, spelling, handwriting, shorthand, and dictionaries as they evolved in dozens of cross-pollenating languages over dozens of centuries. This was when John became acquainted with the work of the German philologists Jacob Grimm, Franz Bopp, G. H. Balg, and Hermann Paul, as well as the Englishmen Henry Sweet and A. J. Ellis and the Scot Alexander Melville Bell, father of the inventor of the telephone. While their work was widely praised, one dissent came from Friedrich Nietzsche, who at the age of twenty-four had been named a professor of classical philology at the University of Basel and went on to deride his German colleagues for being inadequately versed in Greek and Roman antiquity. Worse, he charged, the field of philology was being overrun by men who had lost their way in abstraction and minutiae, men he called "windbags and triflers, hairsplitters and screech owls."

This was also most likely when John discovered *American Journal of Philology*, a quarterly founded in 1880 at the Johns Hopkins University in Baltimore by a Latin and Greek scholar with the unlikely name of Basil Gildersleeve, another American who had studied in Berlin, a former Confederate soldier who remained an unapologetic believer in the Lost Cause. In its decade of existence the journal had become a prestigious megaphone for scholarly writing, and John decided the way to get on the map would be to get published in its pages. But what to write about?

The key came from Henry Sweet and G. H. Balg, who had both written on a subject that was obscure outside the academy but something of a hot topic inside it: the evolution of English diphthongs. This was when the Danish linguist Otto Jespersen, a contemporary of John's, was trying to parse what he would eventually dub the Great Vowel Shift, the melding of vowels into new sounds that would mark the transition from Chaucer's Middle English to Shakespeare's Modern English. With his fluency in German, English, French, Latin, and Greek, John was equipped to tackle even the densest texts—and philologists frequently write in a language so unintelligible to the uninitiated that it borders on the screeching of owls, as Nietzsche had charged. John's grasp of German, in particular, positioned him to explore how the Indo-European Germanic languages had splintered and produced a spongy dialect known as English, which freely absorbed bits of everything from French to Latin, Greek, and homegrown slang. If John admired the elasticity of English, he positively adored the predictability of German, which is what we would now call a what-you-see-is-what-you-get language, a purely phonetic construct in which every letter is sounded and the pronunciation of words is precise and consistent. There are no superfluous or unvoiced letters. There is no confusion over how to pronounce such English words as *through, thorough, tough, thought, trough, thou*. In German, the joint in the human leg is a *knie*, pronounced k-NEE. John had discovered what he was meant to study—the history and evolution of words, their pronunciation, and spelling—and as a result of this discovery his life at last began to come into focus.

In *Humboldt and the Modern German University*, the historian Johan Östling wrote: "This was a time of expansion and dynamism in many areas of society; it was a time when faith in the future and ambitious dreams were tied to science and scholarship. But it was also a time of growing discontent and increasing bewilderment."

John found himself at the intersection where faith in the future collided with discontent and bewilderment. This collision allowed him to see the similarities between Germany's national mission—the struggle to find its footing as a unified nation—and his own personal mission. As Östling said of German scholars: "Within a number of the human sciences—Germanic philology, sociology, folklore studies, linguistics, history—a basic idealist stance was coupled to a mission of defining what constituted a common German identity. Under pressure from technological, economic and scientific advances, many humanists claimed that this was where they had an essential national task."

John, no stranger to discontent with technological advances, realized that this was where he had an essential *personal* task. He needed to decide where to set up his academic shop. Would he pursue scholarship that grew from and fed into the widespread faith in the future? Or would he take the opposite route, burrowing into the past, into subjects that were of little use to the technocrats and scientists and engineers who were coming to dominate the modern world—but, for that very reason, subjects that were all the more alluring to a man with deep misgivings about that hurtling world? Yes, John realized in Berlin, the study of philology could be his harbor and his fortress, his way into the life of the mind that he had yearned to pursue since boyhood. The Misfit had found his perfect fit.

Among the Americans in Berlin at that time were two men on opposite ends of the road to fame. Mark Twain, adored by the Germans, was in town with his family reveling in the life of the international literary celebrity—attending lectures and banquets, breakfasting with duchesses, dining with diplomats, granting interviews, looking after his business affairs, and even managing to do a little writing. Twain found much to admire in Berlin and its people. In one of the letters written during his European tour and published in numerous American newspapers, he marveled at the order and cleanliness of Berlin, the wide streets "as straight as a ray of light," the courteous police, the abundance of newspapers, the lamps of darting cabs, which he likened to "the rush and confusion and sparkle of an invasion of fireflies." He seemed to have only one quibble: "I don't believe there is anything in the whole earth that you can't learn in Berlin except the German language."

The letter from Berlin ends with an account of an elaborate celebration to honor the seventieth birthdays of two intellectual titans—the physician and polymath Rudolf Virchow and the physicist and physician Hermann von Helmholtz. The event attracted a raucous crowd of 4,000, including more than 1,000 students, and it's possible, even likely, that John was among them. It's doubtful he would have missed the chance to see the immortal Mark Twain, whose novel *The Gilded Age* had helped spur his intellectual awakening. Twain was impossible to miss. He was seated at the table with the two guests of honor, dressed in his trademark white suit, his hair and bushy moustache looking like rust turning to cotton. He appeared to enjoy the boisterous toasts and singing and speechifying—he called it "a stupendous beehive"—and it culminated with the arrival of the revered classicist Theodor Mommsen: "Then there was an excited whisper at our table—'MOMMSEN!' and the whole house rose. Rose and shouted and stamped and clapped, and banged the beer mugs. Just simply a storm! Then the little man with his long hair and Emersonian face edged his way past us and took his seat. I could have touched him with my hand—Mommsen!— think of it!"

John, standing nearby, was surely thinking, *I could have touched him with my hand—Twain!—think of it!*

Also in Berlin at that time and just setting out on the road to fame was an unknown American graduate student named W. E. B. Du Bois. After graduating from Fisk University in Nashville and earning a master's degree from Harvard, Du Bois had come to Berlin on a grant, hoping to complete his doctorate in history and, like John, soon discovering that much of his education would take place outside the classroom. Du Bois, an articulate, dapper, light-skinned Black man, dated several German women, even came close to a marriage proposal with one—an unthinkable and potentially lethal breach of social norms in his native country that barely merited notice in Germany. To an American Black man, the absence of an uproar came as a shock. "This is the land," he would write in his autobiography, "where I first met white folk who treated me as a human being."

A prime influence on Du Bois during his two-year stint in Berlin was the economic historian Gustav von Schmoller, who rejected the claims of classical economists that social progress was the product of time-less natural laws and unfettered individualism. Along with the German anthropologist Franz Boas, Schmoller also rejected any correspondence between race and mental aptitude. These ideas, which ran counter to everything Du Bois had absorbed in America, were immensely attractive to him, and they helped set him on the road to his career as a leading Black intellectual. Under the influence of Schmoller and his own personal experiences, Du Bois's thinking about race became more nuanced in Germany. He moved beyond a harsh and simplistic chiaroscuro—a Black world separated from a White world by an inviolable color line—and came to embrace a worldview that could accommodate complex shades of gray. "(In Germany)," he wrote later, "my whole attitude toward the world and toward white people began to change." That's not to say that there was no racism in Germany or that the treatment he received there led him to embrace White people as brothers; rather, the early stirrings of Jim Crow in the South and the racism he'd encountered in Tennessee and Boston were now seen as universal facts of American life, not universal facts of human life. At the University of Berlin, Du Bois had an epiphany of his own: he came to see that his mission was to reveal the truth about American racism not through polemics but through rigorous scholarship and science. "The Negro problem," he wrote in his autobiography, "was in my mind a matter of systematic investigation and intelligent understanding . . .

The ultimate evil was stupidity. The cure for it was knowledge based on scientific investigation."

The lessons he learned in Germany would echo throughout his long career. In Schmoller's scholarship on German class conflict, Du Bois saw a vivid parallel to his abiding subject, American race conflict. This link was revealed in his final research project for Schmoller, a systematic analysis of indebtedness among tenant farmers in the American South. Historians and biographers have noted Du Bois's other borrowings from German scholarship and culture. Nietzche's *Übermensch*—a superman willing to risk all to enhance humanity, someone grounded in life in this world and not distracted by preparations for some mythical afterlife—helped give birth to Du Bois's idea of the Talented Tenth, the educated elite among Black Americans who, he believed, were responsible for leading their race out of the wilderness. Lines from Faust that John would have known by heart—"Two souls, alas, reside within my breast / And each withdraws from, and repels, its brother"—inspired the title and were a central argument of Du Bois's most celebrated work. There's a direct line from Goethe's two souls to these words by Du Bois:

> It is a peculiar sensation, this double consciousness, this sense of always looking at one's self through the eyes of others, of measuring one's soul by the tape of a world that looks on in amused contempt and pity. One ever feels his twoness,—an American, a Negro; two souls, two thoughts, two unreconciled strivings; two warring ideals in one dark body, whose dogged strength alone keeps it from being torn asunder.

A decade after his departure from Berlin, Du Bois produced his German-inflected masterpiece, *The Souls of Black Folk*. The first noun in the title is, in homage to Goethe, plural. The singular *Folk* is also borrowed from the German—*Volk* is not a collection of individuals, but a unified people. Du Bois would spend the rest of his long career feeding off his epiphany in Berlin.

Du Bois, John, and the thousands of other Americans who studied at universities in Germany, France, and Great Britain in the late nineteenth century were transformed by their time abroad. As the historian Richard White put it: "They returned to the United States with a wider sense of the world and new vocabularies for talking about events in their own country."

Those events were increasingly violent and bloody. The country they returned to was not the Gay Nineties of legend but a land riven by the very conflicts of race and class they had studied from afar in Europe. Those conflicts, fueled by widening economic and racial inequality, were playing out in the factories and the streets and the farms, and they would have been hard to ignore even for a man like John, whose top priority was to secure a snug university berth that would allow him to pursue his new passion.

These conflicts were impossible for a Black person to ignore. As his boat from Southampton neared New York, Du Bois felt his euphoria giving way to a sense of dread. "As a student in Germany . . ." he wrote, "I dreamed, I loved and wandered and sang and then after two years, I dropped suddenly back into Nigger hating America." John dropped along with him, and he soon realized that the White South was busily refining two new ways to vent its oldest hatred: the Jim Crow law and the lynching bee.

Ida B. Wells.

SOUTHERN HORRORS

John's dream of securing a berth on a university faculty did not come true—yet. He surely applied for a job at the University of Georgia, no doubt with a good word from his venerable father, probably at Randolph-Macon and William & Mary, possibly at the University of Virginia as well. But no one was hiring a candidate whose résumé boasted just one year of teaching experience, a bachelor's degree, a law degree, and a year abroad at a prestigious university. No matter. John had an idea for his first scholarly article, a credential he hoped would put him on the map, and he could do the research and writing just about anywhere. He wound up doing it in Petersburg, Virginia, where he took a fallback job teaching

Latin and Greek at Southern Female College. The school, in a curious coincidence, had advertised in the Randolph-Macon catalogue during John's senior year, boasting of "a high grade of scholarship" at an institution that was "free from debt" and whose prospects were "never more encouraging."

If that sounded like an adman's overreach, John didn't care. His time in Petersburg was different from his years in Atlanta and Birmingham. He was no longer drifting. Now he dove into the notes he had amassed in Berlin, set about dissecting them, trying to figure out how to stitch their parts into a coherent, wholly original idea. It was an act of synthesis, not unlike a surgical procedure, and it soon produced these opening lines:

> In a paper on the 'The i-Sound in English' (Am. J. Phil. vol. VI, p. 13), Dr. Balg says: "Concerning the nature of the diphthongization of *i* into *ai*, it must be remembered that the first element of the diphthong does, or originally did, not have the sound of *a* (= *a* in *far* or *man*) but that of close *e* (= *a* in *name*), which afterward became open *e* (= *a* in *man*, or nearly so), and is now often heard as *a* in *far*."

Feeling disoriented? It gets better. John's opening continues:

> I think, however, that it will be agreed that the first element of the Modern English diphthong, as heard in America, lies between the *a* in *far* and the *a* in *man*, and corresponds to Sweet's low-mixed-wide vowel; that is, American *i* is about equivalent to Mod. Ger. *ei*.
>
> Just what the pronunciation of this English diphthong maybe, it is not as easy to ascertain as one might think . . .

What *is* this? This is linguistics, and John had taken his first step along its twisting pathways through thickets of Old English and Modern German, pronunciations and diphthongizations, closed and open and low-mixed-wide vowels. John may not have known it yet, but with these lines he had begun to write his ticket to that cherished berth on a university faculty.

———

As John settled into a rhythm of teaching and working on his article in Petersburg, he could not escape news from the wider world. The ground was shifting under his feet. As labor unrest spread across the country, a potentially explosive fight between capitalists and unionized labor was brewing at Andrew Carnegie's Homestead steel mill six miles upriver from Pittsburgh. Determined to break the union, Carnegie had brought in Henry Clay Frick, a fellow millionaire and anti-union man, to head the company's contract negotiations. Frick made an unappetizing offer: work twelve-hour days seven days a week for a wage tied not to the company's (rising) profits but to the (declining) price of steel. The union, as Frick had hoped, rejected the offer. He promptly locked down the heavily fortified mill, known to the workers as "Fort Frick," and brought in Pinkertons to secure it. This led to bloody gun battles that left seventeen dead and dozens wounded. But Frick succeeded at getting Black and White scab workers into the mill and resuming limited production. At the peak of the strike, a Lithuanian anarchist with no union affiliation burst into Frick's office and shot him twice in the neck, then stabbed him four times. Frick declined to die. A week later he was back at his desk as public sentiment swung against the union and its violent tactics. Thousands of state militiamen, members of the new National Guard, were sent in by Carnegie-financed governor Robert Pattison to restore order. The strike was broken. Once again, big money had won.

Though John was not known to have strong pro-union sentiments, he surely would have sided with the steelworkers over ruthless tycoons like Carnegie and Frick and been receptive to the notion, put forward by the anti-monopolist and leading public intellectual Henry George, that America was sinking from democracy toward plutocracy. As the Homestead riot vividly illustrated, money was increasingly controlling the nation's affairs, and it was controlled by an ever-smaller slice of the populace. Bad trends all around, as John saw it. Or, as George put it: "Most of us—99% at least—must pay the other 1% by week or month or quarter for the privilege of staying here and working like slaves."

The Homestead riot was just one of hundreds of incidents in which National Guard units were sent in to quell worker unrest during the decade. But the unrest was not confined to factories in urban centers. The agricultural economy was mired in an ongoing recession, especially in the South, where cotton was fetching historically low prices. From the cotton-growing South to the grain-growing Midwest to the citrus-growing West Coast, dissatisfaction fed the rise of the Farmers' Alliance, a precursor to the Populist Party. The alliance appealed to the rural populace by providing an immaculately loathsome enemy: the money men of the North—Wall Street—and the railroads and monopolies and tariffs that made them rich. More than 100,000 men in the South, mostly sharecroppers and tenant farmers, joined the Farmers' Alliance, drawn by the words of its southern leader, Charles Macune, whose goal was "to organize the cotton belt of America so that the whole world of cotton raisers might be unified for self-protection." To this end Macune proposed a plan that would provide low-cost credit to farmers by building government-owned commodity warehouses where crops could be stored until they fetched the best prices. The idea thrilled debt-burdened tenant farmers in the South.

However, this plan terrified landowners and Democrats and that peculiar southern invention, the supply merchant. This last was a fixture at every southern crossroads, a hybrid banker-shopkeeper who was able to secure enough northern capital to supply destitute farmers with guano and phosphate fertilizers, mules, implements, food, and other necessities on credit that carried crushing interest rates, sometimes as high as 80 percent.

Thus the "time price" of a mule was many times the actual worth of a mule. This was, in the words of W. J. Cash, "one of the worst systems ever developed" because it made a handful of men rich by locking poor farmers in eternal debt while, for good measure, ensuring the exhaustion of the southern soil.

The alliance had a powerful ally in Tom Watson, a Georgian who'd been elected to Congress as a Democrat, then switched to the nascent Populist Party. John saw much to admire in Watson, who sought to "allay the passions and prejudices of race conflict" by uniting Black and White farmers against their shared enemy. Like many southern politicians before and since, Watson had a way with words. Here's how he portrayed the sharecropper's plight: "By the time he pays for that mule, and the store account, and the guano, he has not enough money left to buy a bottle of laudanum, and not enough cotton to stuff his old lady's ear." Watson also opposed lynching and convict leasing, a system inaugurated in Mississippi shortly after the war by which states leased their convicts to private businessmen, who clothed, housed, and fed the prisoners, then pocketed the profits from their labor in coal mines, saw mills, turpentine stills, and cotton fields—"under conditions," the historian David M. Oshinsky wrote, "far worse than anything they had ever experienced as slaves." As far as many White southerners were concerned, this was a signal virtue of convict leasing: it was actually worse than slavery. Unlike slaves, who were valued property, the convicts were a burden worth nothing to anybody except the businessmen who grew rich off their forced labor and the states that profited from turning a major expense into a robust revenue stream. If one Black convict died—and they were almost always Black—another was there to take his place. And so they died at ten times the rate of convicts in non-lease states from gunshot wounds, disease, torture, and overwork.

To John's surprise, there was no outcry from the North against lynching or convict leasing. Quite the opposite. The national magazines he was able to find in the college library—*The North American Review, Harper's*

Weekly, The Atlantic Monthly—had once been full of calls for the abolition of slavery and the equal treatment of freedmen; now they were publishing articles that praised White southerners for reasserting their supremacy in the wake of Reconstruction's collapse. The North, John could see, was following the South's shift to the right, all in the name of reconciliation, all at the expense of Black people.

A trained lawyer like John would have followed the machinations of the US Supreme Court, much as some men follow the progress of a favorite sports team. If John had a favorite player, it was surely Justice John Marshall Harlan of Kentucky, known as "the Great Dissenter," a lone voice of reason on a court that in the last quarter of the nineteenth century was, like the presidency, dominated by conservative mediocrities who favored business, resisted federal intervention in states' affairs, upheld the Chinese Exclusion Act, blocked antitrust actions, and struck down the income tax. The court's rulings were almost invariably good news for the businessman and/or bad news for Black people. Having ruled in 1877 that states could not prohibit the separation of races on public conveyances, the court went a step further in 1890 and ruled that states could *require* it. Emboldened, Louisiana and Mississippi promptly passed laws requiring separate cars for Blacks and Whites on intrastate railroads and streetcar lines—two of the early separate-but-equal Jim Crow laws and soon to be the basis for one of the most momentous decisions in the court's history. Southern legislatures now moved to disenfranchise Black voters through poll taxes, literacy tests, and a bit of chicanery known as the grandfather clause, which allowed the grandsons of voters—that is, poor, illiterate White men—to vote even if they couldn't pay the poll tax or pass the literacy test. Of course, very few Blacks had a grandfather who had ever voted. By holding Blacks and Whites to the same standards, southern legislatures were cleverly adhering to the letter of the postwar constitutional amendments while brazenly ignoring their spirit. The hellhounds, to John's dismay, were finally off the leash.

John did see one reason for hope: Ida B. Wells was back in the news, and she was no longer teaching school or tilting at windmills. After her victory against the Chesapeake & Ohio Railroad was overturned on appeal by the Tennessee Supreme Court, Wells, undaunted, had set up as a journalist based in Memphis and dedicated herself to chronicling the wave of lynching spreading across the South, fueled by proliferating Jim Crow laws and the unchecked fury of White supremacists.

Wells's anti-lynching crusade had deeply personal roots. It grew out of an innocent game of marbles between a mixed group of Black and White boys outside People's Grocery Store in Memphis, which led to a dispute that soon drew in adults and ended with the whipping of one of the Black boys. Later, armed White men descended on the Black-owned store and were met by armed Black men who opened fire, wounding three of the attackers. They retreated. As rumors of a Black uprising spread through the city, a White mob returned to the store. Finding it abandoned, they looted it, terrorized the neighborhood, and hustled more than thirty Black people to the city jail. Days later, three of the prisoners—including Thomas Moss, a proprietor of People's Grocery Store and a close friend of Wells's—were spirited from the jail and shot dead. Then the mob mutilated their corpses.

Before the Memphis campaign of terror, Wells had tended to see lynching as an abhorrent but tolerable response to the rapes of White women by Black men, which was supposedly becoming so widespread that *Harper's Weekly* dubbed it "the new Negro crime." But Wells was nagged by doubts. Her friend Tommie Moss had not even been present during the shootout in his store, and he certainly had not been accused of rape. Wells began to suspect a simpler and darker truth: Moss's crime was that he had built a successful business that competed with a White-owned business across the street. Lynching, Wells now began to suspect, had little to do with protecting the delicate flower of White womanhood; it was, as she would write in her autobiography, something far more sinister: "an excuse to get rid of Negroes who were acquiring wealth and property and thus keep the race terrorized and 'the nigger down.'"

But the journalist in Wells was not satisfied with mere speculation, so she set about investigating every lynching she heard about. The results appeared in the *New York Age* in the summer of 1892, then were collected in pamphlet form and published, with an introduction by Frederick Douglass, shortly after John's return from Berlin.

Reading *Southern Horrors: Lynch Law in All Its Phases* would have filled John with revulsion—and a creeping sense of shame. Wells didn't merely dismiss White southerners' rationale for lynching as "the same old racket—the new alarm about raping white women." She also flung a dangerous dart by pointing out the undeniable fact that many interracial sexual liaisons were consensual: "White men lynch the offending Afro American, not because he is a despoiler of virtue, but because he succumbs to the smiles of white women." Wells had already leveled this charge a year earlier in an unsigned editorial in her newspaper, the *Memphis Free Speech and Headlight*, adding a freighted warning: "Nobody in this section of the country believes the threadbare lie that Negroes rape white women. If Southern men are not careful, they will over reach themselves and public sentiment will have a reaction; a conclusion will be reached which will then be very damaging to the moral reputation of their women."

This had so outraged White Memphis that a mob stormed the *Free Speech* offices—Wells, luckily, was out of town at the time—and shut the paper down permanently. This, it turned out, was a dress rehearsal for a similar, but far bloodier, assault by a White mob on a Black-owned newspaper in Wilmington, North Carolina, six years later.

Wells suggested several ways for Blacks to respond to the wave of violence. First: "a Winchester rifle should have a place of honor in every black home." Second was to leave the South, as thousands of Black Memphians, including Wells, did in the aftermath of the triple lynching. And third was to boycott streetcars and trains in Memphis and other jurisdictions that imposed Jim Crow separation of the races—a protest that presaged the Montgomery bus boycott and the ensuing civil rights movement by more than half a century.

Wells, like Du Bois, believed that the cure for stupidity and ignorance was knowledge based on scientific investigation. And so in *Southern Horrors* she laid out the hard numbers produced by her legwork: "the dark and bloody record of the South shows 728 Afro-Americans lynched during the past 8 years . . . (and) only *one-third* of the 728 victims to mobs have been *charged* with rape." (Italics hers.) So much for the "rape myth." She added that no fewer than "one hundred and fifty have been known to have met violent death at the hands of cruel bloodthirsty mobs during the past nine months."

John's sense of shame came from this stinging rebuke by Wells: "The men and women in the South who disapprove of lynching and remain silent on the perpetration of such outrages are *particeps criminis*, accomplices, accessories before and after the fact, equally guilty with the actual law-breakers."

John felt not only shamed, but paralyzed. Was it really true that if a man opposed to lynching did nothing to stop the practice, he was as guilty as the man who tied the noose and lit the bonfire? And what could a single man do to stop an armed White mob in the grip of bloodlust? John would wrestle with these questions for the rest of his life.

———

As John fleshed out his article on diphthongs, he drew on the works of dozens of scholars he had discovered in Berlin. The two he mentioned in his opening paragraphs, Sweet and Balg, were particularly powerful influences. After steeping himself in Anglo-Saxon, Old English, and Old Icelandic, Henry Sweet left home in London while still a teenager to study Germanic and Comparative Philology at the University of Heidelberg. Then, barely out of his teens, he began writing a vast dictionary of Old English. *A twenty-year-old compiling a dictionary of a dead language!* Such ambition would have staggered John. I believe it also planted a seed.

Sweet's first paper was titled "The History of *Th* in English"—an inspiration for the title of the article John had begun to write. Sweet went on to study phonetics under Alexander Melville Bell, who had developed a system called Visible Speech, a set of graphic symbols that depict the position of the organs of speech—tongue, lips, throat—as they articulate sounds. Bell had devised his system as an aid to help deaf people learn to speak, but it revolutionized the study of phonetics by giving it the foundation of a hard science. Sweet was also drawn to A. J. Ellis, who had produced the first large-scale history of English dialects and invented an intricate system of phonetic notation. Sweet, who would soon produce his own *Handbook on Phonetics* and a system of shorthand writing, called Ellis "the pioneer of scientific phonetics in England." John's eyes, already opened to the rich, if obscure, intricacies of philology, now began to see the possibilities of phonetics, which was built on the alluring premise that the way words are written should flow from the way they are spoken. But, as John had already discovered, it's no simple matter to determine exactly how words are spoken. *Just what the pronunciation of this English diphthong may be, it is not as easy to ascertain as one might think* . . . And it's equally difficult to ascertain how that pronunciation should be rendered in writing. John had stumbled onto an open, fertile field.

Henry Sweet was a prickly personality, a perfectionist, a lone wolf who did not suffer fools gladly and who, in the words of one admirer, exhibited a "Satanic contempt for all academic dignitaries and persons in general who thought more of Greek than of phonetics." This admirer called Sweet "a man of genius with a seriously underrated subject."

The admirer was George Bernard Shaw, the Irish playwright and future Nobel laureate who, in a few years, would use his interest in phonetics and spelling reform—along with his admiration for Henry Sweet—to fashion the central character of one of his most popular plays, *Pygmalion*. The protagonist, Henry Higgins, is a professor of phonetics who makes a bet in the opening act that he would need just six months to rid the flower girl Eliza Doolittle of her "kerbstone" Cockney accent and pass her off as a duchess. "Pygmalion Higgins is not a portrait of Sweet," Shaw wrote in an introduction to the play. "Still, as will be seen, there are touches of Sweet in the play." To wit: Higgins makes use of Bell's Visible Speech in his work, and in Shaw's words he's "a middle-aged bully . . . but he is so entirely frank and void of malice that he remains likable even in his most unreasonable moments." Higgins has difficulties in social settings, lacks empathy, jiggles coins in his pockets, says whatever pops into his mind, and dismisses all women as "idiots" and Eliza as a "bilious pigeon." But he doesn't *mean* to be monstrous. This is simply the way he is. One scholar has gone so far as to suggest that Higgins—and, by extension, Sweet—exhibited the classic symptoms of a form of high-functioning autism that wasn't identified until 1944 and that we know today as Asperger's Syndrome. It's a plausible theory.

John's other influence was G. H. Balg, a German linguist who'd been educated at Freiburg and Heidelberg and then emigrated to America, where he studied at the University of Wisconsin before settling in the hamlet of Mayville, midway between Madison and Milwaukee, home to many German and Swiss immigrants. In this unpromising backwater, Balg taught Latin and German at the local high school and in his spare time, with minimal resources, set about producing works of astonishing erudition.

Balg had just come out with a new version of the first Germanic Bible, translated from the Greek in the fourth century by Wulfila, bishop of the Goths, who also invented the Gothic alphabet. Balg edited Wulfila's Bible and added an introduction, a guide to syntax, and a glossary. Balg, in keeping with the preachings of Sweet and Ellis, dropped unnecessary letters and spelled words phonetically—*becum, thuro, sumtimes, filology, typografical,* and *difthongs.*

Even more impressive to John than Balg's phonetic spelling and wide-ranging scholarship was his ability to compile a Bible and a 638-page glossary under conditions that, in Balg's telling, included "the deplorabl fact that in its preparation I hav had no personal help whatsoever." John thought back to Berlin, where Schmoller and Wagner and the other professors had squads of graduate students at their disposal, eager to assist with research, cataloging, correspondence, and other chores. As for his research sources, Balg added, "I found too soon that that my library was insufficient . . . nor was ther any other library near me that might hav been consulted. In cases of absolute necessity I applied to the University of Ann Arbor, Mich., and, upon the kind endorsement of Prof. Wm. Allen of the University of Wisconsin, my requests wer in every possibl case kindly and promptly complied with by its librarian, Prof. R.C. Davis. Furthermore, several scientific works hav appeared during the preparation of my book, sum of which I hav not seen at all, while others reacht me comparatively late."

John made a vow. If Balg could flourish in a remote backwater like Mayville without assistants or colleagues, far from a suitable library or any archives, then, John told himself, he could flourish in the far less brackish backwater of Petersburg, Virginia, where he had access to his Berlin notes and to superb libraries at Charlottesville and Washington, DC. And that's what he did. Given the long lead time of scholarly journals, John must have finished his article on diphthongs by the time his year at Southern Female College came to an end because the article was accepted by Basil Gildersleeve for publication in the spring 1894 issue of *American Journal of Philology*. This was the credential John's résumé had been lacking. He reapplied for a job at the University of Georgia, and this time he was hired as an instructor of English. It was a humble beginning, but John was finally on his way. As it happened, Sylvanus was hired at the same time as a professor of law. If Charles had pulled levers behind the scenes to promote the hiring of his sons, which was how things worked in the Gilded Age, it proved to be one of the last things he did.

The World's Columbian Exposition in Chicago.

A DEATH IN THE FAMILY

On April 27, 1893, his sixty-seventh birthday, Charles Morris attended a speakers' contest held outdoors on the Athens campus. The day was unseasonably chilly. In addition to occasional visits from the "blue devils," Charles had been a lifelong sufferer of neuralgia, a painful nerve disorder, and he had always been highly sensitive to cold weather. After the speakers' contest he went home and, feeling tired, took to bed. Within a week he contracted pneumonia, and on the morning of May 3, he died at home.

The eulogies that poured forth were as overwrought as the Gilded Age itself. A local historian named Augustus Longstreet Hull extolled Charles as "a gentleman of the old school, a Virginian of Virginians, courteous and brave." Then Hull took it up a notch: "Major Morris was a man of broad culture . . . He had traveled abroad and mingled with men and rubbed against the world, and he was free from the dogmatism which is so apt to clothe the lifelong teacher. Major Morris professed to be a typical 'old fogy,' and clung to the manners and traditions of the *ante-bellum* days with a tenacity that never relaxed. He was a declared foe of 'science' so-called, and all its pretensions. He planted by the moon, and insisted that wheat could turn to 'cheat' and tobacco degenerate into mullein. Plain and unaffected in manner, but always a gentleman, sincere and tender-hearted, he was greatly beloved by all his students and esteemed by all who knew him."

When you cut through the gas, this is actually a revealing snapshot. It tells us that Charles was a proud member of the old school who clung to the manners and traditions of the prewar years, which is surely shorthand for saying that he was not inclined to apologize for having owned slaves or having served in the Confederate Army, and that he embraced the myth of the Lost Cause. Hull's placing the word "science" between quotation marks reveals that Charles took a dim view of the technical and medical breakthroughs shaping the modern world. When he was running Taylor's Creek, he had planted by the moon—folk wisdom that claims it's best to plant corn, pole beans, sweet peas, and other above-ground flowering crops when the moon is full. Some people swear by it; others think it's hokum. Hull may have been hyperventilating when he wrote his eulogy, but there is an undeniable ring of truth to his closing claim that Charles was beloved by his students.

Proof of this came the year after his death, when the student yearbook, *Pandora*, was dedicated to Charles. The book opens with these words:

To the Memory of the noble Gentleman.
Professor Charles Morris,
who, for twenty-eight years, instructed the students of the

University by the example of his lofty character, as
much as by his eloquent discourse from the
chair, this volume is dedicated with
all love and veneration.

In an introduction, the student authors tie themselves in knots trying to outdo Hull and Charles's other eulogists. These students favored center-parted hair and three-piece suits with watch chains; they're clean-shaven and look like they smell good. But these fops do manage to produce a few insightful sentences: "No sycophancy or deceit ever found lodgment in this heroic soul. Others might cringe to a sickly public opinion, others might bow the knee to false gods of a degenerate time, but he would abide by his convictions . . ." What's that I'm hearing? It's an uncanny echo of John Blair Dabney's portrait of earlier generations of Morrises: *"They abhorred all disguise & dissimulation . . . (and) they wore no mask over their opinions, & were too frank & open, too indifferent to the censure of the world, to conceal their feelings. . . . They had no spice of that politic hypocrisy, which consults appearances in every action . . ."*

The only person who dared to utter something close to a criticism of this noble, courteous, brave, unaffected, tenderhearted, and heroic old-school colossus was his eldest son, Sylvanus, who allowed that the Old Roman did exhibit "one flaw." It was this: "He sometimes yielded to gusts of temper, and lost control of himself." Did the man ever exist who exhibited just one flaw? Surely not, but don't bother trying to point that out to the hagiographers when a man like Major Charles Morris is fresh in the ground.

⸺

The newspapers and magazines were trumpeting an eye-popping display of American progress and technical achievement that had just opened in Chicago. The World's Columbian Exposition, also known as the World's

Fair or simply the White City, was intended to be a celebration of the four hundredth anniversary of Christopher Columbus's arrival in the New World, but it turned out to be more a celebration of the nation's proliferating cornucopia of consumer goods, an inadvertent expression of hardening racist sentiments, and a reminder that the war of the currents still had a spark of life.

The array of neoclassical buildings at the heart of the fairgrounds embodied chief architect Daniel Burnham's ideas for the City Beautiful movement, which would inspire urban planners for years to come, most notably in Chicago and Washington, DC. The temporary buildings at the heart of the fair exhibited Beaux-Arts flourishes—anathema to such modernist architects as Louis Sullivan and Frank Lloyd Wright—and they were made of plaster, cement, and jute fiber, which was painted white so their facades glowed like sugar cubes under electric lights powered by alternating-current generators provided by George Westinghouse, who had underbid Thomas Edison to get the lighting contract. This so-called White City featured temples to the engines that drove the American economy: Railroads, Manufacturers, Agriculture, Mining, Machinery, Electricity. This last building contained a model home equipped with fixtures that conjured a future of convenience: electric stoves, hot plates, carpet sweepers, washing machines, fire alarms, and lamps. Also on display were various generators, transformers, motors, incubators, seismographs, and phonographs. Notably absent were the promised prototypes of Edison's highly anticipated Kinetoscope, a machine that was said to allow a single viewer to peer through a peephole and witness yet another miracle: moving pictures. Two years before the World's Fair opened, Edison had riffed on what would happen when—not if—he perfected his Kinetoscope and his moving-picture camera, known as the Kinetograph, and figured out how to synchronize moving pictures and sound. As he told a Chicago *Tribune* reporter: "Such a happy combination of photography and electricity that a man can sit in his own parlor and see depicted upon a curtain the forms of the players in an opera on a distant stage, and hear the voices of the singers. When the system is perfected, which will be in time for the Fair, each little muscle in the singer's face will be seen to work; every color of his or her attire will be exactly reproduced, and the stride and positions will be as natural and varied as those of the live characters."

Edison's rhapsody was premature but not inaccurate. The Kinetograph made its debut on May 9 at the Brooklyn Institute of Arts & Sciences, where a physicist named George M. Hopkins explained its workings to an audience of four hundred scientists. It was a very un-Edisonian event in that it lacked dazzle, Thomas Edison, or a single newspaper reporter or photographer. After Hopkins gave his talk, it took the scientists three hours to file past the varnished box and peer, one by one, through the peephole at a loop of black-and-white film that showed three blacksmiths silently hammering a piece of hot iron on an anvil, then silently passing around a bottle of beer, then silently hammering some more. The show lasted all of twenty-seven seconds, but the stunned scientists understood that they had been given a tantalizing glimpse of the future. Synchronized sound and projecting machines would arrive soon. An unprecedented revolution in entertainment was poised to begin.

Outside the White City was the sprawling Midway, a shameless mash-up of escapism and intellectual uplift. Here it was possible to travel on a moving sidewalk without lifting your feet or climb aboard a 264-foot wheel, designed by George Ferris, equipped with thirty-six cars, each larger than a railroad car and able to hold up to sixty people. At any time, more than 2,000 fairgoers were being spun giddily into the sky. Down on the ground, other diversions were provided by belly dancers, body builders, a 1,500-pound Venus de Milo sculpted from chocolate, replicas of Columbus's three ships, and an eleven-ton block of cheese. Buffalo Bill Cody had set up his Wild West show just outside the fairgrounds and was doing brisk business. For those seeking more cerebral fare, Eadweard Muybridge delivered lectures and, using a device called a zoopraxiscope, showed his sequential photographs of animals in motion. There were miles of new consumer goods on display, including baby carriages, zippers, bathroom fixtures, and telephones, along with new brands of food and drink such as Cracker Jack, Shredded Wheat cereal, Juicy Fruit gum, and Pabst Blue Ribbon beer. There were displays of ethnic cultures from Egypt, Turkey, Samoa, Java, Japan, Alaska, and the African kingdom of Dahomey, as well as artifacts of Indigenous people, including Native Americans and Eskimos. Yet there was little evidence of African American contributions to American progress other than a display of Hampton Institute's educational program and "Women's Work in Savagery," which included examples of African, Polynesian, and Native American artifacts. This should not have been surprising given that Black people were barred from the fair's planning commission, a club of prosperous White men who dreamed up the extravaganza while dining on green turtle consommé and woodcock on toast. Black people were also blocked from the construction or staffing of the fair, other than menial jobs. One notable exception could be found at the R. T. Davis Mill Co.'s exhibit, where a portly former slave from Kentucky named Nancy Green, decked out in a head kerchief, was merrily singing spirituals and flipping pancakes made with self-rising Aunt Jemima pancake flour. The company's promotional materials described its new pitchwoman as "a simple, earnest smiling mammy." Green would die in 1923, but her smile would radiate from boxes of Aunt Jemima pancake flour and bottles of Aunt Jemima syrup for more than a century—until the company's owners retired the brand after acknowledging that the character Green portrayed had been based on "a racial stereotype."

That wasn't the end of the fair's racist slights. The staff of *Puck*, the popular satirical magazine, composed and published twenty-six special weekly editions on the grounds during the fair. When fair organizers designated August 25th "Colored American Day," to appease Black people angry over their treatment, *Puck* responded by publishing a full-color two-page chromolithograph that was a printer's marvel and a racist's dream. The drawing, titled "Darkies' Day at the Fair (A Tale of Poetic Retribution)," showed a throng of Black people, dressed either as members of a marching band or an African tribe, lining up to get slices of free watermelon. The caricatures all have thick lips and simian features. One caption reads:

> *With one loud whoop, with one fell sweep,*
> *They swarm down on the stand;*
> *The sons of Ham in the foremost jam,*
> *With a big slice in each hand.*

All of this ignited the wrath of Ida B. Wells, who was on hand to urge a boycott of Colored American Day and contribute to a pamphlet called *The Reason Why the Colored American Is Not in the Columbian Exposition*. Some 10,000 copies of the pamphlet were distributed from the Haitian pavilion. Though Wells's contributions were largely a rehash of her earlier writings on lynch law and the convict leasing system, Frederick Douglass, in an introduction, did get to the heart of the question posed on the pamphlet's cover. The purpose of the White City, he wrote, was simple: "to exhibit the Negro as a repulsive savage." He added: "The enemies of the Negro see that he is making progress and they naturally wish to stop him and keep him in just what they consider his proper place." In a speech before thousands of listeners, Douglass thundered that America didn't have a "Negro problem," America had a "national problem."

Though no one knew it at the time, a dark subplot was unspooling out beyond the bright lights of the White City. A handsome blue-eyed medical doctor named Herman Webster Mudgett, using the alias H. H. Holmes (in honor of Sherlock), was running an establishment called the White City Hotel three miles west of the fairgrounds. It featured some unusual amenities, including secret passageways, airtight rooms equipped with gas, a walk-in vault, and a greased chute that led to the basement, which was equipped with surgical equipment and a human-sized kiln. Holmes's victims, usually young women, wound up in the basement, where he harvested their organs and skeletons for sale to medical institutions, then disposed of the unsalable bits by burning them or submerging them in pits of lime or acid. Holmes would eventually confess to twenty-seven murders, though the precise number is unlikely ever to be known. So in addition to serving as a showcase for uniquely American strains of ingenuity, technical prowess, jingoism, artistry, and racism, the Columbian Exposition also gave birth to a uniquely American strain of monster: the serial killer.

Eugene Debs.

"DEBS! DEBS! DEBS!"

John was about to learn a lesson his late father had learned two decades earlier while teaching at Randolph-Macon: the value of a steady paycheck, even a modest one, in hard times. Five days after the Columbian Exposition opened and two days after Charles died, panic swept the New York Stock Exchange. Cotton and wheat were by far America's two biggest exports, and an anemic cotton harvest in 1892 had put rippling strain on the nation's finances. Under the crop-lien system, so despised by Tom Watson and his fellow Populists, debt-strapped southern tenants and sharecroppers were forced to sell their harvested crops immediately, regardless of the prevailing price. Any profits went into the pockets of landowners, supply merchants, shipping companies, and the web of agents who sold and financed the crop—that is, Wall Street. Meanwhile, wheat farmers were also being squeezed by punishing debt payments at a time of declining prices.

Henry Adams coined a vivid metaphor for the American economy in the twilight of the Gilded Age: "Our bladder has been blown up till it must burst someday." There was no shortage of forces working to burst the bladder. The amount of new railroad track opened yearly had peaked in 1887, and it was now apparent that railroads were overbuilt, poorly managed, and, in more than half the cases, unable to pay dividends to investors. Falling investment in railroads, in turn, hurt the iron and steel industries. Building construction had peaked in 1892 and would decline for the rest of the decade, which pinched the industries that produced lumber, bricks, and other building materials. The American economy had become complex, interconnected, global. As much of Europe slid into recession, foreign investment in the American industries, especially from the United Kingdom, dried up. In need of hard money, many Europeans sold their American stocks, depleting the US gold supply and increasing the cost of credit while depressing prices. Having produced more goods and services than markets could absorb, businesses cut production. Deflation worsened. The bladder finally burst on May 5.

Within days of the panic at the New York Stock Exchange, depositors stormed banks across the country demanding cash. By the end of the year, 360 state and national banks would fail. The iron industry would suffer the worst year in its history. The humming looms in textile mills fell silent. More than 15,000 businesses went bankrupt, and 119 railroads went into receivership. Employers responded by firing workers and cutting the wages of those they kept on. For most of the decade, the unemployment rate was in double digits, climbing as high as 20 percent by some estimates. The nation seethed with strikes, walkouts, lockouts, and bursts of bloody violence. It would come to be known as the Panic of 1893, and its aftermath was every bit as grim as the Great Depression that would descend forty years later, maybe even grimmer because instead of a president with vision and political muscle, Americans were saddled in 1893 with Grover Cleveland.

Yet, John noticed, the suffering was not universal. For the lucky few—Henry George's "1 percent"—the Nineties still had a pronounced glow of gaiety. John had read enough novels and newspapers to have a picture of the upper crust. As the rest of the nation sank into economic depression, they were busy building palaces from San Francisco to Asheville, North Carolina, from Fifth Avenue to Newport, Rhode Island, ornate Beaux-Arts and neo-Italian Renaissance and Gothic wedding cakes that had electric lights and smelled of beeswax and brown soap and had only one purpose: to announce to the world that the owner of the house possessed a staggering amount of money, possibly old, more likely new. Such people ate jellied plover and drank Turkish coffee from filigree cups and sailed for Europe on a whim and thought nothing of spending $300 on a single bridesmaid's dress. John found nothing in their lives to envy.

Just as they had done during the downturn of the 1870s, the rich kept getting richer. Agile Andrew Carnegie, for instance, reacted to the falling price and demand for steel railroad track by setting up open-hearth furnaces at Homestead and providing structural steel and armor plate for a deep-pocketed new client: the U.S. Navy. Carnegie profited handsomely from the growing fleet of battleships commissioned by Congress, including the *USS Maine*, which in a few years would play a watery role in a pivotal chapter in American history. Never content with one lucrative contract, Carnegie got his friends in Washington to grease the sale of his steel armor to Russia. Once again, bad times turned out to be very good for men named Carnegie, Vanderbilt, Pullman, Morgan, and Frick.

Few employers embodied the best and worst impulses of the age more vividly than the railroad car tycoon George Mortimer Pullman. He contained multitudes: benevolence and avarice, vision and myopia, a social conscience and overweening self-interest. Pullman amassed a fortune leasing his luxurious dining and sleeping cars to railroads, not by following Andrew Carnegie's model of low costs and high volume, but by feeding the Gilded Age's appetite for opulence and comfort. And so his cars featured improved suspensions, plush carpets and upholstery, chandeliers, double-glazed windows, and fine cuisine served by Black waiters in starched white jackets. The Pullman Palace Car Company was the nation's largest employer of African Americans, yet they were relegated to jobs as cooks, porters, or waiters and paid so poorly that only through hustle and tips could they make a living wage. Pullman's treatment of his workers, both Black and White, sprang from a conviction that contained the seed of his ruin: the paternalistic belief that the 1 percent knows what's best for everyone else.

Nowhere was this more evident than in the creation of the workers' utopia known as Pullman, Illinois, a planned community south of Chicago engineered by its founder to provide decent housing for his workers, an orderly, self-contained universe free of saloons, brothels, gambling dens, and other pits of urban vice. Each home was sunny and well-ventilated, equipped with running water, gas for lighting and cooking, and indoor water closets. Pullman owned everything—the houses, schools, parks, market, church, library, sewage system—and his agents visited workers' homes to make sure they were complying with his forty-two-page manual of regulations that covered everything from how to dress to how to clean house. By 1893, the population of Pullman had reached 12,600.

There was, however, a serpent of discontent in this workers' paradise. Rents were relatively high. Some found the town dull. Many resented the constant surveillance by Pullman's minions almost as much as they resented the inability to buy their homes. Even William Stead, a visiting British reformer who largely praised Pullman's experiment in community planning, admitted the town had an air of "paternal despotism."

When the deepening depression cut the demand for Pullman's plush train cars, he responded by firing workers and cutting the wages of those he kept on by as much as 50 percent while refusing to reduce the costs of their utilities, groceries, or rent. Some workers ended up owing Pullman money on payday. Resentment turned into anger, anger into outrage. After Pullman laid off members of the American Railway Union's (ARU) negotiating committee, the new union formed by the fiery labor leader Eugene Debs, 90 percent of Pullman's workers did something the paternalistic despot found unimaginable: they walked off the job. He responded not by negotiating with his disaffected workers but by laying off the remaining 10 percent.

Debs had insisted that the ARU be open to all workers—skilled and unskilled, male and female, Black and White. It was an emblem of his belief that workers needed to stand together as one because the fault line in America was class, what he called "caste," and America, as Debs saw it, had two of them: "the producing classes and the money power." He thought George Pullman was "as greedy as a horse leech," but he advised against a strike because he understood that the deck was stacked against organized labor—the federal courts and the corporations, in his eyes, were now "synonymous." But the ARU membership ignored him and voted to back the wildcat strike by refusing to handle any train that included a single Pullman car. (Members also voted 112–110, over Debs's objections, to bar Blacks from joining the union.) The strike radiated outward from Chicago, and once it began to gather steam Debs was all in. Within a month, 125,000 workers were on strike and twenty railroads were paralyzed, from Detroit to the West Coast. Passengers were stranded. Mines, mills, and factories, unable to obtain fuel or transport their goods, shut down. Prices soared. Antimonopoly sentiment—that is, anti-railroad sentiment—swung public opinion firmly behind the strikers. Pigheaded Pullman had succeeded in turning a local brushfire into a national conflagration.

John would have been fascinated by Eugene Debs, as were millions of Americans. Newspaper accounts told of throngs waiting for him at train stations, and as his train approached they would roar his name like a mantra: "Debs! Debs! Debs!" Then they listened to him, rapt, for hours as he laid out his vision of how corporations and monopolies, aided by the courts, were unmanning the American worker. He leaned toward his audience as he spoke, his voice climbing and dipping, his hands chopping the air, the veins bulging on his bald skull. This man, this Moses, was preaching a gospel John was willing to believe in. But could Debs possibly lead the producing classes to victory over the money power?

Not if Richard Olney had anything to say about it. After he was named US Attorney General by President Cleveland, Olney didn't bother to resign as general counsel for two railroads, a conflict of interest that typified the Gilded Age. Olney made more from his railroad jobs than he did from his government job, so it's no surprise that he was ready to work fist-in-glove with the powerful General Managers' Association, which represented the twenty-four railroads that used the Chicago hub, and he was determined not merely to end the strike but to crush the union. Using an earlier legal opinion, Olney decreed that any train carrying a single mail car was a mail train, and to interfere with such a train was a breach of federal law. Federal marshals were forced to intervene when strikers tried to block trains that contained a mail car and a Pullman car. Then Olney got the courts to issue an injunction forbidding ARU leaders from promoting the boycott in any way. They couldn't even talk about it. It was getting hard to argue with Debs's claim that the courts and the corporations had become synonymous.

If Pullman had lit the fire, President Cleveland now poured a generous dose of gasoline on the flames. Heeding Olney's unsubstantiated claim that the only way to keep the mails moving was to send federal troops to Chicago, Cleveland sent in troops and federal marshals over the objections of the governor of Illinois and the mayor of Chicago. The troops were met by mobs—apparently only a sprinkling of strikers or railroad workers among them—that destroyed property in the Union Stockyards and torched buildings on the deserted grounds of the Columbian Exposition. Mobs then blocked tracks and burned hundreds of railroad cars. With the situation sliding toward chaos, the 14,000 armed men were given the order to open fire. Some thirty people died in the Chicago rioting, another forty nationwide. Within days order was restored in Chicago and the national strike soon fizzled.

Of course Debs had ignored the injunction to stop promoting the strike or talking about it. He never seemed to stop talking. He and seven other ARU organizers were promptly tried and convicted of violating the federal injunction against "ordering, directing, aiding, assisting or abetting" the boycott. The Sherman Antitrust Act, which had been designed to break up monopolies, had now been turned on the producing classes by the money power. In a 9-0 ruling, the US Supreme Court upheld the verdicts. Debs was sentenced to six months in prison, which he served in the county sheriff's elegant Victorian house in Woodstock, Illinois. During his incarceration, Debs wore tweed suits and starched shirts and was frequently invited to supper at the sheriff's table. He also read *Das Kapital* for the first time, the beginning of his conversion to socialism. When he'd served his six months, he boarded a train for Chicago, where a hundred thousand people waited at the station in a downpour to greet him with the familiar roar: "Debs! Debs! Debs!"

Man entering the colored section of a theater.

SEPARATE AND UNEQUAL

John was grateful for more than his steady paycheck. Though the university had not yet made any concerted effort to modernize and was still little more than a glorified academy, John was pleased to see that Athens was keeping step with the changing times. The town's population had now reached 10,000, the downtown streets were paved with macadam, and electric streetcars had replaced the mule-drawn trolleys. Telephone service had expanded, four railroads now serviced the town, and the New Athens Opera House had replaced Deupree Hall, where John had fallen in love with Gilbert and Sullivan as a boy. To power the trolleys and feed the rising demand for electricity in homes and businesses, the Athens

Electric Railway Company was building a dam and hydroelectric plant on the Oconee River.

In addition to the various private academies, the town had belatedly opened its first public schools in two identical brick structures—one for Black students, the other for White students—separate and, supposedly, equal. Meanwhile, in the west end of town, a promising educational experiment was taking place. Public education in Georgia may have been far behind the rising national standards, but there was a dawning realization that the state desperately needed to train teachers. Peabody Institutes had become a fixture in Georgia, segregated summer enclaves sprinkled throughout the state to train aspiring teachers, Black and White. They were named after George Peabody, a northern financier and philanthropist who'd given J. P. Morgan his start and set up the $3.5 million Peabody Education Fund after the Civil War to promote public education in the South. The fund was now headed by the Georgian J. L. M. Curry—the same man who had observed the integrated Virginia Assembly in session in the 1870s and concluded that freedmen's precarious rights and liberties would survive only if well-raised White gentlemen stood up to the poor White lower class. In 1889 Curry, a gifted orator, had electrified the Georgia Legislature with a speech imploring the lawmakers to fund a state normal school. They agreed with the need but declined to put up any money, so summer sessions were begun in Athens on a shoestring, with money from the Peabody Fund and other sources. Textbooks and paid teachers were unaffordable luxuries, so the university chancellor and numerous faculty members volunteered to teach courses without compensation. It's not known if John was among them. These summer sessions—segregated by race, of course—were such a success that the parsimonious legislators soon appropriated a staggering $10,000 for the fledgling Normal School. So many students flocked to Athens that the overflow had to be housed in tents.

John would have been heartened by this development, but he was never allowed to forget how tightly even such modest signs of progress were circumscribed by inviolable southern customs. Curry was also an agent for the Slater Fund, which promoted industrial education for Black people along the lines of Booker T. Washington's Tuskegee Institute in Alabama, but his hope was never that education would result in equality of the races, or even the mingling of the races. Curry had owned slaves and served in the Confederate Army, and he regarded the Fourteenth Amendment as "the blunder of the centuries." His modest hope was that by educating both races, White people would avoid being dragged down to "the neth-ermost hell of poverty and degradation." This sentiment put him in line with other southerners who promoted the education of White and Black students in segregated schools, notably Charles Aycock of North Carolina and William Henry Ruffner of Virginia. W. J. Cash sketched the cynical calculation behind their support for Black education: "It will enable us to make sure that he (the Negro) acquires no dangerous notions, to control what he is taught, to make sure that he is educated to fit into, and to stay in, his place." John had no choice but to come to terms with a cruel con-tradiction at work here: in Georgia and in the South at large, any "reform" must be designed, first and last, to preserve the status quo.

Another irony was the high cost of the state's stinginess on education spending. As a lowly instructor of English and Modern Languages (French and German), John was required to teach basic English composition to all incoming freshmen, and he soon learned that the state's patchwork public schools had left many freshmen woefully unprepared for college work. In extreme cases, John's task was remedial, which the course catalog freely admitted: "A course is given in the fundamental principles of Grammar, including the analysis and synthesis of English sentences, and the art of speaking and writing the language correctly. Owing to the poor prepara-tion of many students, it is necessary to devote special attention to this work." I'm guessing John suspected that some of his more countrified charges were wearing their first pair of shoes. Yet he had little tolerance for incompetence and none at all for unruly behavior, lack of effort, or inattention. In these early years of his long teaching career, he developed a tic that would become a trademark: if a student was fidgeting or whispering or daydreaming, or if his lack of preparation led him to blurt out a breathtakingly wrong answer, John would fire a chalkboard eraser at the blockhead. Possibly because of his time as a baseball player, John had a wickedly accurate right arm. As one student recalled, "He hit me smack in the head one time. Not because I was not paying attention—I was much too afraid of him to get out of line. Actually he was aiming at the boy in front of me, who ducked." This was the first, but not the last, mention of John's ability to instill fear in his students—and in others who failed to meet his exacting standards. He was not a man you wanted to disappoint.

This was also when John saw his byline in print for the first time, a magical moment for every writer. His debut article in *American Journal of Philology* appeared under the headline, "On the Development of Diphthongs in Modern English from OE. *î* and *û*." After his opening mentions of G. H. Balg and Henry Sweet, John posits that to understand the diphthongized *î* in Modern English, one needs to take into account the way it was pronounced in his native Virginia, which itself was a relic of the English pronunciation in the seventeenth century. To prove his point he veers from writing prose into composing something that looks like a mathematical equation: "Thus the development of a diphthong from OE. *î* was as follows: OE. *î* > *ei* (= Romic ei) > *ei* (= *er* in *better* + *i* in Fr. *si*) > American *ei* (Romic *äi*, Ger. *ei*) > Irish *oi* (as in *loike* [?])." That parenthesized question mark seems to suggest that John was at least a little mystified by what he had written. Or maybe his knowledge of Irish was on the thin side. But he marches gamely to this conclusion: "That the *û* was diphtongized after the development of the *ó* into *oo*—which, we may remark in passing, is not heard as a diphthong in this country—will be seen upon a careful examination of the phonetic authorities quoted by Sweet in his Hist. Eng. Snds. (§§832, 833, 834, 827). The same result as in the case of *î* followed. The territory of the *û* being encroached upon, an attempt was made to make the sound more distinct, and an obscure sound was unconsciously uttered before it."

In just three dense pages, John established the template for how he would go about pursuing the life of the mind. He would travel tangled, willfully obscure back alleys that could be navigated only by someone who had mastered scholarship that was baffling to most mortals. He was not the only scholar working those back alleys. His debut article appeared alongside such fare as "On the Authorship of the Leptinean Orations Attributed to Aristotle" by J. E. Harry and "The Dramatic Satura and the Old Comedy of Rome" by George L. Hendrickson. In joining such company, John would risk becoming one of Nietzsche's despised hairsplitters and screech owls. John saw it as a risk worth taking. He agreed with George Bernard Shaw that all of it—the origins, evolution, pronunciation, and spelling of words—was a "seriously underrated subject." To John it was highest heaven.

Traveling to Chicago for the World's Fair had proved too ambitious, so John would have been determined not to miss the Cotton States and International Exposition in Atlanta in the fall of 1895. He likely read the official guide, which announced that the fair, though smaller than the White City, would have a "Negro Building," built by Negro contractors using Negro laborers and designed to showcase the achievements of numerous Negro schools and colleges and banks, as well as displays of needlework and art. "This," the guide boasted, "is the only building ever erected at an exposition for the sole purpose of demonstrating the progress of the Negro in the arts of civilization." The entrance was flanked by plaster sculptures designed to illustrate just how far Black people had come in the past fifty years. On one side was a log cabin and, as the guide put it, "the face of an old negro mammy, her head covered with the characteristic bandana"—Aunt Jemima herself. On the other side was "a representative negro of this day and generation"—the old lion himself, Frederick Douglass, who had died of a massive heart attack earlier that year. Inside, John saw a work by a former slave from Athens named Harriet Powers—an ebullient quilt made of cutout shapes sewn into a large fabric, the *appliqué* technique imported from West Africa. The workmanship was dazzling. During the fair's three-month run, there would be days dedicated to the Women's Christian Temperance Union, the Daughters of the Confederacy, Poets, Brick Makers, and a three-day Congress on Africa. The staff of *Punch* magazine would not be on hand to satirize this last event.

Though the fair, like everything in Atlanta, was driven by money—it was intended to show the world, and especially the nations of Latin America, that the South was a beacon of social progress and therefore a worthy trading partner—John would have been delighted by the inclusion of Black achievements, a laudable advance over what had happened in Chicago. John wanted to see it all with his own eyes, and he especially wanted to hear one of the speeches scheduled for the opening-day ceremonies.

Before the fair opened, John spent a relaxing summer at Taylor's Creek with his widowed mother, his sisters, brother Jim, who was serving as a missionary in Brazil, and baby brother Charles Ed, who was beginning to make a success in the blossoming profession of accounting in New York City. After returning to Athens at the end of the summer, John took the train to Atlanta on September 18 and made his way to the fairgrounds at Piedmont Park, where he took a quick tour, passing through buildings devoted to Manufacturers, Agriculture, Machinery, Transportation, Electricity, and, of course, the Negro. There were Mexican, German, Chinese, and Indian villages, vaudeville shows, an ostrich farm, and a Ferris wheel. Then John stepped into a small building dubbed "Living Pictures." In a dark room with a couple of dozen seats, he gazed at a curtain where a machine called a Phantascope beamed pictures that moved. The subject matter of those moving pictures is unknown, but it could have been anything—two people dancing, a man riding a horse, a ship approaching a dock. What matters is that John was transfixed by these fluid little miracles. On that day, though the expression did not yet exist, a movie lover was born.

The 3,000-seat auditorium was nearly filled to capacity when John arrived—a largely White crowd with a contingent of Blacks seated near the stage. Everyone, Black and White, rose to applaud as the featured speaker strode onto the stage, a Black man with regal bearing and a smile that John read as a mix of self-assurance and gratitude. The audience fell silent as Booker T. Washington, president of Tuskegee Institute and heir apparent to Frederick Douglass, began to speak in an accent John recognized from his native Virginia—clipped Elizabethan curlicues imported from England in the seventeenth century. John had come here expecting to hear a call for equal rights and a bold program for Black advancement, but that, to his disappointment, was not what he was hearing. His disappointment soon turned into despair as the words poured out of Washington's mouth: "Our greatest danger is that in the great leap from slavery to freedom we may overlook the fact that the masses of us are to live by the productions of our hands, and . . . we shall prosper in proportion as we learn to dignify and glorify common labor."

It got worse: "No race can prosper till it learns that there is as much dignity in tilling a field as in writing a poem. It is at the bottom of life we must begin, and not at the top . . . The opportunity to earn a dollar in a factory just now is worth infinitely more than the opportunity to spend a dollar in an opera-house."

Now came the hammer blow: "In all things that are purely social we can be as separate as the fingers, yet one as the hand . . . The wisest among my race understand that the agitation of questions of social equality is the extremest folly, and that progress in the enjoyment of all the privileges that will come to us must be the result of severe and constant struggle rather than of artificial forcing."

John must have been dazed. This Black man was *capitulating* to the deepest wishes of the White man. Unlike Douglass or W. E. B. Du Bois or Ida Wells, he was agreeing to abandon the struggle for social equality and accept the notion that the Black man's place was the field and the factory, working with his hands, free of the nonsense that he had any business aspiring to write a poem or appreciate an opera—or, by extension, to vote or hold elected office or serve on a jury. The organizers of the exposition must have been in ecstasy: their gospel of racial separation and White supremacy was now being preached by the most influential Black person in America! John was jolted from his daze. Every White person in the room was rising, applauding, shouting Washington's name. John, like all the Black people, remained seated and silent.

John's gloom would have deepened the following year when the US Supreme Court delivered one of the most cataclysmic decisions in its history. The case was brought by a French-speaking Creole shoemaker from Louisiana named Homer Plessy, who contained one-eighth African blood and frequently passed for White. He decided to challenge Louisiana's Separate Car Law on unconventional legal grounds: his lawyers, led by Albion Tourgée, contended that the law deprived Plessy of his property in the form of his *Whiteness* because it forced him from White train cars into colored cars. The Supreme Court rejected this argument on the basis of the one-drop rule—that anyone with a single drop of Negro blood, including an octoroon like Plessy, was a Negro. Writing for the 7–1 majority, Justice Henry Billings Brown stated: "We are unable to see how this statute deprives him of, or in any way affects his right to, such property. If he be a white man and assigned to a colored coach, he may have his action for damages against the company for being deprived of his so-called property. Upon the other hand, if he be a colored man and be so assigned, he has been deprived of no property, since he is not lawfully entitled to the reputation of being a white man."

Brown then addressed Plessy's contention that two separate things cannot possibly be equal: "We consider the underlying fallacy of the plaintiff's argument to consist in the assumption that the enforced separation of the two races stamps the colored race with a badge of inferiority. If this be so, it is not by reason of anything found in the act, but solely because the colored race chooses to put that construction upon it." Finally, fatally, Brown removes courts and legislatures from matters of racial equality: "Legislation is powerless to eradicate racial instincts or to abolish distinctions based upon physical differences, and the attempt to do so can only result in accentuating the difficulties of the present situation. If the civil and political rights of both races be equal, one cannot be inferior to the other civilly or politically. If one race be inferior to the other socially, the Constitution of the United States cannot put them upon the same plane."

The lone dissenting voice belonged, as usual, to John's hero, John Marshall Harlan, who sets the table by stating that "there is no caste here" and "our Constitution is color-blind" and "all citizens are equal before the law." Then he serves up his main course: "The arbitrary separation of citizens on the basis of race while they are on a public highway is a badge of servitude wholly inconsistent with the civil freedom and the equality before the law established by the Constitution. It cannot be justified upon any legal grounds."

But it was justified by the legal opinion of the Supreme Court. Two years later, echoing Brown's contention that legislation is powerless to eradicate racial instincts, the court upheld the Mississippi state constitution's poll tax, literacy test, and grandfather clause, plus its stipulation that only registered voters could serve on juries. Though it effectively disenfranchised almost all Black people, the constitution was allowed to stand because on paper it treated both races equally. Discrimination, if it existed, came from the people who enforced the law, and they were beyond the reach of both legislatures and courts. In these two rulings, the Supreme Court gave its formal blessing to Jim Crow. He was now free to cleave the South into two separate but unequal worlds, and he would do so with zeal, ingenuity, and terrible efficiency for the next half-century—until the penultimate year of John's life.

PART TWO
THE MIND OF THE SOUTH
(1898-1922)

The USS Maine.

LITTLE BIG WAR

T he so-called American Century began two years ahead of schedule, on February 15, 1898, when a pair of mysterious explosions splintered Andrew Carnegie's impregnable steel armor and sent the USS *Maine* to the bottom of Havana Harbor.

The battleship had been dispatched to Cuba at the request of the US consul in Havana, a nephew of Robert E. Lee's named Fitzhugh Lee, amid rising tensions between Cuban freedom fighters and their colonial masters from Spain. As the *Maine* steamed toward Havana, other American warships were shifted to the Florida Keys and the Gulf of

Mexico and also to Hong Kong, close to Spain's holdings in the Pacific. Possibly seeing a reflection of their forebears' rebellion against an imperial European power, Americans were solidly behind the Cubans in their struggle for independence. A vigorous "Cuba Libre" propaganda machine in Florida helped fan public support, while American newspapers reported extensively—and often inaccurately—on Spanish atrocities, including the imposition of martial law and squalid camps where civilians were herded to rob guerilla fighters of their cover, which supposedly resulted in the deaths of tens of thousands of civilians from malnutrition and disease. President William McKinley resisted calls for war and worked to negotiate a settlement with Spain, which pleased American business interests. After monopolizing Cuban sugar markets and developing heavy export traffic to the island—and after finally emerging from the depression—American businessmen were leery of anything that might disrupt their long-awaited return to profitability. McKinley, yet another pro-business president, was sympathetic to their pleas.

The sinking of the *Maine* changed the equation. The more sensational-istic American newspapers, especially those owned by Joseph Pulitzer and William Randolph Hearst, reported as fact that the ship had been blown up by Spain. Headlines, all based on hearsay, blared: "Spanish Treachery," "Destroyed by a Torpedo," "Blood-Thirsty Spaniards," and "Maine Explosion Caused by Bomb or Torpedo?" At least the writer of this last headline, which appeared in Pulitzer's *New York World*, had the decency to add a qualifying question mark. But such even-handedness was the exception. Hearst offered a $50,000 reward to anyone who could identify "the perpe-trators of the *Maine* outrage." While awaiting the findings of a US Navy court of inquiry, Congress, firmly in the grip of war fever, appropriated $50 million to build up the nation's military. On March 22 the court of inquiry delivered its verdict: the explosions originated *outside* the *Maine*'s hull, most likely triggered by a mine or torpedo, which caused ammunition magazines onboard to explode. The report stopped short of assigning blame:

"The court has been unable to obtain evidence fixing the responsibility for the destruction of the *Maine* upon any person or persons." Given the nation's pro-war froth, however, a rush to judgment was inevitable. America needed a culprit, and Spain was it. Within days an American blockade was in place and the two nations were at war.

The frenzy soon reached Athens. The US Army had just 25,000 soldiers in uniform when war was declared, but young men across the nation rushed to volunteer. They, along with National Guard units, would soon swell the nation's fighting force to more than a quarter of a million men. Many of John's students left school to volunteer for the fight, just as Charles and many of his students had left William & Mary in the days after Fort Sumter. John would have been aghast when a new tent city sprouted on the west side of Athens—not to house an overflow of aspiring teachers but to house an overflow of aspiring warriors. So many of them were from the North, especially New York, that the encampment was dubbed Brooklyn. A. L. Hull, the banker turned amateur historian who had so mellifluously eulogized John's father, was in the crowd the day the recruits paraded up College Avenue. Standing nearby was a Confederate veteran named Woods who had lost his right arm at Spotsylvania. Hull asked him what he thought about the spectacle of federal troops parading through downtown Athens. "I think if I had a gun," Woods replied, "I would like to shoot into them."

The raging jingoism—both pro ("Remember the *Maine!*") and con ("Forget, hell!")—appalled John. Just as the news of William Kemmler's botched electrocution had galvanized John's opposition to the death penalty, the war fever now galvanized his pacifism. He had never embraced the romanticism of war, thanks to the stories his father and others had told of watching friends die in agony, serving under idiotic politicians and officers, watching civilians riot over price gouging and food shortages, watching cities burn. Now, with memories of Civil War horrors still fresh, America was jumping right back in, even though the question that led to the war—why did the *Maine* sink?—had not been definitively answered and remains in doubt to this day.

This was both the death of American isolationism and the birth of a still-evolving national character. In their rush to war in Cuba, Americans showed themselves to be willful, impulsive, and heedless—unwilling to let inconvenient facts derail their desires, eager to jump into a far-flung conflict despite dubious justification, an incomplete understanding of local history or conditions, and no idea how to get out. Hints of this character, particularly impulsiveness, had been on display in the Americans' treatment of the Native populace and in the South's doomed secession from the far more powerful Union. But those were domestic dramas, their consequences contained by national borders. The consequences of the Spanish-American War were global. It lasted all of ten weeks, and just 332 Americans died in combat (many more died from typhoid, yellow fever and malaria), which led Secretary of State John Hay to famously call it "that splendid little war." To John, it was neither splendid nor little. Within a year it would lead to a much larger and uglier war in the Philippines that would drag on until 1913, cost more than 4,000 American lives, and lead to the slaughter of hundreds of unarmed Indigenous women and children by American soldiers. Though John had no way of knowing it, the justification and execution of these two wars would reverberate for years to come and, in a very real sense, remain in play today.

Yet there is no denying that John Hay's splendid little war had one immense consequence. It transformed the United States overnight from a big, bawling, self-absorbed baby into a formidable world power. By the end of 1898, the United States had acquired a global empire with eight million new subjects, stretching from Puerto Rico to Guam to the Philippines, and there was never any doubt, given recent court decisions and prevailing racial attitudes, how Americans would treat these "colored" people. They were, in the words of *The Nation*, "a varied assortment of inferior races which, of course, could not be allowed to vote."

Possibly worse, from John's point of view, was the way the war accelerated a race among world powers to arm themselves with ever more destructive weapons. Once again he was seeing the dark side of technological progress. Great Britain and Germany were already in a race to build the deadliest navy. Now the United States, suddenly in the spotlight on the world stage, eagerly joined the race.

Meanwhile John was busy climbing the academic ladder, rising from instructor to adjunct professor to professor in just a few years, and now his teaching duties included a course called English Language and Teutonic Philology. The second half of this pairing was surely not a big draw in *fin-de-siècle* Georgia, yet I think John deserves credit for persuading the administration that one of his more obscure passions would give the university a bit of the intellectual heft it was lacking. The catalog stated: "This course is designed to introduce the systematic study of the English language from the historical and philological standpoint; to give the student an opportunity to do for his own language and literature what he is required to do in the ancient languages and literatures—viz: to study them scientifically, to trace their growth and development from earliest beginnings to the present day." The operative words here are *systematic* and *scientifically*, clear echoes of John's time at the University of Berlin. The final semester of the three-year course was devoted to the comparative philology of either classical or Teutonic languages. For a late–nineteenth century southern university, this qualified as heavy lifting.

When he wasn't teaching, John was busy writing. His second byline appeared in *American Journal of Philology*'s last issue of the century, above his article titled "Sidney Lanier and Anglo-Saxon Verse-Technic." John opens with breezy sentences that show he is capable of wearing his erudition lightly. Here's his opening: "When Tennyson pointed out to Hallam those portions of Henry VIII which a later, accurate scholarship agreed with him in ascribing to Fletcher, he was guided by no rules for metrical tests, but was led to his conclusions simply by his natural ear for melody, which immediately perceived the difference of cadence."

This sentence requires some unpacking. Hallam was Arthur Hallam, an aspiring poet who befriended another aspiring poet, Alfred Tennyson, when they were students at Cambridge. Among their classmates was James Spedding, who, although unnamed here by John, would become the first among many scholars to demonstrate that John Fletcher, William Shakespeare's designated heir as head playwright of the King's Men theater company, almost certainly wrote more than half of the late Shakespeare play *Henry VIII*. While John's opening marvels that Tennyson's "natural ear for melody" enabled him to anticipate Spedding's scholarship by some twenty years, this sentence's true purpose is to introduce what comes next: "Similarly, when Sidney Lanier, in his lectures on poetry at the Johns Hopkins University, laid down the fundamental principles of A.S. (Anglo-Saxon) versification, he was chiefly indebted for his perception of the truth to the delicate rhythmical sense of a poet and an accomplished musician. Such testimony is not to be lightly disregarded . . ."

This is remarkable. John's erudition has enabled him to see the link between two very unlike men: the major English poet Alfred Tennyson and the minor American poet Sidney Lanier, who was an ardent admirer of the Anglo-Saxon poets, an accomplished musician, and the author of the 1880 book, *The Science of English Verse*, which John surely was familiar with. A rich exploration of the similarities between musical phrasing and poetic meter, the book describes the "rhythms" and "tunes" and "colors" of verse. Circling back to Tennyson, Lanier produces a clever illustration of the parallel importance of accents and silences in both music and poetry. First he offers this rhythmic scheme:

"Upon hearing this strain," Lanier writes, "every ear will accept it as a substantial reproduction of the rhythmic movement of voice in reciting the following stanza (from Tennyson):"

> Break, break, break,
> On thy cold gray stones, O sea:
> And I would that my tongue could utter
> The thoughts that arise in me.

This leads John to agree with Lanier that verse, like music, cannot exist without a beat. John uses a German word: "(T)here is no verse, spoken declaimed, or sung, which can dispense with *takt*. This is what makes verse verse; the lack of this makes prose."

Having stated his case so clearly, John now wanders off into the muddy weeds of textual analysis—remember, this is *American Journal of Philology*, not *Punch*—and the reader is bombarded with terms such as "anacrusis," "hemistich," "arsis," and "scansion." The article ends with a tantalizing footnote: "I desire to announce that I have prepared, and will soon have published, a small book elaborating and illustrating the views presented here."

Though he was immersed in his teaching and writing, John could not have been unaware of the grim events taking place beyond the cozy campus. It was the peak of lynching fever in the South. During the last decade of the century, there was an average of more than one lynching per month in Georgia, a number that peaked with twenty-seven people lynched in the state in 1899, a performance surpassed only by Mississippi. The one small consolation John could find in this horrific news was that most of the lynching took place in the cotton and peanut flatlands in the southwestern corner of the state, far from hilly enlightened Athens in the northeast. So far there had not been a single lynching in surrounding Clarke County.

Elsewhere the news was even grimmer. In Wilmington, North Carolina, White mobs intimidated Black voters, stuffed ballot boxes, overthrew an elected Fusion government, then burned the offices of the city's Black-owned newspaper and shot dead more than sixty Black citizens. One of the lead fomenters of this bloodbath—it was nothing less than a coup—was Josephus Daniels, the respectable editor of the Raleigh *News & Observer*. Of course the paper reported that the White men of Wilmington had done a great civic service to rid their city of its corrupt Black rulers and their White enablers. Five days after the killing stopped, Daniels's paper offered this tidy summation of what racist violence had brought to Wilmington: "Victory, White Supremacy and Good Government."

When John was awarded his second sabbatical in 1900, he returned to Europe, this time to the universities in Freiburg and Copenhagen, eager to plunge back into his philological research. But he found something new and unsettling in the European air: anti-American sentiment. Where he had been warmly welcomed on his initial visit, in the coffee houses and bars and lecture halls of Berlin, he now got a chillier reception. Newspaper articles excoriated

America—and, by extension, Americans—for overreach in the invasion of
Cuba and the annexation of Spain's far-flung territories. The parades and mili-
taristic displays John had dismissed as amusing on his first visit to Germany
now seemed ominous in light of the fact that the German navy was in a furious
building phase, trying to surpass the French and Russians in firepower while
playing catch-up with the still-superior British Royal Navy. John even heard
beer hall talk that Germany was planning to invade the United States—possibly
the shipyards at Hampton Roads, Virginia, possibly New York or Boston—but
he figured this was the beer talking. However, there was no dismissing the
newspaper reports about a new class of warship under construction in Britain,
vessels that were going to be the swiftest and deadliest ever built. Their speed
would come from quiet, efficient steam turbines instead of the old steam piston
engines, which turned engine rooms into wet, noisy hells. Their firepower
would come from massive twelve-inch guns that were guided by electronic
range finders and able to fire armor-piercing shells more than fourteen miles.
Underwater tubes would fire torpedoes. The German newspapers marveled
at the ingenuity and efficiency of this coming generation of killing machines,
and though the first one would not be launched for several years, it already
had a name. The name was designed to reassure, but it had the opposite effect
on John. The words H.M.S. *Dreadnought* filled him with dread.

Before John left for home, he paused at the spa in Wiesbaden, Germany,
where he was put on a regimen that rid him forever of his tobacco and
coffee habits. His health noticeably improved, and he returned to Athens
as the University of Georgia was preparing for its centennial. (Though
chartered in 1785, the university did not hold its first classes until 1801.)
Chancellor Walter Hill had asked each faculty member to fill out a brief
biographical questionnaire, and John's responses offer some intriguing hints
about the state of his life. The space to provide *Facts relating to marriage* is

left yawningly blank, a reminder that John is still a bachelor as his fortieth birthday looms. Was this a source of social awkwardness? In the space to list his *Writings*, John offers this: "Brief articles on technical subjects in the *American Journal of Philology* and in *Englische Studien: 'Anglo-Saxon Metre'* (unpublished)." This study of meter must have been the forthcoming book he'd mentioned in the footnote to his article on Sidney Lanier in *American Journal of Philology* two years earlier. What became of it? Was it abandoned? Rejected by publishers? Burned? It's unlikely the answer will ever be known, but it's impossible to miss the note of self-deprecation in the words "brief articles" and "technical subjects." Was John being modest, or was he simply giving a clear-eyed appraisal of his willfully obscure pursuits?

Now comes the major surprise in the questionnaire: the ardent anti-joiner has finally found an organization worth joining. In the space for *Member of learned societies*, John wrote: "Modern Language Association of America." This group had come together in 1883, the year the Brooklyn Bridge opened, a few months after Charles Francis Adams Jr., Henry's father, delivered a scathing commencement address at Harvard deploring the way modern languages were taught in American secondary schools and colleges. Adams was classically educated like John, meaning Greek and Latin were the foundation stones of all his learning, and yet he bridled at the fixation on dead languages at the expense of far more useful living languages in a rapidly industrializing and modernizing world—"this active, bustling, hard-hitting, many-tongued world," as Adams put it. Though he went easier on Latin because of its uses in philosophy, medicine, and science, Adams branded the study of Greek as a college entrance requirement "a positive educational wrong." And in an echo of W. J. Cash's mockery of the Old South's "superstitious awe of the classics" and Andrew Lipscomb's dismay that the preference for classical languages over modern ones had created an "aristocracy of pretensions to culture," Adams dismissed the fixation on classical literature as intellectual posturing: "There is in what are called the educated classes, both in this country and in Europe, a very considerable amount of affectation and credulity in regard to the Greek and Latin masterpieces." Adams closed with a preference that surely spoke to John: "I would rather myself be familiar with the German tongue and its literature than be equally familiar with the Greek."

Forty professors of modern languages gathered in New York City in the last week of December that year to discuss the sorry state of their profession and what could be done to improve it. Adams's address was on everyone's mind as they hashed out a manifesto. It turns out these language professors weren't the only group holding a convention that week. In what had become a Gilded Age trend, the week between Christmas and New Year's Day was now unofficially convention season for all sorts of organizations, leading one historian to dub this the "Guilded Age." While the modern language professors were meeting in New York City, Freethinkers were gathering in upstate New York, the Ohio Liquor Dealers came together to protest taxes on their wares, the American Society of Professors of Dancing was meeting in Philadelphia, and representatives from eight eastern colleges were huddling in New York to promote amateurism and prevent money from contaminating intercollegiate sports.

John's membership in the Modern Language Association demolished my simplistic assumption that he had locked himself in the past. He was turning out to be more complicated than that. He was torn between two warring worlds, and his life was becoming a struggle to resolve the tensions between the familiar comforts of the past and a future that presented a terrifying tangle of contradictions—medical breakthroughs alongside executions and an arms race, rising educational standards alongside lynchings, increasing convenience and comfort alongside increasing inequality—all of it happening faster every day. It was now possible to transmit Morse code across the Atlantic without wires. Shortly after winning reelection, William McKinley had become the third president assassinated in John's lifetime. A wave of business mergers had come in the aftermath of the depression, creating vast, faceless conglomerates that were beginning to dominate the economy and turn America into a country of middle managers. John saw his first automobile—a little carriage puttering through the streets of Athens. His answer to all this accelerating change was not a wholesale embrace of one world and a wholesale rejection of the other; his answer was a selective embrace of the best of each world and a rejection of the worst. John still had his Latin and his Greek, but he would soon become a dedicated teacher of German. He still read Tacitus and Cicero, but he admired Mark Twain and was drawn to such emerging modern writers as Theodore Dreiser and Upton Sinclair, Edith Wharton and W. E. B. Du Bois. He was ripe for the coming advances in moving-picture technology and other forms of popular entertainment, just as he was prepared to oppose the coming waves of wars. Of course he deplored the horrors of lynching and the impulse to turn the latest inventions into weapons. He was in a murky No Man's Land between two worlds, unsure what was coming, uneasy and groping, but at least he could console himself that he was far from alone.

Despite his misgivings about the Spanish-American War, John had to admit that one positive thing came out of it. Here in the twilight of Pasteur's Revolution, researchers had determined that both yellow fever and malaria are transmitted by mosquitoes that have bitten an infected host. Thus the diseases were transmissible but not contagious by contact, and a team of Americans in occupied Cuba, led by surgeon general Walter Reed, launched a campaign to eradicate yellow fever by eliminating its preferred mode of transport: the *Aëdes aegypti* mosquito. Once again, prosaic measures would trump technical wizardry in a campaign to improve human health. Dr. William Gorgas, the army's chief sanitary officer, took advantage of the martial law then in place and imposed strict protocols: the city was divided into twenty districts, and people known to have the disease were quarantined in mosquito-proof rooms with window screens; all arriving ships and motor vehicles were inspected; standing water and stagnant ponds were drained; pyrethrum powder was burned to fumigate the homes of known carriers; all cisterns and water receptacles were mosquito-proofed. The results were nothing short of miraculous. In seven months, yellow fever was wiped out in Havana, never to return. Based on his triumph in Cuba, Gorgas would soon be summoned to another incubator of yellow fever and malaria, the isthmus of Panama, where the United States was hatching colossal schemes.

Gretchen McCurdy Gallagher.

A PLEASING STAGE PICTURE

At about this time, a young musician from upstate New York named Gretchen McCurdy Gallagher accepted a teaching position at the Lucy Cobb Institute in Athens. The school had been founded in 1858 by T. R. R. Cobb, who would die fighting for the Confederacy at Fredericksburg, and it was named after his daughter Lucy, who had died of scarlet fever shortly before the war. The school prided itself on being more rigorous than the finishing schools then dotting the South, schools that aspired to do little more than prepare young women for their preordained roles as wife and mother. The Lucy Cobb Institute aimed higher. When he was chancellor at the university, Andrew Lipscomb came to give lectures on

Shakespeare, and many notable speakers were brought in over the years, including the poets Carl Sandburg and Vachel Lindsay. The students spoke French at the dining table. The curriculum included mathematics, art, literature, French, English, and Latin, as well as phonetics, elocution, Bible studies, "conduct and manners," and music. It was this last offering that brought Gretchen McCurdy Gallagher to Athens.

She had grown up in Dansville, New York, the granddaughter of Irish farmers from County Mayo who'd fled the Potato Famine in 1847 and lost their infant child on the Atlantic crossing. As a teenager, Gretchen's father, Thomas Gallagher, had gone to work as a clerk in a grocery store and then opened a wholesale grocery business, but eventually he realized he had a gift for selling insurance and could make real money at it. He also realized he wanted to provide finer things for his children than he had known. Gretchen showed early musical promise, especially on the violin, and after attending local Catholic schools, she was sent to Rochester to study with the Dutch violinist Henri Appy. She then attended the Conservatory of Music in Cincinnati, where her father had been transferred, and by the time she was a teenager, she was signed with a booking agency and performing at Chatauquas and on a loose circuit that ranged from Cincinnati to Youngstown, Buffalo, and Rochester, with at least one foray into New York City. Audiences were enthusiastic and the press notices were flattering. In Youngstown, one reviewer was moved to comment on Gretchen's striking appearance: "Of graceful presence, the young player made a pleasing stage picture in her light concert gown, with the touch of color lent by the rose at her throat and the buds in her hair." Other reviewers praised her playing for its "flawless execution," "rich coloring," and "admirable fluency." In addition to glowing reviews, she began collecting letters of recommendation—possibly realizing, as her twenty-fifth birthday approached, that she was no longer in child prodigy territory and needed to start thinking of a fallback if her performing career didn't pan out. One of her teachers at the Conservatory, P. A. Tirindelli, wrote: "On the many occasions I have heard you play the violin, I have found you possessed of a studious temperament, and, above all, of a remarkable depth of feeling and an exceedingly smooth technique. I believe also that you are admirably adapted for teaching."

And so in 1903 she arrived at the Lucy Cobb Institute, where she began teaching violin, viola, piano, and mandolin while directing the student orchestra. John, a music lover, regularly attended concerts by students and faculty in the elegant Seney-Stovall Chapel on the Lucy Cobb campus, where many of his friends and colleagues sent their daughters. Did he see Gretchen for the first time performing on the chapel's stage? Or possibly on the conductor's podium, guiding her charges through one of the pieces she had performed many times, Henri Vieuxtemp's "Ballade et Polonaise"? Was she wearing a rose at her throat and buds in her hair? Surely not, because she was no longer the star of the show; she was now an employee whose job was to help bring up the polish on well-to-do southern girls. Yet John noticed her—she was not stunningly beautiful, but she was handsome and she had poise—and a spark glowed inside him. My father offered this vague version of how their first meeting might have happened: "John was just a lonesome bachelor around town. He'd gone to recitals and heard Gretchen play, and he screwed up his courage and asked her for a date."

She accepted, and soon a courtship took flight. Gretchen was living with the other single teachers in a house on the Lucy Cobb campus, and it was a short walk there from the house where John was living with his widowed mother and unmarried sister Louise. What an odd couple Gretchen Gallagher and John Morris must have made! The twenty-four-year-old Irish Catholic violinist from the Far North and the forty-year-old agnostic scholar, the son of a former slave owner from the Old South. Yet those differences were the source of a strong attraction, and given what lay ahead it's not hard to imagine that they spent hours mesmerizing each other with stories of their families and their schooling, their travels and their careers. Since her arrival in Georgia, Gretchen had been struggling to adapt to the South's hardening racial divide, and John was able to give her insights into the sources of that divide—what it was like to grow up around freed slaves, people who reacted to their bondage with acts ranging from raw vengeance to undying loyalty, and why certain White people were clinging so viciously to a world that was long lost. She also heard about how unhappy John had been in the grasping boomtowns of Birmingham and Atlanta, what a joy it was to travel and study in Europe, how he was thinking about tackling a major work of scholarship, possibly a German-English dictionary.

He, in turn, heard Gretchen tell what it had been like to attend parochial schools in the small upstate New York hamlet of Dansville, where Clara Barton had founded the Red Cross. Then came the discovery that Gretchen had a musical gift, which was nurtured by her doting father and devoted teachers and soon led to the untouchable thrill of finishing a performance and watching a roomful of strangers jump to their feet and shout "Bravo!" She told John she was at peace with the fact that she would never be a great performer—a reckoning that eventually comes to most aspiring artists. She was not quite good enough, not quite driven enough. Then, too, she was up against the ethos of the Victorian age. As the art historian Linda Nochlin would write in the 1970s about the historical obstacles to women artists, the late nineteenth century insisted upon "a modest, proficient, self-demeaning level of amateurism as a 'suitable accomplishment' for the well-brought up young woman, who naturally would want to direct her major attention to the welfare of others—family and husband." And yes, Gretchen said, she was enjoying her job teaching at Lucy Cobb, even though the director, a niece of the founder named "Miss Millie" Rutherford, had a personality that sometimes crossed the line from forceful to domineering.

John also heard about Gretchen's gregarious father, Tom, who never met a stranger and was almost never at home, always on the road selling insurance and staying in a string of hotels in second-rate towns that must have triggered memories of John's boarding-house purgatory in Birmingham. For Tom Gallagher it was the Powers Hotel in Rochester, the Leland in

Syracuse, the Delavan in Albany. Tom, to hear his daughter tell it, had a peculiarly American zeal for a life that would have driven John mad. But Tom Gallagher couldn't get enough of it—the personal bonds with customers, the hotel lobbies, the bad roads and the bad food, the banquets, the camaraderie of his fellow salesmen. Tom even learned to speak a little German so he could communicate with his German clients. He loved his life, and it was making him rich.

Her uncle Jim, according to Gretchen, was a very different kettle of fish. He was the youngest of the four Gallagher children, and from an early age he'd been attracted to the underside of life—saloons, racetracks, card games, boxing rings, and women of dubious virtue. He'd lately been living in the town of Auburn, in the Finger Lakes district, with a woman named Cordelia Moulton who ran what the newspaper poets alternately referred to as a "sporting house," a "disorderly house," or a "bagnio" where "Cyprians" and "punks" named Mary, Eva, and Ida plied their trade. In plain English it was a brothel, and Cordelia Moulton was its madam. Jim had scrapes with the law early and often, and back in 1884, when Gretchen was just entering school, he'd pleaded guilty to forging another man's signature on a note payable to his brother Tom. Jim was sentenced to three years in the reformatory in Elmira. Even as a young girl, Gretchen found it hard to believe that two brothers could be so unalike.

Eventually the black sheep of the Gallagher family went all the way over to the dark side. The newspapers covered the story extensively, and Gretchen was able to retell it in vivid detail. Her uncle Jim was selling pools at the trotter tracks sprinkled around central New York, earning $30 a day, and he found he liked to gamble but was hobbled by a handicap. "He is a poor judge of horseflesh," according to one newspaper account, "and is said to have lost heavily at the races." Heavily, as in $1,500 on one occasion, a small fortune.

Alongside his deep love for gambling, Jim had developed a deep loathing for an Auburn hack driver named George Siebert. On one of many woozy nights in the saloons that dotted downtown Auburn, a debate about the merits of various wrestlers led to Siebert challenging Gallagher to step outside and see who was the superior wrestler. The challenge was accepted, and the two men, accompanied by a gaggle of giddy drinking buddies, rode to a nearby park, where the rivals stripped to the waist and had at each other. It was no contest. Jim Gallagher, with hands like a pair of Belfast sinks, whipped George Siebert. The bad blood between the men thickened.

On the night of July 29, 1901, Cordelia Moulton quarreled with two of her "inmates," Alice Davis and Josephine St. Dennis, who packed their things and prepared to leave the house and find work elsewhere. Ferrying customers to and from the establishment was George Siebert's bread and butter, and now he was summoned to pick up the two escapees. While he was loading their luggage onto his hack, Siebert bombarded Cordelia Mouton with the "vilest epithets" and "severe accusations" against Jim Gallagher. When Jim returned to the house later, Cordelia told him: "If you are a man, you will give Siebert a good sound thrashing. If you don't do it, you are no longer a friend of mine."

Jim Gallagher took the bait. He walked to the Waldorf Café and asked to borrow a gun from the saloonkeeper, James Gaynor, claiming he needed protection when he walked out of town to the farm Cordelia Moulton had recently bought. Jim said he'd been robbed a couple of times on the dark country roads. Gaynor, thinking nothing of it, loaned him a revolver. Instead of walking out of town, though, Jim walked around the corner to White's Saloon, where he saw George Siebert's hack parked in front. Perfect. With the revolver in his right hip pocket, Jim walked in and found Siebert alone at the bar. Doubly perfect. The barman, Fred Leader, was washing a glass.

"Good evening, George," Jim said as he walked past Siebert. Siebert turned. Jim said, "Have you got good evidence of what you're saying about me?"

"What's that?"

Jim's voice rose a notch. "I said, have you got good evidence of what you're saying about me?"

Siebert, sensing trouble, reached into his right coat pocket and took out a piece of metal that Jim believed was a knife. Siebert grabbed Jim's right shoulder and lunged at him. As they tussled, Jim drew the revolver and fired a shot over Siebert's head, hoping to scare him off. Now Fred Leader put down the glass he was washing and hurried around the bar, calling, "Don't, Jim! Don't, Jim!"

The two men continued tussling, and Jim started striking Siebert on the head with the revolver. The gun fired again. This time the bullet entered Siebert's skull behind his left ear and lodged in his brain. He fell in the doorway that led to the back room.

Jim walked out of the saloon without a word. On the street he was met by the proprietor, William White, who had been alerted about the ruckus inside. "My God, Jim," White said, "what have you done?"

"Ain't that awful," Jim said. He handed the gun to White and walked toward City Hall to find a policeman. On the way he met a detective named Callahan and turned himself in. George Siebert was already dead. The "knife" he had used during the fight turned out to be a fingernail file.

While awaiting trial on a charge of murder in the first degree, Jim was rarely lonely. He was visited in jail by a colorful parade of characters that included his brother Tom, Cordelia Moulton, a powerful Syracuse alderman, saloonkeeper, and horse trainer named Frank Matty, and "Diamond" George Cochran, a "horseman" who sported six diamonds imbedded in his front teeth, diamond shirt studs and vest buttons, and a watch with thirteen diamonds set in the shape of a horseshoe. The man was the avatar of bling. Riffraff from the racetracks also came to visit—"most of them being horsemen and gamblers," one newspaper sniffed.

Jim Gallagher pleaded self-defense, but in January of 1902 a jury convicted him of manslaughter. He showed no emotion when he heard the verdict or when the sentence was read: fifteen years in the state prison at

Auburn, the same grim fortress where William Kemmler had been executed by electrocution a dozen years earlier. His lawyers announced their intention to appeal the verdict and seek a new trial, but their appeal was denied.

John was transfixed. This refined young woman was descended from Irish peasants and had a convicted murderer in the family, and yet she played the violin like a dream and was elegant and eloquent, a born storyteller, an accomplished artist, the most fascinating jumble of contradictions John had ever met. And she was delightful company. And her father was rich. The Misfit had finally found his match.

While John and Gretchen were busy falling in love, writers, inventors, engineers, and politicians were busy adding to America's growing store of marvels and horrors. John had seen trains in the sky in Berlin, but now trains were running beneath the streets of New York City, a traffic-reducing innovation called the subway. Diphtheria could now be treated with an antitoxin, which would soon lead to mass immunizations of school children. Led by Theodore Roosevelt, its new president with bullish global ambitions, the United States was angling to pick the carcass of the failed French effort to dig a massive ditch through the midriff of Panama. The mastermind of that debacle was Ferdinand de Lesseps, who had overseen the successful completion of the Suez Canal and then proposed digging a similar canal in Panama, at sea level, without locks, that would connect the Atlantic and Pacific Oceans, put an end to the treacherous trip around South America's Cape Horn, and revolutionize international trade. But the French were doomed by hubris, by rococo corruption, and by a murderous, mountainous jungle. More than 20,000 people died during the French expedition, including the cream of the nation's engineers, many of their family members, and countless laborers imported from Jamaica. One cartoon suggested that de Lesseps wasn't digging a massive canal;

he was digging a mass grave. People died primarily from malaria and yellow fever because the role of the mosquito in the transmission of these diseases had not yet been established. The massive excavating machines created new swamps ideal for breeding mosquitoes, and at the overflowing French hospital outside Panama City, crockery rings filled with water were placed around plants to protect them from umbrella ants, providing another superb incubator for deadly mosquitoes. The jungle was a versatile killer. People also succumbed to typhoid fever, dysentery, smallpox, pneumonia, snakebite, and sunstroke. A French painter named Paul Gaugin had come to the Caribbean hoping to escape stifling France and "live on fish and fruit for nothing." After arriving in Colón, broke, he took a job on a canal-digging crew, grueling pick-and-shovel work that led him to write home to his wife: "I have to dig . . . from five-thirty in the morning to six in the evening, under tropical sun and rain. At night I am devoured by mosquitoes." He added that he felt "poisoned" by the gummy heat. But Paul Gaugin, unlike many thousands of others, managed to survive.

Theodore Roosevelt wasn't concerned with such human suffering or with the staggering financial losses and political scandals of the French failure. He was concerned with seizing an opportunity—to complete and control an isthmian canal that would connect America's new holdings in the Caribbean and the Pacific and, in the bargain, cement the nation's status as a major world power. Roosevelt insisted he was not an imperialist; he was merely in favor of expansion and progress. But many people, John and Gretchen surely among them, felt uneasy when they heard Roosevelt proclaim, "I wish to see the United States the dominant power on the shores of the Pacific Ocean." The newspapers were full of disconcerting stories about behind-the-scenes American efforts to ensure that Panama broke free from Colombia. In time the infant Panamanian government agreed to a canal treaty that, in the words of one senator, "sounds very much as if we wrote it ourselves."

In the Midwest, meanwhile, men named Buick, Olds, and Ford, following the lead of Karl Benz and other Europeans, were putting together rudimentary automobiles, working to perfect engines powered by gasoline, diesel, electricity, and steam, while designing systems that would enable them to manufacture their creations in quantity. One of Ford's early racing models was driven onto the ice of frozen Lake St. Clair in Detroit and wound out to the impossible speed of ninety miles per hour. It was dubbed the 999 in honor of the world's fastest locomotive. In Brooklyn, New York, an inventor named Willis Carrier had installed his new cooling system, the Apparatus for Treating Air, in the offices of the Sackett-Wilhelms Lithographing and Publishing Co. By blowing air over cold coils, the device lowered the temperature and, just as important, reduced humidity. It kept the company's papers from wilting and its inks from smearing. Four years would pass before Stuart Cramer, a textile mill engineer in North Carolina, would coin the enduring term for Carrier's invention: *air conditioning*. Oddly enough, Cramer's system *added* humidity to the air in textile mills, which made yarn easier to spin and less likely to break—and worsened the already hellish working conditions. Several more years would pass before Carrier's invention began to revolutionize the comfort levels inside factories, offices, stores, theaters, and homes.

It was then that W. E. B. Du Bois finally published his masterpiece, *The Souls of Black Folk*. It's likely John had followed Du Bois's career since their days at the University of Berlin, and if so he would have been delighted to discover that Du Bois shared his misgivings about the ascendancy of the nation's most influential Black leader. In his essay "Of Mr. Booker T. Washington and Others," Du Bois wrote: "This 'Atlanta Compromise' is by all odds the most notable thing in Mr. Washington's career." This was not a compliment. Du Bois proceeded to excoriate Washington for his "submission and silence as to civil and political rights." John shared Du Bois's belief that the two things required for Blacks to rise were education and the right to vote. And by education Du Bois did not mean the narrow industrial and agricultural training preached by Washington; he meant "the well-equipped college and university" able to train "the best of the Negro youth as teachers, professional men, and leaders." We're back to the Talented Tenth, which could not hope to thrive under Washington's obsequious system. But surely the lines in this essay that spoke most directly to John were Du Bois's taxonomy of the different classes of White southerners: "the ignorant southerner hates the Negro, the workingmen fear his competition, the money-makers wish to use him as a laborer, some of the educated see a menace in his upward development, while others—usually the sons of the masters—wish to help him rise." John prided himself in belonging to this last group. Yet a huge question loomed: Given the iron rule of Jim Crow, was it possible for John—or any other White man in the South—to help Blacks rise?

Not if Thomas Dixon could help it. When *The Souls of Black Folk* was published, the reigning hit on Broadway was *The Leopard's Spots*, an adaptation of the best-selling debut novel by Dixon, a Baptist minister, lecturer, novelist, and playwright from North Carolina who weaves a story of virtuous White men rising up to crush the Black beasts who seek to control them and rape their women. The novel's unsubtle subtitle says it all: *A Romance of the White Man's Burden*. A central character, Rev. Durham, is so intent on the total subjugation of Blacks that he opposes even Booker T. Washington's tepid push for industrial and agricultural education. The book was a fictional replay of the actual White supremacist coup in Wilmington five years earlier—and a mere taste of what was to come from this brazenly racist writer. And he was hardly working alone. Robert W. Shufeldt had just published *The Negro, a Menace to American Civilization*, and Charles Carroll had come out with a book whose title read, in part, *The Negro a Beast, but created with articulate speech, and hands, that he may be of service to his master—the White man*. Atlanta newspaper editor John Temple Graves toured the country preaching the necessity of lynch law as the only reliable deterrent to the Black rapist. The gifted Black writer Charles W. Chesnutt, who had just published *The Marrow of Tradition*, his own novel based on the Wilmington coup, was driven to despair: "The rights of the Negroes are at a lower ebb than at any time during the thirty-five years of their freedom, and the race prejudice more intense and uncompromising." And it was not only southerners who condoned disenfranchisement of Blacks. In 1900 the *New York Times* wrote: "Northern men . . . no longer denounce the suppression of the Negro vote (in the South) as it used to be denounced in the Reconstruction days. The necessity of it under the supreme law of self-preservation is candidly recognized."

Finally, on a more uplifting note, two brothers named Orville and Wilbur Wright were making history on the remote Outer Banks of North Carolina. The brothers were bicycle mechanics from Dayton, Ohio, clever and industrious high school dropouts who had taught themselves enough about engineering and aerodynamics to build the world's first wind tunnel, design propellers, and create an engine with a lightweight aluminum block that they fitted into an aircraft with wings made of muslin stretched over wooden ribs. Their first successful motorized flight, with Orville at the controls, lasted just twelve seconds. But by the end of that historic day, December 17, 1903, the brothers had flown two times apiece and kept their delicate bird aloft for more than a minute. Man now owned the heavens.

John and Gretchen were married on June 23, 1904—John's forty-first birthday—at her parents' home in Cincinnati's fashionable Mt. Auburn district. The marriage certificate listed the groom's occupation as "teacher," the bride's as "none." The newlyweds paused at the Greenbrier Hotel in Hot Sulphur Springs, West Virginia, on their way to New York, where they sailed for Europe.

After stopping in Ireland to visit Gallagher relatives in County Mayo, they made their way to Italy for an idyllic week on the island of Capri.

They bathed in the turquoise Mediterranean, visited Roman ruins, and hired a boat to take them into the Blue Grotto, a dome-roofed chamber with electric blue water miraculously lit from below. The Roman emperor Tiberius used the grotto as a swimming hole, John told Gretchen, and Mark Twain wrote about it in *Innocents Abroad*, claiming the water was the most "ravishing" blue he had ever seen. Gretchen must have been impressed by John's knowledge of history, his fluency in numerous languages, and how easy it was to travel with him. For John, this might have been the first time in his life that he tasted true happiness. One thing that requires no speculation is that the newlyweds got straight to business. Gretchen was already pregnant.

Le Petit Journal*'s depiction of the Atlanta riot.*

EPIPHANIES IN ATLANTA

When they returned from their European honeymoon, John and Gretchen moved into a rented house on Milledge Avenue and settled back into their teaching duties. There were signs, both superficial and substantial, that the university had begun to get in step with the dawning Progressive Era. On a superficial note, the chancellor who had been installed just before the turn of the century, Walter B. Hill, was the first since the Civil War who did not sport elaborate facial hair. The "Guilded Age" had also been the Golden Age of Facial Hair, and Hill's sleek grooming and forward thinking announced that the old ways were gone and change was in the air.

On a more substantial note, Hill was the first chancellor in a century who was a layman, a distinct signal that the university was finally ready to escape the suffocating grip of the state's powerful religious—that is, Protestant—denominations. Hill believed Black people should have access to higher education, he supported Prohibition, and he believed the university should not be a cloistered academy but should dedicate itself to addressing the state's social problems. In this he was in line with progressive reforms taking place at the state universities in Michigan, Wisconsin, and California. Hill cajoled the legislature to increase education funding, and he wooed the philanthropist George Peabody when he visited the campus in 1902. It worked. State appropriations increased steadily during Hill's tenure, and Peabody, who was already supporting the Normal School, agreed to fund one of Hill's dreams: a new library that came equipped with the university's first professional librarian. Hill also worked to expand the faculty of the law school and course offerings in education, engineering, forestry, pharmacy, business, medicine, and architecture.

This infusion of money, energy, and ideas must have delighted John, and it began attracting educators of stature, such as the sociologist Howard W. Odum, who returned from Columbia University to his native Georgia to join John on the faculty for a few years before getting whisked away to the University of North Carolina, where he would produce his monumental work of social analysis, *Southern Regions in the United States*. The influence of such men, even if they paused only briefly in Athens, lingered with faculty and students alike.

Progressive ideas were taking root far beyond Athens. Libraries and laboratories were sprouting on campuses large and small. As the states' spending on education increased across the South, old country schoolhouses were giving way to solid consolidated schools—segregated, of course—and illiteracy rates were falling sharply. The more enlightened element was suddenly emboldened to speak out in opposition to entrenched notions and in favor of unsettling modern ones. William Poteat, after studying at the

University of Berlin, returned to his alma mater, Wake Forest College in North Carolina, and began to teach Darwin's findings on evolution as fact, not theory. Poteat not only survived the predictable uproar at the Baptist school but eventually was named its president. Meanwhile, Dr. Andrew Sledd, a professor at Emory College in Georgia, had the audacity to publish an article in *The Atlantic Monthly* attacking Jim Crow laws in general and lynching in particular. The article included this incendiary sentence: "There is nothing in a white skin or a black to nullify the essential rights of man as man." Sledd was promptly fired, but the University of Florida offered him a job, and after Emory relocated to Atlanta, he was rehired there and remained on the faculty for the rest of his life. At Trinity College, the starchily Methodist school in North Carolina that would become Duke University, a history professor named John Spencer Bassett suggested in the *South Atlantic Quarterly* that next to Robert E. Lee, the greatest man born in the South in a century was Booker T. Washington—a *Negro*! Leading the backlash was the Raleigh newspaper publisher Josephus Daniels, one of the White supremacists who had helped foment the recent coup in Wilmington. Daniels saw to it that the offender's name always appeared in print as "bASSett." But the Trinity College faculty threatened to resign if the trustees fired Bassett, and the trustees, after a fiery debate, allowed him to stay. These and other events showed that progressive ideas and dissent against southern pieties were no longer unthinkable.

Another change at Georgia was that John's brother Sylvanus had been named dean of the law school. The faculty of that school, like the others, was still small but growing, which led to a development that John most likely viewed with his characteristic mix of scorn and amusement. As the university historian Thomas G. Dyer put it: "For Georgians as for Americans generally during the so-called Progressive Era, education was becoming an enterprise, a business to be managed efficiently like any other sound venture, complete with the trappings of a bureaucracy." Americans, John mused, could turn anything—even a university—into a business, then stock it with technicians and middle managers. A writer then emerging in Baltimore, H. L. Mencken, would coin a delightfully derisive term for these pedagogical bureaucrats. He would dub them "educationists." Perfect, John thought, with a bittersweet laugh.

For reasons unknown, Gretchen traveled alone late in her pregnancy to be with her family in Cincinnati. In Christ's Hospital, she gave birth to a daughter on March 22, 1905—nine months, almost to the day, after the wedding. They named the girl Margarethe, a German-inflected moniker that delighted John but would present serious problems in years to come. John had hired a Black nanny named Fimmie because it was understood that Gretchen was going to return to her teaching job as soon as she felt up to it. She was not going to be one of those typical well-brought-up young Victorian women who abandoned herself to the welfare of others. She loved her music and her students and had no intention of sacrificing them at the altar of convention. Within a few weeks of her return from Cincinnati, she was back at Lucy Cobb, where preparations were already underway for the school's looming fiftieth anniversary celebration.

That winter a novel was published that did something almost unheard-of in American fiction, at least not since *Uncle Tom's Cabin*: it struck such a nerve with the public that it changed the course of the nation's history. Upton Sinclair's *The Jungle*, a lightly fictionalized account of his own reporting, was a portrait of the horrific working and living conditions of the people, mostly immigrants from Eastern Europe, who toiled in Chicago's meatpacking industry. The story follows the downward spiral of Jurgis Rudkus, who has come from Lithuania seeking a better life and finds himself working in an inferno where the cattle are fed waste from breweries that causes their hides to erupt with boils, where men fall into rendering vats and get sent through meat grinders and become ingredients in canned meat, where the waste from the square mile of packing houses drains into an arm of the Chicago River, known as "Bubbly Creek" because gigantic bubbles of carbonic acid burst on its surface, which is caked so hard that chickens can walk across it. From time to time the river catches fire. Though unrelievedly grim, the novel was a sensation, selling more than 25,000 copies in the six weeks after publication. It horrified some readers and infuriated others. It caused beef exports to plummet. It was pulled from the shelves of the public libraries in the meatpacking cities of Chicago and St. Louis, and it led President Roosevelt, fresh off a landslide election victory, to dispatch investigators to the Chicago packing plants. He then summoned Sinclair to the White House but found him a "crackpot," largely because of his socialist leanings. Nevertheless in June, just four months after the novel's publication, Roosevelt eagerly signed the Pure Food and Drug Act and the Meat Inspection Act, pieces of legislation that had languished for years before Sinclair's novel galvanized the nation.

John surely read the book, possibly on winter nights while his wife and infant daughter slept, and he would have found much to admire in Sinclair's ambition and his cause, though his prose tended to be mechanical and didactic. And while John surely applauded the new laws—who wouldn't, other than the owners of a meatpacking plant?—he was by nature distrustful of people like Theodore Roosevelt who claimed they wanted to improve the world. John had seen the "improvements" Henry Grady had helped bring to the South, the ugly red-brick mills, the shabby housing huddled around them, and the human wrecks who issued from that housing, children who were put to work at the age of six and worked fourteen-hour days and grew up, starved of sunlight and fresh air, into adults with fish-white skin and sunken chests, stringy hair and scrambled teeth, worn to exhaustion by the age of forty. Yes, John distrusted American do-gooders because his classical education had led him to a primitive, nearly pagan, vision that was closer to Homer than to Henry Grady—that the race was essentially unimprovable and every man was engaged in an eternal war between his noble and venal impulses, between the angels and the beasts that dwelled inside him. No politician or booster or law could ever change that.

For his part, Sinclair, suddenly a rich celebrity, was dismayed by his book's astonishing impact. He had set out to expose and rectify industrial capitalism's exploitation of workers, but readers couldn't stop thinking about all that tubercular meat. "I aimed for the public's heart," Sinclair complained bitterly, "and by accident I hit it in the stomach."

The 1906 Georgia governor's race, as far as John and Gretchen were concerned, was a tussle between two troglodytes. It was downright embarrassing. The two leading candidates, both Democrats of course, had ties to Atlanta newspapers that were spreading inflammatory lies about Black misdeeds and schemes, just as the White papers had done in the run-up to the coup in Wilmington eight years earlier. The frontrunner was Hoke Smith, a former publisher of the *Atlanta Journal* who favored the formal disenfranchisement of Black people and had won the support of former Populist leader Tom Watson, who'd made a U-turn and become a vocal White supremacist. Writing in Watson's magazine, Smith asked: "What does Civilization owe the Negro? Nothing! *Nothing!* NOTHING!" Not to be outdone, his rival Clark Howell, editor of the *Atlanta Constitution*, countered that the poll tax had already silenced the Black vote and the real issue was that Hoke Smith, while serving as secretary of the interior under President Grover Cleveland, had appointed Black people to federal posts—and therefore he couldn't be trusted to uphold White supremacy in Georgia. Smith denied the charge. And so the campaign boiled down to a dispiriting question: Which candidate was the more immaculate White supremacist?

Atlanta's Black population had quadrupled since John's year teaching at Morehead Military Academy, and it was now sharply stratified, ranging from scuffling day laborers to an educated, property-owning middle class all the way up to such men as Alonzo Herndon, a former slave who had been minted the city's first Black millionaire. White resentment of this rising community was thorough and relentless. The new Black arrivals competed with Whites for jobs, housing, and services, and the rough saloons along Decatur Street, known as "Atlanta's Bowery," were said to be nests of vice and crime frequented by the "shiftless Negro" element. Some of the dives had pictures of naked White women on the walls! Equally repugnant to Whites were middle- and upper-class Blacks, who were guilty of acting "uppity" and "self-important" and "bumptious." Every day the newspapers were publishing a drumbeat of sensational stories—most of them completely fabricated—about "brutish" outrages by Black men against White women. These were leavened with stories about Black people who had so thoroughly forgotten their place that they were striving to attain social equality with Whites. The drumbeat culminated with reports of four separate attacks on White women on Saturday, September 22. As newsboys barked the headlines on downtown street corners in the heat of an Indian summer afternoon—*"Extra! Third Assault on White Woman by Negro Brute!"* and *"Extra! Bold Negro Kisses White Girl's Hand!"*—a surly White mob began to coalesce near the downtown hub of Five Points. An editorial in the *Evening News* was typically inflammatory. "With his yellow lips forming insulting phrases," it read, "Luther Frazier, a young Negro, attacked Miss Orrie Bryan, the pretty eighteen-year-old daughter of Thomas L. Bryan, in her home." *Yellow* lips! To this bit of poetic license the paper added a call to arms: "Men of Fulton, what will you do to stop the outrages against the women? . . . Shall these black devils be permitted to assault and almost kill our women, and go unpunished?"

The mob soon swelled to 10,000 men, many of them lit up with liquor. The inevitable bloodletting began when the mob dragged two Black men off a Marietta Street trolley, stabbed one, and beat, kicked, and stomped the other to death. A lame Black bootblack leaving one of Alonzo Herndon's barbershops was chased down Peachtree Street and beaten to death with fists and clubs. Now it was open season. Armed with guns, knives, iron bars, bricks, hatchets, and hatred, White mobs fanned through the city, randomly killing Black people by hanging, shooting, stabbing, and beating. Three Black corpses were dumped at the foot of the Henry Grady monument on Marietta Street, a telling tribute to the great promoter of progress in the New South. The police did little to stop the violence, and sometimes even assisted the mob. Finally, when rain began to pelt the streets early Sunday morning, the bloodlust fizzled. But it was far from extinguished.

The next day something remarkable happened: Black Atlanta fought back. It began with small acts, as when a Black postal worker named George White was making his Saturday rounds downtown in a tiny cart pulled by a Texas mustang. Along for the ride on that unseasonably warm day was one of White's sons, Walter, a thirteen-year-old boy with blond hair, blue eyes, and skin so fair that he, like his father and mother, could have passed for White. As they made their rounds, father and son sensed something wasn't right. They saw the clots of men gathering on street corners. Then they watched, horrified, as the mob chased a Black man and knocked him down and beat him savagely until someone shouted, "There goes another nigger!" and the mob left the dead man in a pool of blood and went off in search of fresh prey.

After that, father and son stuck to back streets until they arrived at the family's tidy two-story frame house on Houston Street, on the borderline between a White neighborhood and a Black neighborhood that were both shading toward shabby. George's wife, Madeline, a college graduate and schoolteacher, implored him to get guns to protect the family. Reluctantly, he agreed.

The next day, Sunday, there were rumors that the White mob planned to sweep from downtown past the Whites' house and into nearby Darktown "to clear out the niggers." This, George realized, was war, and now he was glad he had procured two guns. With his wife and five daughters secure in the rear of the house, far from the street, George handed Walter a gun and prepared to stand vigil by the parlor windows as night fell. The lights in the house were turned off and the streetlights had been shot out. Father and son spent anxious hours peering into the darkness, across the front porch and the tidy lawn to the freshly painted picket fence. Finally, toward midnight, they heard a roar, dim at first but growing steadily until flickers of torchlight appeared on Houston Street as a White wave came surging downhill toward its target. Suddenly the wave froze as a voice cried out, "That's where the nigger mail carrier lives!" George and Walter tensed. They recognized the voice instantly; it belonged to the son of the grocer where the family had shopped for years. "Let's burn it down! It's too nice for a nigger to live in!" In the next minutes, young Walter White, still straddling the color line, still not sure which world he belonged to, experienced an epiphany. Years later he would recall it:

> In the flickering light the mob swayed, paused, and began to flow toward us. In that instant there opened up within me a great awareness; I knew then who I was. I was a Negro, a human being with an invisible pigmentation which marked me a person to be hunted, hanged, abused, discriminated against, kept in poverty and ignorance, in order that those whose skin was white would have readily at hand a proof of their superiority . . .

As the revelation was sinking in, the mob kept moving toward the house. Now Walter's thoughts were interrupted by his father's voice:

> In the eerie light father turned his drawn face to me. In a voice as quiet as though he were asking me to pass him the sugar at

the breakfast table, he said, "Son, don't shoot until the first man puts his foot on the lawn and then—don't you miss!"

Miraculously, no one stepped over that picket fence. The sound of gunshots split the night—neighbors of the Whites, barricaded in their house, had begun firing at the mob. Black Atlanta was fighting back. There were more gunshots from the house. The mob, startled like a school of fish, hesitated, jittered, then retreated back up Houston Street. On that night a young man had learned that he was ready to kill men who were willing to hunt, hang, and abuse him because of an invisible pigmentation in his skin. As the mob melted away, Walter White had a second epiphany:

> In the quiet that followed I put my gun aside and tried to relax. But a tension different from anything I had ever known possessed me. I was gripped by my knowledge of my identity, and in the depths of my soul I was vaguely aware that I was glad of it. I was sick with loathing for the hatred which had flared before me that night and come so close to making me a killer; but I was glad I was not one of those made sick and murderous by pride.

Less than a mile away, another epiphany was taking place. W. E. B. Du Bois, then on the faculty of Atlanta University (now Clark Atlanta University), had been on a research trip in Alabama when word of the riot reached him. He hustled home on a train, and on the way he bought a Winchester double-barreled shotgun and two dozen shells filled with buckshot. He had finally heeded the credo of Ida B. Wells—*a Winchester rifle should have a place of honor in every Black home.* Like George and Walter White before him, Du Bois now stood vigil, in his case on the steps of a campus building that sheltered his wife and their six-year-old daughter and other terrified Black people. As with young Walter White, something had awakened inside the bookish Du Bois. Years later he would describe the change: "If a white mob had stepped on the campus where I lived I would without hesitation have sprayed their guts over the grass."

The mob did not come onto the campus. Instead, on Monday evening a group of county policemen and armed White civilians descended on a nearby section of the prosperous Black neighborhood known as Brownsville, alerted to a rumor that Black people were meeting to arm themselves and prepare a counterattack. The policemen were not mounted, and in the dusky light some Black people claimed they mistook the men for another mob. Many of the Black people were indeed armed, but they, like the Whites and Du Bois, were intent only on protecting their homes and businesses. The police began arresting any Black person who carried a gun, and while some of the policemen guarded the prisoners, a small group split off to investigate a crowd of armed Black people gathering nearby. The police fired first, and the Black crowd fired back. The exchange left one policeman dead, another wounded, and three Black men dead in the street. The arrested men were transported to downtown. On the way, two of them were shot dead in police custody.

Now, inflamed by the killing of a policeman, three companies of heavily armed state militia swept into Brownsville, arresting Black people wholesale and confiscating guns and ammunition. More than 250 men were arrested as rioting flared throughout the city.

By Tuesday morning the killing was over. It's estimated that three dozen or more Black people were killed in the violence while two White people died—the policeman in Brownsville and a pregnant woman who saw a mob outside her house and dropped dead of a heart attack. A White writer from the North named Ray Stannard Baker offered a telling postmortem: "It is significant that *not one of the negroes killed and wounded* in the riot was of the criminal class." (Italics his.) The *New York Times* agreed with Baker's assessment. "As a matter of fact," the paper noted, "no one believes that a single guilty Negro was killed."

Yet White Atlanta was not inclined to repent. Like the White supremacists in Wilmington, the leaders of Atlanta got busy rewriting the narrative. "Mayor Blames Negroes," read a headline in the *New York Times*. The article quoted Mayor James Woodward: "As long as the black brutes assault our white women, just as long will they be unceremoniously dealt with."

When pleas for federal intervention reached the White House, President Roosevelt did precisely what President McKinley had done in response to the coup in Wilmington: nothing. The southern states were free to do as they pleased.

John and Gretchen were appalled by the news out of Atlanta, which was making headlines around the world. The coup in Wilmington may have seemed like a distant aberration, but this nightmare was playing out next door and it was impossible to ignore. Which leads to the question that must be asked, and not for the last time: If John and Gretchen were as progressive and open-minded as I have come to believe they were, why didn't they get out? Why didn't they join the tens of thousands of southerners, Black and White, who saw that the federal government had capitulated to the states, who saw that Jim Crow was now both unquenchable and unstoppable, who saw that the chasm between the races kept growing wider, and who, seeing these things, gave up on the South and moved away?

The answer is complicated. First, we have to go back to George Washington and Thomas Jefferson and Patrick Henry, men who may have been philosophically opposed to slavery but were able to live with their misgivings because it was so "convenient" to do so—not to mention profitable—and because to do anything else would have required upending the entrenched social order. If a man is powerless to change his world, these men concluded, then he must figure out a way to live in it. Similarly, John and Gretchen may have been appalled by the recent events in Atlanta, and they may have despised the reign of Jim Crow, but even under such a cloud, they were managing to carve out a life that was not merely convenient, but also decent. They were starting a family, they had jobs they loved, they enjoyed a wide social circle in one of the South's more enlightened towns, where the Morris family name counted for something. Their life was, in a word, convenient. Comfortable. Besides, they were able to tell themselves, their conduct—treating Black people fairly, banishing racial epithets from their home, other gestures large and small—was an antidote to the poisons emanating from Jim Crow. And that antidote, small as it may have been, would have vanished if they had packed up and left.

But I believe it goes much deeper than that. Gretchen had grown up in the North, John had traveled extensively, and neither of them harbored any illusions that the North or the Midwest or the Far West—or Europe, for that matter—were oases of racial tolerance and harmony. Events were about to confirm such a cold-eyed assessment. In the next decade and a half, there would be bloody race riots across the country, not only in the South but in Chicago and Springfield, Illinois (Abraham Lincoln's hometown!), Philadelphia, Washington, DC, Indianapolis, Omaha, Tulsa, and New York City. The grass was no greener north of the Mason–Dixon Line or west of the Mississippi River. Maybe it was best to stay put and try to live a decent life and hope that small acts of kindness and tolerance might actually make a difference. It strikes me as a reasonable—and morally defensible—choice. Another factor had come to light that would have cemented their decision to stay put. Gretchen was pregnant again.

The Morris house on Mell Street, the first commission for the architect Fred J. Orr.

ARTS AND CRAFTS

W hile the riot was convulsing Atlanta, Andrew Carnegie was trying to figure out how to give away his fortune. He had sold his steelworks to J. P. Morgan for more than $200 million, which made Carnegie the richest man in the world and made it possible for Morgan to cobble together the largest corporation in the world, U.S. Steel. And now Carnegie, retired, in his sixties, richer than God, was trying to live up to the obligation he had set forth in his "Gospel of Wealth" essays: After providing for his family, Carnegie believed, it was the duty of every rich man to give away his fortune while he was still alive. Inherited wealth produced nothing but sloth and misery.

Giving away such a pile proved to be a full-time job. Education and world peace were Carnegie's abiding passions, and he endowed more than two thousand free public libraries as well as schools, museums, churches, teacher pensions, universities on both sides of the Atlantic, and a Peace Palace at the Hague. All but lost in this orgy of largess was Carnegie's belief, one shared by John Morris, that English could be made into the world language if knotty spellings were simplified through the omission of "silent and useless letters." Carnegie also believed that a unified international language would foster world peace. To achieve this seemingly simple but devilishly complicated goal, Carnegie put up the handsome sum of $250,000 in 1906 to create the Simplified Spelling Board.

Among the board's original thirty members were renowned scholars, editors, lexicographers, educators, and writers, including Mark Twain. Within a month, the board had produced an initial list of three hundred words with new phonetic spellings. The *-ed* suffix was shortened to *t*, so that a dead person was *deceast*. Catalogue became *catalog*, surprise became *surprize*, and through became *thru*. It's an echo of the German linguist G. H. Balg's description of the obstacles he had to overcome in backwoods Wisconsin while producing magisterial works of scholarship: *"several scientific works hav appeared during the preparation of my book, sum of which I hav not seen at all, while others reacht me comparatively late."*

As it happened, Americans had been pushing for spelling reform as far back as Benjamin Franklin's 1768 book, *A Scheme for a New Alphabet and Reformed Mode of Spelling*. Noah Webster, bristling at the outsize influence of the British lexicographer Samuel Johnson, came out in 1783 with *The American Book of Spelling*, his attempt to "purify" the language by ridding it of British corruptions. The book and its subsequent editions would become one of the best sellers in American publishing history, yet only a few of Webster's Americanisms survived when his *American Dictionary of the English Language* appeared in 1828. Then one of John's heroes, the British linguist A. J. Ellis, published *A Plea for Phonetic Spelling*, and, working with the shorthand proponent Isaac Pitman, persuaded the public schools in Waltham, Mass., to teach his phonetic system, which he called *Fonotypy*. The schools in St. Louis adopted a modified system.

Soon afterward, the Spelling Reform Association came together and, with the backing of the National Education Association, preached the merits of phonetic spelling to a receptive audience of reformers that included President Theodore Roosevelt. In 1906, the year the Simplified Spelling Board was formed, Roosevelt ordered the Federal Printing Agency to adopt some phonetic spellings in government documents, and he announced that he would use reformed spelling in his official communications and messages to Congress. The move backfired. People were outraged that spellings they had used all their lives were suddenly in danger of being tossed out the window. Newspapers mocked the reform movement. The *Baltimore Sun* suggested that rather than spelling his own name "Rusevelt," the president should go with "Butt-in-Sky." A popular postcard showed a caricature of Roosevelt in full Rough Rider regalia, along with a ditty that invoked the nineteenth-century humorist Josh Billings, who'd used slang and phonetic spelling to get laughs. The card read:

> *Az Ruzvelt sez—*
> *Never mind your Qs and Ps—*
> *But go ahed—spel az yu pleez—*
> *Lay Noah Webster's book aside,*
> *And let Josh Billings be yur gide.*

A red-faced Roosevelt soon rescinded his order, and the Spelling Reform Association faded away just as the Simplified Spelling Board was getting down to work. Its future did not look bright. For once, it appeared that habit and tradition were destined to trump the Progressive Era's craving for all things efficient and new.

All families generate myths. Most grow from a germ of historical fact—an act of heroism during wartime, a brilliant investment, a quirk of personality—that then gets magnified, sanitized, or otherwise distorted through repeated retellings. One Morris family myth had it that John was a vigorous proponent of phonetic spelling. My father told me many times about his father's preference for spelling words the way they sounded and his support for the campaign to rid the language of silent and useless letters. There is evidence that this myth has some substance. John served with other academics on one of the advisory groups that met regularly with the Simplified Spelling Board. Though there is no surviving record of his contributions to the cause, it's known that John adopted phonetic spelling in his daily life. A letter written to one of his children during the First World War, for instance, contains spelling that drew on G. H. Balg and the Simplified Spelling Board's original list of three hundred phonetic spellings. The letter reads in part:

> I hav had at least two dear letters from you, which I enjoyed reading very much. I am so glad to hear that you are going to hav the nice trip to Va. Beach. That wil be the first time you hav seen the ocean, altho, for that matter, Lake Michigan is big enuf. Stil the surf is much higher at the seashore, and you hav to be careful how you dive into the billows, or they wil knock you hed-over-heels and make you drink quarts of salt water.

Wize werds.

As Gretchen's due date drew near the following spring, she and John had reason to be alarmed. Despite the breakthroughs in discovering the sources of infectious diseases and in developing ways to prevent and treat them, infant mortality rates had actually increased during the last decades of the nineteenth century. A leading cause was "summer diarrhea," an affliction that peaked in the warm months thanks to diluted and adulterated milk that was erratically refrigerated on its journey from farm to market to home. Tainted milk also caused typhoid, scarlet fever, diphtheria, and tuberculosis. Babies who had recently stopped breastfeeding, including Margarethe, were particularly vulnerable. In New York City in 1885, the infant death rate was a shocking 273 per 1,000 live births.

But there was also reason to hope. More than forty years after Louis Pasteur discovered that heating beer and wine would prevent the growth of organisms that led to spoilage, pasteurization was finally being used to treat numerous foods and beverages, including milk. Pasteurized milk was introduced in Pittsburgh in 1907, and soon afterward Chicago, possibly still smarting from the fallout of *The Jungle*, became the first American city to enforce compulsory pasteurization of milk. A typhoid epidemic convinced New York City to follow suit. These decrees, coupled with improvements to urban water supplies and sewer systems, had dramatic results. By 1920, the number of infant deaths per 1,000 live births would plunge to seventy-one, a drop of nearly three-quarters in thirty-five years.

Gretchen gave birth to a healthy boy on March 24, 1907, two days after Margarethe's second birthday. They named their firstborn son Charles, after John's father. Though no one knew it at the time, he was to be the troubled child.

John's and Gretchen's social circle was widening, and it had come to include a gifted young artist named Fred J. Orr, who'd grown up in Athens and earned a degree in engineering from the university before studying at Drexel University in Philadelphia and Columbia in New York City, then coming back home to Athens to teach what he called "manual arts" at the

Normal School. With his impish grin and infectious energy, Orr threw himself into the teaching of drawing, design, color study, woodworking, and handicrafts. He also taught interior design and furniture making and had his students design simple country houses, stressing the importance of natural light and proper ventilation so that the houses provided "comfort and convenience combined with beauty."

Like John, he was a demanding teacher, a perfectionist with a lighter side. When a student moaned that completing one of Orr's grueling assignments would be the death of her, he promised he would personally pick out an artistic casket. He also cautioned his students against crying onto a watercolor—because salt water would make the pigments run.

On a more serious note, Orr was something of a one-man outpost of the Arts and Crafts movement then flourishing in Europe. Led by such artists and writers as John Ruskin and William Morris (no kin to John), proponents of the movement sought to counter the depersonalizing mechanization of the second Industrial Age by developing independent workers who designed the things they made. Starting from a fascination with medieval art and its guild culture, Morris in particular worked to improve the level of workmanship in a dizzying array of disciplines, including architecture, weaving, calligraphy, printing, metalworking, woodworking, pottery, and embroidery, with applications for the makers of everything from wallpaper to dyes, upholstery, stained glass, lamps, leather, ceramics, tapestries, furniture, houses, and books. Accomplished in all these fields, Morris, a true product of the Victorian era, was also an acclaimed poet, novelist, essayist, artist, architect, and translator, as well as an ardent socialist. While he railed against capitalists for turning workers into machine tenders, he was not opposed to machines if they could produce high-quality goods. He was willing to concede that in the Industrial Age, the designer could not always be the maker. What Morris despised was the *division* of labor—divorcing the worker from the finished product by making him or her a performer of ever more precise and repetitive tasks. He also despised any design that was ornate and artificial.

These ideas spoke to Fred Orr who, much as he enjoyed teaching, had bigger aspirations. He wanted to be an architect, he told John, and to that end he had begun building a house, largely of his own design, on seven bucolic acres near the western city limits. The house, heavily influenced by the Arts and Crafts movement, had sloping roofs, southern exposures, spacious terraces, high ceilings, uncluttered lines, and meticulous workmanship. The house had no ornate or artificial flourishes. It seemed to grow out of the land. Behind it was a forest, an orchard, flower and vegetable gardens, and a pond stocked with bream. Orr and his wife kept chickens. As Orr explained in an article in *Country Life in America* magazine: "Economy was obtained by eliminating the superfluous. There is scarcely a piece of molding in the entire construction. Beauty was gained from structural lines and simple treatment of materials." Beauty was also wedded to function. With pasteurization not yet widespread and electric refrigerators not yet available, Orr came up with an ingenious solution for preserving food in a hot climate. "Between the butler's pantry and the kitchen is a refrigerator porch," he wrote. "Its northern exposure reduced ice bills, while a screened safe for meat and milk above the refrigerator makes ice unnecessary during most of the year." It was, Orr concluded proudly, the best of both worlds: "a country home in the city."

John was awestruck by Orr's achievement. He surely let Orr know that the Morris family had outgrown the rented house on Milledge Avenue and that he and Gretchen were thinking of buying a house. Eventually the two men struck a deal: John gave Orr his first commission to design a private house. It would rise on a treeless lot on Mell Street, about a mile from the campus.

Commissioning an architect, even a relatively untested one, to design a one-of-a-kind house is the sort of thing rich people do. How did John and Gretchen manage it on their teachers' salaries? I have a hunch that this was the first time—and I know for a fact it was not the last—Gretchen turned to her father for help.

By now Tom Gallagher had been transferred by the Aetna insurance company from Cincinnati to Chicago, where he was a much bigger fish in a much bigger pond, the sole agent for a territory that spanned the Midwest. John didn't see that trips to Des Moines and Duluth were a big step up from trips to Schenectady and Syracuse, but he was told his father-in-law was in heaven. Tom was welcomed by Chicago's business elite as a public speaker and raconteur, a veteran of the lunch club and the banquet hall, where he was in demand as a toastmaster who delighted audiences with yarns about a concocted Irish character named Casey. "The first bird I ever shot was a squirrel," one Casey yarn begins, "and I missed him altogether. Then I shot him again in the same place. Then I threw a stone at him, knocked him out of the tree and he fell into the water and was drowned. That's the first bird I ever shot." Audiences ate it up.

Tom Gallagher was also an avid joiner. He, like many devout Catholics, belonged to the Knights of Columbus and also to a fraternal order modeled on King Arthur called the Round Table, to a national club of insurance executives called the Honorable Order of the Blue Goose, and he had just been named president of a whimsical outfit known as the Cook County Association of Concatenated & Conglomerated Order of the Grandfathers. If Gretchen called to announce that another grandchild was on the way, due in the summer of 1908, and, oh, by the way, she and John could use a little help paying for their first house, then Tom Gallagher, a soft touch known to his growing brood of grandchildren as Bompa (his wife, Sarah, was Mama Wee), probably didn't hesitate. Anything for his children and grandchildren. Anything to keep them off the road his brother Jim had traveled.

However Fred Orr got paid, he designed a remarkable house for his first clients. It had distinct Arts and Crafts notes, including long, sloping roofs, ample porches, high ceilings, and an asymmetrical composition that allowed for the free flow of light and air. There were echoes of his own house, including sliding doors between dining room and living room and a workspace outside the north-facing kitchen, with clean lines and meticulous workmanship throughout. Like Orr's house, it, too, seemed rooted to the ground. And in a sign of Orr's sense of humor, he labeled a storage space off the front porch the Plunder Room. John, a fan of Norse epics, must have been delighted.

Imagine a scene with me. Construction of the house is nearly complete, and one day John and Orr meet at the site to watch workers spreading the last swaths of stucco on the exterior walls. The yard is still dirt. Suddenly a weird little black box on four wheels goes muttering up Mell Street. The driver waves at the two men, and the black box honks like a goose. It's one of Henry Ford's new Model Ts, and John remarks that the damn things seem to be proliferating like guinea pigs. Orr agrees with a laugh, then offers the opinion that Henry Ford is the anti–William Morris. Henry Ford is busy dividing labor into ever smaller and more precise increments. Henry Ford, Orr admits sadly, is also the future. The two men watch as the black box disappears and the muttering dies. Then they turn to admire the new house that will soon bring the best of the past to life.

American soldiers with massacred Moros at Bud Dajo in the Philippines, March 7, 1906.

A BRILLIANT FEAT OF ARMS

The news out of Panama was bad, the news out of Washington was worse, and the news from the Philippines was the worst of all.

In Panama, Dr. William Gorgas's campaign to replicate his Havana miracle was foundering. For starters, he was trying to eradicate yellow fever and malaria not in a contained city but throughout the fifty miles of mountainous swampy jungle that lay between Panama City, on the Pacific coast, and the fetid port of Colón, on the Caribbean. He was also hampered by inadequate staff and supplies, fruits of a nearly religious bureaucratic fervor to avoid the graft and waste that had helped doom the French effort. The result was an impenetrable jungle of red tape, including forms in triplicate that delayed the delivery of vital supplies for months. But Gorgas's chief handicap was that many of his superiors dismissed the new science that had established, beyond all doubt, that yellow fever and malaria were transmitted by mosquitoes. Admiral John Walker, head of the canal commission, went so far as to declare the science "balderdash." He advised Gorgas to forget about mosquitoes and instead pave the streets, paint the houses, and get rid of all the dead cats. John Wallace, the chief engineer, announced that he was "distrustful" of the mosquito-control program, including Gorgas's demand for window screens. The project's chief architect, M. O. Johnson, added that he had "little faith in the modern ideas pertaining to yellow fever transmission." Gen. George W. Davis, governor of the Canal Zone, cabled Washington that newspaper stories about scattered outbreaks of yellow fever were "cruelly exaggerated" and that conditions were actually improving.

The results were predictable. Davis was soon so sick with yellow fever that he was unable to carry out his duties, which, apparently, included attacking the press and lying about conditions in the Canal Zone. Those discredited news reports were not exaggerated, cruelly or otherwise. As cases of yellow fever mounted and hospital wards filled, panic set in among the American workers, administrators, and military personnel. Daily funeral processions began to thread through the streets of Panama City and Colón. Then came the terrifying news that a Barbadian dockworker had died of bubonic plague. Gorgas sprang into action. The dock area in Panama City was cordoned off, buildings and ships were fumigated, animal pens and latrines were torn down and burned, and a ten-cent bounty was offered for every dead mouse or rat. The rats were often as big as guinea pigs and many were infected with bubonic plague. Meanwhile, incidents of yellow fever, though rising, were outstripped by fatal cases of malaria, dysentery, tuberculosis, and pneumonia, especially among Black workers. Now simmering panic turned into raw terror. Three-fourths of the Americans on the isthmus hurriedly packed up and headed for home.

It's not likely that John cheered this news of governmental myopia and duplicity—or the suffering and death it caused. But my guess is that he was secretly pleased that the canal effort was faltering, because he saw it as an act of hubris. It was, despite official denials, part of a campaign to build an American empire—the key to Roosevelt's dream of seeing the United States dominate the Pacific Ocean. It was, to John's classically educated mind, the Greek myth of Icarus played out in modern times: the Americans had flown too close to the sun, and they got burned.

Which brings us to the news out of Washington. Andrew Carnegie had promoted a second Hague Conference to foster world peace, but like the first one, eight years earlier, it failed to prod the world powers to pursue disarmament. The nations wouldn't even agree to future limits on their arsenals. When Britain proposed curbs on new naval armaments, Germany rejected the idea because it would limit its ability to develop new weaponry and thus would solidify British naval superiority. In a sign of hardening attitudes, no government would agree to give up any armaments it believed necessary to its national security—though they did make a half-hearted promise not to use poisons or poisonous weapons in warfare. The arms race continued at its brisk pace.

With President Roosevelt leading the way, the United States kicked into a new gear. Roosevelt, a big-navy man who remained optimistic about the Panama Canal despite the recent setbacks, ordered the construction of six ships of the dreadnought class. Possibly more disturbing to John was the news that independent inventors were devoting more and more of their creative energy to projects that attracted the interest of the military, including gyroscopes, wireless telegraphy and telephony, gunnery, fire-control systems, searchlights, even airplanes. The Wright brothers, who until now had seemed indifferent to making a financial profit off their invention, were aggressively pitching their plane to military officials in the United States and Britain, arguing that controlling the skies would soon be as important as controlling the seas. Their pitches landed with a thud—until they didn't. After the Wrights had made successful demonstration flights in Europe, the US War Department relented and sent out bids for airplanes with specifications that matched those the Wrights had unsuccessfully pitched earlier. The Wright Company soon opened lavish offices in New York City. One of its backers, a man who knew profit when he smelled it, was Cornelius Vanderbilt.

John was surely aware of the ancient Roman adage *If you wish for peace, prepare for war.* It may have sounded good on paper—who wants to take on a superior military force?—but John distrusted it because his reading of history had taught him that when people develop a weapon, they invariably use it for its intended purpose—that is, to inflict violence, not prevent it. As he saw it, America's enthusiasm for the global arms race could only end badly.

In fact, the nation was already sinking into a deepening quagmire halfway around the world. After Americans had ousted the Spanish from the Philippines at the end of the Spanish-American War, the indigenous insurgency against Spanish rule had morphed into a war against the new American occupiers. Though American forces claimed victory over the insurgents by 1902, in truth the war was far from over. Muslim Moros in the south had been fighting the Spanish for years, and now they resisted American attempts to occupy their islands, part of the campaign to prepare the nation for full independence. The Moro were known as fierce fighters. Every adult male carried a blade and, if possible, a gun. They kept slaves. There were constant internecine conflicts between tribes in the dense island jungles. Moro acts of banditry and scattered attacks on American sentries led to retaliation, which led to more banditry and attacks, which led to ever-more-brutal retaliation. Many in the rotating cast of American commanders had fought in the Indian Wars, and they saw the Moro as just another breed of savage to be subdued. One exception was Captain John Pershing, who learned local dialects and traveled unarmed to villages, where he met with tribal leaders, chewed betel with them, listened to their problems, and tried to solve them without bloodshed. Much more typical was his successor, General Leonard Wood, who set out to civilize the Moro through subjugation. He outlawed slavery, imposed an American-style system of justice, and taxed the Moro to pay for improvements to roads, schools, and other infrastructure that they didn't need or want. Wood, in the words of one subordinate officer, exhibited "a sheer lack of knowledge of the people, of the country." Predictably, Wood's efforts to Americanize the Moro failed and, just as predictably, he resorted to force. He would bombard a fortified village with artillery, then send infantry to mop up. Since prisoners were rarely taken, women and children were inevitably part of the lopsided body counts. In one campaign on the island of Jolo, some 1,500 Moro died compared to seventeen Americans. "While these measures appear harsh," Wood was quoted in the American newspapers, "it is the kindest thing to do."

John and millions of other Americans were about to learn the true extent of Wood's kindness. When hundreds of Moro took refuge in the crater of an extinct volcano called Bud Dajo, Wood rejected the advice to wait them out and, against orders from Secretary of War William Howard Taft, prepared to attack. He ordered soldiers to hack their way through the jungle that bearded the steep slopes of the volcano, and after two days of meeting limited resistance, they arrived at the rim of the crater. Then, on Wood's order, artillery, machine guns, and hundreds of riflemen took up positions around the rim of the crater and began firing down on the huddled Moro, who were armed with knives and rocks. When the shooting stopped, all but a few of the Moro were dead—various reports put the number killed between six hundred and a thousand—while eighteen America soldiers died in the campaign. President Roosevelt sent Wood a wooden cable: "I congratulate you and the officers and men of your command upon the brilliant feat of arms wherein you and they so well upheld the honor of the American flag."

Mark Twain, as staunch an anti-imperialist as John, did not send congratulations to Leonard Wood. He wrote so acidly about the massacre at Bud Dajo that many of his words were withheld from publication until a century after his death. He called the American soldiers "uniformed assassins." He added sarcastically: "The enemy numbered six hundred—including women and children—and we abolished them utterly, leaving not even a baby alive to cry for its dead mother. *This is incomparably the greatest victory that was ever achieved by the Christian soldiers of the United States.*" (Italics Twain's.) He concluded with another sarcastic flourish: "I was never so enthusiastically proud of the flag till now!"

President Roosevelt came to regret his cable to Leonard Wood. A photographer snapped a picture of American soldiers posing around a trench stacked with the corpses of Moro men, women, and children after the massacre at Bud Dajo—a gruesome image that might have reminded Roosevelt of the many times he'd posed with big-game trophies in Africa. The picture made the front pages of newspapers around the world. W. E. B. Du Bois called the shocking image "the most illuminating I've ever seen."

But the shock and outrage didn't last long. Six weeks after the massacre in the Philippines, a devastating earthquake rocked San Francisco. Tremors were felt as far away as Nevada. The city burned for three days, leaving more than 3,000 people dead and nearly half a million homeless. Overnight, the massacre at Bud Dajo became old news and the war was all but forgotten. Mark Twain would live another four years, and the war would drag on aimlessly, pointlessly, for three years after his death. No one seemed to notice. A splendid little war, indeed.

Henry Ford's Highland Park assembly line.

A CAR FOR THE GREAT MULTITUDE

Gretchen gave birth to a second daughter on July 31, 1908—Sarah McCurdy Morris, named after Gretchen's mother. Shortly after the delivery, Gretchen was, as usual, back at work, giving music lessons and finalizing the musical entertainment for the looming fiftieth anniversary celebration at the Lucy Cobb Institute.

The growing family settled into Fred J. Orr's capacious Arts and Crafts creation on Mell Street, which became a hive of activity. Gretchen had given birth three times in four years, and she and John would have been overwhelmed without the help of Black domestics—maids and cooks and nannies willing to work for low wages. In a sign that she was adapting to southern ways, Gretchen referred to the nannies as "black mammies" and marveled at their efficiency and devotion. Black domestics' pay was so low that they developed a blacklist of White employers in Athens who bristled at paying even rock-bottom wages or treated their help badly. While the archives contain no mention of John and Gretchen on such lists, I don't take this to mean they paid their help more than the going rate. For one thing, money in the household was always tight. For another, John and Gretchen were no revolutionaries. They were intent on treating others decently, not on upending the social order.

Illness seemed to come in flurries, and at various times the children suffered from tonsillitis, inflamed adenoids, and a condition described as "intestinal indigestion," which was probably severe diarrhea, possibly the dreaded summer diarrhea. Cases of dysentery were treated with opiates administered four times daily, day and night. Charles knocked a pot of boiling water onto his feet, and the burns took three agonizing months to heal. When his tonsils had to be removed, he nearly suffocated from the chloroform. All three children were stricken with measles at the same time. John put his faith in the doctors; Gretchen put hers in God. Though John had no use for organized religion, he acquiesced to Gretchen's insistence that the children be baptized as Roman Catholics. At the time there were so few Catholics in Georgia outside Atlanta and Savannah that a priest had to travel to Athens once a month to say Mass and perform baptisms at St. Joseph Church, which had been housed since 1881 in a small wooden structure on the estate of the late Thomas R. R. Cobb, founder of the Lucy Cobb Institute.

Athens, like the Morris family, was growing. More and more motorized cars and trucks were seen on the streets, darting between the trolleys and horse-drawn buggies and wagons. The Southern Mutual Insurance Company building punched an impressive seven stories into the sky above downtown, part of a regional trend to build vertically that made no sense economically. Land was still cheap and plentiful in the larger towns and cities of the

South—unlike in Chicago or New York—yet the princes of progress tried to outdo one other with ever-taller monuments to their success at manufacturing furniture and textiles, soft drinks and cigarettes. And so skyscrapers sprouted in Winston, Greensboro, Atlanta, Spartanburg, Columbia, and other southern cities which, as W. J. Cash wryly noted, "had little more use for them than a hog has for a morning coat." Few of these tall buildings were ever fully occupied. Nevertheless, two years after the Southern Mutual building opened in downtown Athens, it was eclipsed by the nine-story-tall Holman Hotel.

Meanwhile, a new county courthouse opened downtown with a feature that marked it as a product of its time. The first, second, and third floors were taken up by offices and courtrooms, while Sheriff Walter Jackson lived on the fourth floor, which also housed the jail and a rooftop exercise area for prisoners. With its fortified doors, thick plate-glass windows, and thick cell bars, the jail was proclaimed "mob-proof"—meaning the prisoners were supposedly safe from any lynch mob that might try to break in and spirit one or more of them away to a gruesome death. The new state-of-the-art jail in Athens was, to John, a sick sign of a sick time: it was no longer enough for jails to keep people from breaking out; now jails had to prevent people from breaking *in*.

Yet the lynch mobs and the race riots making headlines across the nation had led to one positive development. Incensed by the bloody 1908 riot in Springfield, Illinois, which left dozens of Black homes and businesses in ashes and two Black men dead, a group of reformers, social workers, suffragists, journalists, socialists, and proponents of racial equality came together the following year in New York City to form the National Association for the Advancement of Colored People (NAACP), which vowed to fight lynching and promote enforcement of the postwar amendments to the Constitution. Sprinkled among the mostly White attendees at the founding conference were a few Black people, including Ida B. Wells, now Ida Wells-Barnett, and W. E. B. Du Bois, who would soon begin editing the group's influential magazine, *The Crisis: A Record of the Darker Races*. In an editorial in the inaugural edition, in November 1910, Du Bois vowed that the magazine would "show the danger of race prejudice." The print run of that issue was 1,000. Within a year circulation had jumped to 16,000, and within a decade it reached 100,000 readers. During the Harlem Renaissance, the magazine would publish a galaxy of influential Black writers, including Countee Cullen, Jean Toomer, and Langston Hughes.

While John found such developments heartening, they always seemed to get overshadowed by fresh horrors. Three years after the NAACP came together, a White teenager named Mae Crow was found lying in a ditch in Forsyth County, Georgia, fifty miles northwest of Athens. She'd been raped and brutally beaten and was barely alive. The response of the White community was by now predictable: a noose was snugged around the neck of a young Black suspect named Ernest Knox, who provided the expected confession. For his protection, Knox was transported to the jail in Atlanta, which infuriated a growing mob of vengeance-hungry White citizens in Forsyth County. The mob soon seized a Black field hand named Big Rob Edwards, who had been seen with Ernest Knox on the day Mae Crow was attacked. But the sheriff appeared to thwart their plans by locking Edwards in the jail in Cumming, the Forsyth County seat, then conveniently dis-appearing. Members of the mob, which now numbered more than two thousand men, splintered the jail's barred outer door with sledgehammers, overpowered the lone deputy inside, and led Edwards out into the sunshine, where they were greeted with lusty cheers. While Edwards kept muttering prayers and pleading for mercy, the men tied a noose around his neck and beat him until he was unable to walk. They then dragged him up to the town square, stones and gravel tearing his flesh. The rope was thrown over the cross arm of a phone pole, and Edwards's bloodied body, possibly still alive, was hoisted into the air. The mob opened fire. "Pistols and rifles cracked," a witness told the *Atlanta Georgian*, "and the corpse was mangled into something hardly resembling a human form." The bullet-riddled pulp was left there overnight, dangling and dripping, as a warning to the county's already terrorized Black populace.

After Mae Crow died from her injuries, Ernest Knox and another young Black suspect, named Oscar Daniel, were brought under heavy guard from the Atlanta jail to Cummings, where they were tried on trumped-up charges and convicted of rape and murder. Before an enthusiastic throng, the men were executed by public hanging not far from the spot where Rob Edwards was murdered. Jim Crow justice had been served.

But the story didn't end there. As the *New York Times* reported, the White men of Forsyth County mounted a terror campaign designed to rid the county of every one of its more than one thousand Black residents. It was called a racial cleansing, and it was accomplished by White men on horseback—night riders—armed with rifles, shotguns, stoppered bottles of kerosene, and sticks of dynamite. By torchlight they posted notices on the doors of Black homes, ordering the residents to leave at once. They fired bullets into those doors, threw rocks through windows, torched countless homes and churches. They even threatened to burn down the houses and barns of White farmers who continued to employ and protect Black field hands. It worked. Within months, there was not a single Black person living in Forsyth County, Georgia.

W. E. B. Du Bois sent a White reporter named Royal Freeman Nash to Forsyth County to investigate the terror campaign for *The Crisis*. Reports by Nash and others must have had a numbing effect on John, and yet he was able to find a small solace. Wilmington, Atlanta, Forsyth County, and dozens of other southern locales had been turned into blood-soaked killing fields, but Athens and surrounding Clarke County remained an island of civility in a sea of backwardness. It had not been touched by the insanity. Not yet.

John, meanwhile, had been named the professor of Germanic languages at the university, and he started making periodic trips back to Germany to pursue scholarly research that was becoming both broader and more tightly focused. Even as he explored obscure new back alleys—Norse epics, the origins of family names, the construction of medieval armor—he embarked on a project that would consume him for decades to come: he had begun to write a German-English dictionary.

This project became a central family myth—and it would become a source of misunderstanding and great disappointment to me. For years I operated under the belief that John had set out to write a *phonetic* dictionary, which my father might have told me, or which might have been the result of my conflating John's interest in phonetic spelling with his passion for word origins and definitions, then assuming that the two came together when he wrote his dictionary. Since German is, as mentioned, essentially a phonetic language, I spent years operating under the assumption that the phonetic spellings would be confined to the English words in the dictionary. A reasonable assumption, perhaps, but only after I was deep in the writing of this book would I learn that it was wrong.

There is, however, no question about the conditions under which John worked as he amassed his dictionary. He had no Boswell, no one to chronicle his epic effort, no contract with a publisher, no guarantee that his efforts would ever get published or find an audience or earn a single dollar. He worked alone, in a bubble of his own making, invisible to the world and, according to several sources, supremely content.

The news out of Panama had improved considerably, thanks to a change in command that freed Dr. Gorgas to pursue his mosquito-eradication campaign, which brought tropical diseases under control and allowed the brutal work of dredging and drilling and blasting to pick up speed. The project also benefited from the unwavering support of President Roosevelt and his successor, the 300-pound colossus William Howard Taft, who grew up in the same Cincinnati neighborhood where Tom Gallagher raised his family and where John and Gretchen were married. John, a close reader of newspapers, surely noticed that the locks in the canal had been widened from 95 to 115 feet so they could accommodate the US Navy's new dreadnought battleships. This canal, as John had suspected all along, was as much about war as commerce. Despite Taft's support for the canal, his one-term presidency would come to be seen as a brief and largely forgettable interregnum between the reigns of a pair of two-term titans, Roosevelt and Woodrow Wilson. Taft, though decent and well-meaning, seemed tone deaf. He was supportive of the despised Mexican dictator Porfirio Diaz. He sent unwelcome US troops to occupy Nicaragua. He removed most Black people from federal appointments in the South. He fought nobly to break the monopolies of Standard Oil, U.S. Steel, International Harvester, American Tobacco, and dozens of other companies, but largely failed. Big as he was, Taft left a small footprint on history.

Something memorable did happen late in his term in office, though, something almost unthinkably horrible. On its maiden voyage from Southampton to New York City, in April 1912, the ocean liner *Titanic* sank after ramming an iceberg. The ship, with state-of-the-art technology and sumptuous appointments, was said to be unsinkable, but more than 1,500 of the 2,224 people on board perished in the frigid waters of the North Atlantic. In this tragedy John heard an echo of the hubris that had caused the Panama Canal project to falter: people had gotten so drunk on technology that they had allowed themselves to forget that there are no absolutes in this life. Hubris always exacts a terrible price.

It was a time when men were jumping out of airplanes and landing softly under billowing parachutes. It was possible to telephone across the Atlantic. A federal income tax was passed. The Armory Show in New York introduced America to the European avant-garde's shocking stew of new styles with new names—Cubism, Impressionism, Fauvism—by unknown artists named Picasso, Matisse, Van Gogh, Duchamp, and hundreds more. The drawn-out war in the Philippines, by now long forgotten by most Americans, finally came to an end in the summer of 1913 when American troops, in five days of vicious fighting, annihilated the last of the Moro resistance. Later that year something happened that few Americans would ever forget. At his sprawling factory in Highland Park, Michigan, a city within the city of Detroit, Henry Ford began producing his popular Model Ts on a moving assembly line—an idea that had come to him while studying the work flows in breweries, canneries, and meatpacking plants. Instead of the worker going to the work, Ford would bring the work to the worker. The result was ever-greater speed and efficiency, and ever-declining costs. The ways Americans worked, traveled, and spent their money were forever changed.

Ford divided the construction of an automobile into eighty-four distinct tasks. By assigning each worker a single task—bolting the same door hinge in place hundreds of times per work shift—Ford completed the divorce of the worker from the thing being made. It was the final dehumanization of industrialized labor that William Morris, among others, had worked so hard to resist. It was the perfection of the replicable event—and it meant there was no limit to how many cars Ford could produce. But his diabolical genius went even further. By paying his unskilled assembly line workers the astonishing wage of five dollars a day, he turned his employees into his customers, dutiful consumers of his affordable product. After four months, the average assembly line worker could afford to buy his own Model T. At first the cars came only in black because black paint dried faster than other colors—an important consideration since speeding up the process, while shaving costs and maximizing volume, was the iron commandment of the

Ford gospel. A Model T traveled the assembly line from start to finish in an hour and a half. Ford described his mission with typical farm boy flair: "I will build a car for the great multitude."

John saw something to admire in Henry Ford that had nothing to do with his knack for making money by reducing workers to machine tenders. It was his attitude toward the gathering war clouds in Europe. Ford, like John, was an avowed pacifist, part of an anti-war movement comprised of some highly strange bedfellows that included Andrew Carnegie, William Randolph Hearst, Secretary of State William Jennings Bryan, social reformer Jane Addams, progressive Wisconsin senator Robert LaFollette, and White supremacist congressman from North Carolina Claude Kitchin, plus platoons of suffragists, socialists, populists, labor unions, German- and Irish-American groups, and clergymen. If Europe was sleepwalking toward war, as John had sensed during his recent visits to Germany, at least he could console himself that America appeared to have no appetite for the looming fight.

⸺⸺

So what kind of parents were John and Gretchen? Anecdotal evidence from their children and grandchildren suggests that they were loving but somewhat distant—the opposite of today's hovering, hands-on parents. They were not strict disciplinarians, which is not to say the Morris children were allowed to run wild. My father told me that he and his siblings were taught to speak when spoken to by adults, and they were expected to be seen and not heard. They all had impeccable manners. John and Gretchen were raising their children at a time when American family life was dividing, largely along class lines, into what the historian Steven Mintz and the anthropologist Susan Kellogg called "cooperative" or "companionate" arrangements. Under the former, typically adopted by immigrant, minority, and rural working-class families, all members of the family were expected to contribute to the family's material welfare, either by doing piecework at home or taking a job outside the home. The children working in the textile mills came from "cooperative" families. So did Isaiah Stroud, who had been forced by necessity to drop out of school to drive the ice wagon. In the "companionate" Morris family, the children were sent to school from kindergarten through college and they were granted greater social freedom, left largely to their own devices. Gretchen was a typical mother in such a family, having pursued higher education and taken a job outside the home while happily turning over many domestic chores to hired help. In essence, the Morris family had been companionate at least since the time of John's grandfather, Great Richard, who had pursued higher education, practiced law, and never spent a day working with his hands.

The most notable exception to this parental distancing appears to have been Gretchen's bond with Margarethe. Gretchen was by now a recognizable type: the failed artist who gets a second chance to live her dream, vicariously through a proxy—better yet, through a proxy she herself has tutored. Under Gretchen's instruction, Margarethe showed early promise on the piano and the violin, and by the age of eight she was performing Schumann at private recitals, much as Gretchen had done in her youth. All the Morris children took piano and violin lessons, but there was never any question that Margarethe was the "special" talent. She was sent to the Academy of the Sacred Heart in Cincinnati, a Catholic school with a strong music program that could groom her for bigger things. Gretchen, an independent woman with a fierce devotion to her daughter's budding career, thought nothing of leaving the family at home and making the twenty-four hour journey alone, by train, to Cincinnati to see Margarethe perform. Anything for Margarethe's career.

The lynching of Leo Frank on August 17, 1915.

THE VOICE OF GOD

The summer of 1914 brought calamity and triumph on the world stage, sorrow and joy at home.

The calamity came first. On June 28, Archduke Franz Ferdinand, heir to the Austro-Hungarian throne, and his wife, Sophie, were assassinated in Sarajevo, the capital of Bosnia. The assassin, Gavrilo Princip, was a member of a team that hoped the assassination would break Austro-Hungary's grip on its South Slav provinces and lead to an independent Yugoslavian nation. After one of his confederates tossed a bomb that failed to kill the intended target, Princip climbed on the running board of the Archduke's touring car and shot him in the jugular vein, then shot Sophie in the stomach. The match had been struck. Austro-Hungary declared war on Serbia, other powers took sides according to long-standing treaties, and within a month Europe had stumbled into the most senseless of its many wars.

Two weeks after the calamity in Sarajevo came the triumphant, long-delayed opening of the Panama Canal. But all anyone could think about or write about was the growing conflagration in Europe, which led to the question on John's mind and everyone else's: How long would President Wilson be able to live up to his vow to keep the United States neutral? News of the opening of the Panama Canal, one of the greatest engineering feats in human history, was shunted to the back pages of the nation's newspapers.

Two weeks after that overlooked triumph, Gretchen gave birth to her second son, John Dabney Morris, who would be known as Jack—another John Morris born during wartime. In addition to its new member, the family acquired a new next-door neighbor, Robert Preston Brooks, a Rhodes scholar who taught sociology and Georgia history at the university. Brooks would come to be known among the neighborhood children as Puny because he was puny. His prose style was as dry as the Gobi desert. He was also, according to my father, "bad to drink." But he was an expert bridge player, a lively conversationalist with a razor wit, and good company. He became a dear friend and a fixture in the Morris house, especially during the sacrosanct Thursday night bridge game.

On September 21, the penultimate day of that momentous summer, John's mother died at her home in Athens "after an illness of several days," according to the *Athens Daily Herald*. She was eighty-one. Mary Minor Morris Morris, like her late husband, got the royal treatment from local obituary writers and was the subject of flowery resolutions by the senior law students at the university and the local chapter of the United Daughters of the Confederacy, of which she was a charter member. After the funeral, John's maiden sister, Louise, packed up the house on Milledge Avenue and returned to Taylor's Creek, where she would live out the last four decades of her life tending to the place and playing the role of the unmarried, untamable, and unrepentant southern eccentric.

—∞—

The reports from the battlefields of Europe were almost beyond imagining. Men were dying by the thousands from rapid-fire artillery, machine guns, tanks, poisonous gas, and flamethrowers. In a single day at the Battle of the Frontiers, 27,000 French soldiers were mowed down. Airplanes flew overhead raining death. German U-boats continued to menace merchant and passenger ships in addition to enemy warships. As the lines hardened and trench warfare expanded, soldiers began digging mass graves before major advances. When the shooting stopped, bodies sometimes lay where they had fallen for months, stacked three and four deep, their lifeless flesh blackened by bluebottle flies. It was far worse than anything John had thought possible. It was the final perversion of technology. It was the first *industrialized* war.

—∞—

Mercifully, there were distractions from these horrors. Moving pictures had become much more sophisticated in the twenty years since John first saw crude ones flickering on a curtain at the Atlanta Cotton Expo in 1895. They were now called movies, and John became a regular at the theaters in downtown Athens which, in addition to hosting operas and dance performances and one-man shows, screened an eclectic diet of silent movies. My father described John as an avid moviegoer late in life, and it's likely his love for the medium was born in the silent era, when he would have been drawn to such early stars as Little Mary Pickford and Fatty Arbuckle and that ingenious rapscallion Charlie Chaplin. It's no contradiction—in fact, it makes perfect sense to me—that a man who immersed himself in the Anglo-Saxon origins of words and other knotty topics would be eager to escape into the theater's welcoming, anonymous dark, where he could be swallowed up in the frenetic slapstick of a Mack Sennett comedy or relive, through moving pictures, the familiar stories of Cinderella and Pinocchio and Robin Hood, even Anna Karenina and Dante's *Inferno*.

Athens began buzzing with anticipation when the Colonial Theater announced it would host the regional premiere of D. W. Griffith's controversial new movie, which had recently electrified President Wilson during a screening at the White House. *The Birth of a Nation* was based on Thomas Dixon's novel *The Clansman*, which was a rehash of the Lost Cause themes of *The Leopard's Spots*—freed Black people are portrayed as animalistic brutes, and the only defense against their lust for White women is the noble night riders of the Ku Klux Klan. Dixon had met Woodrow Wilson when they were graduate students in history at Johns Hopkins University, and early in 1915, Dixon, seeking to win an endorsement that would blunt possible censorship of the movie, offered to screen the movie for President Wilson in the White House, promising he would witness "the birth of a new art—the launching of the mightiest engine for the molding of public opinion in the history of the world." Wilson was intrigued. A Virginian with pronounced racist tendencies, Wilson had allowed his cabinet members to segregate federal workplaces for the first time since the Civil War. He had, in effect, welcomed Jim Crow across the Potomac to Washington. Now he welcomed Dixon and his movie into the White House.

After seeing *The Birth of a Nation*, Wilson was quoted as saying, "It is like writing history with lightning, and my only regret is that it is all so terribly true." There is reason to doubt he ever said those words, but they've been repeated so often that they have become part of the national narrative. And since he didn't condemn the movie, Wilson had in effect given it the endorsement Dixon was hoping for. After premiering in Los Angeles, it began opening in theaters across the country. It was an instant sensation.

Audiences were sharply, even violently, divided. The NAACP called for the movie to be banned. It was banned in Chicago and Ohio but praised as a masterpiece in Utah and Mississippi. People rioted outside theaters. It was the first twelve-reel film, with a running time of over three hours, and it shattered box office records.

On the night of the Athens premier, John and Gretchen, eager to see what the fuss was about, settled into orchestra seats in the packed theater. Gretchen knew most of the musicians in the orchestra pit, having taught more than a few of them. The surrender at Appomattox had taken place exactly fifty years earlier, and a contingent of Confederate veterans was in the house that night, old men dressed in their faded grays who had come, according to one newspaper account, "to see many stirring scenes that will carry them back to the days when they were in the trenches before Richmond, Vicksburg, or Appomattox."

As soon as the house lights began to dim, John felt the familiar thrill. This moment had always been his favorite thing about going to the movies—this sense of the outside world fading away as he was swallowed by soft darkness in a room full of strangers, nobody talking but everybody bound together by the shared ghosts that would soon begin flickering on the screen. As a lifelong agnostic, John might have believed that this was as close as he would ever come to a religious experience, this form of private communion, this marriage of anonymity and intimacy.

The movie was, as advertised by the president of the United States, history written with lighting. The lightning was the movie's stunning artistry. The camera, until now static, was suddenly kinetic, in motion, all-seeing. It gazed down on a panoramic cavalry charge; it was in the smoky midst of combat scenes; it got lost in crowds and mobs; it rode with a column of white-robed Klansmen. Griffith skillfully blended long shots, medium shots, close-ups, and fade-outs, and many of the scenes, including the assassination of President Lincoln, were artfully staged and acted. The movie was undeniably a work of art, a breakthrough, a revelation of the medium's untapped potential.

But the history on the screen, as Wilson had failed to mention, was written not with lighting but with a cartoonist's pen. D. W. Griffith, like

John, was the son of a Confederate officer; unlike John, he was happy to glorify the antebellum South while condemning the depredations of Reconstruction and praising the White man's response to them. The movie included three title cards with quotations from Wilson's five-volume *A History of the American People*, including sentiments about Reconstruction that dovetailed with those of Dixon and Griffith: "In the villages the negroes were the office holders, men who knew none of the uses of authority, except its insolences." And: "The white men were roused by a mere instinct of self-preservation . . . until at last there had sprung into existence a great Ku Klux Klan, a veritable empire of the South, to protect the southern country." A carpetbagger vows: "We shall crush the white South under the heel of the black South." The Ku Klux Klan is portrayed as "the organization that saved the South from the anarchy of black rule." This was not history; this was an elaborate revenge fantasy.

When THE END flashed on the screen, most of the people in the theater stood and applauded. John and Gretchen remained seated. They exchanged a sick look. They realized the people around them were not applauding the film's technical wizardry; they were applauding its appalling message.

A few weeks after John and Gretchen saw Griffith's unsettling movie, the news broke that a German U-boat had sunk the British passenger ship *Lusitania* off the southern coast of Ireland, killing 1,198 people, including 128 Americans. The Germans claimed the ship was carrying war materiel to Allied forces—which proved to be true, despite British denials—and, as such, she was fair game. Now the war fever John had dreaded began to burn across the nation. President Wilson sent a formal protest to the Germans, but the United States remained on the sidelines. For now.

The grim news about the sinking of the *Lusitania* and its powerful pull on public opinion was followed a month later by some good news: Georgia governor John Slaton commuted the death sentence of Leo Frank, a super-intendent at the Atlanta Pencil Co. factory who had been tried, convicted, and sentenced to death by hanging for the murder of a thirteen-year-old factory worker named Mary Phagan. John had followed Frank's trial closely, and to his legal mind the evidence didn't come close to adding up. The prosecution had relied on the testimony of Jim Conley, a Black janitor at the pencil factory, and John detected inconsistencies in Conley's story as well as obvious signs that the barely literate janitor had been coached by prosecutors. What struck John was not that a jury had believed Con-ley's implausible story—but that a Black man had been allowed to testify against a White man. Yet it wasn't hard to read the subtext: if Leo Frank was guilty of a crime, it was that he was a Jew—a college-educated Jew from the North. Southerners saw him, in the words of historian Albert Lindemann, as "a rich, punctilious northern Jew lording it over vulnerable and impoverished working women." American anti-Semites now had their very own Alfred Dreyfus.

When the US Supreme Court denied Frank's appeal on a 7–2 vote, Gov. Slaton spent twelve days reviewing ten thousand pages of docu-ments, visiting the crime scene, and considering letters recommending commutation of Frank's death sentence from the trial judge and from a private investigator who had worked for the prosecutor, Hugh Dorsey. To John's surprise and delight, the governor did the courageous—and unpopular—thing and commuted Frank's sentence to life in prison, citing new evidence that had come to light since the trial. As Slaton told reporters after announcing his decision: "I would be a murderer if I allowed that man to hang."

The predictable mob, numbering five thousand, soon surrounded the governor's mansion in Atlanta. National Guardsmen and county police were called out to disperse the mob while Jews began fleeing the city—much as Black people had fled Forsyth County, Atlanta, Wilmington and the scenes of countless other pogroms. For his safety, Frank had been transported to the state prison in Milledgeville, where his safety turned out to be far from assured. A fellow inmate slashed his jugular vein but failed to kill him.

On the night of August 16, a convoy of eight cars arrived at the prison from Marietta, Mary Phagan's hometown. In a well-orchestrated operation, the men snatched Frank from the prison hospital and drove him more than one hundred miles on darkened dirt roads back to Marietta. There, at dawn the next day, they hanged Leo Frank in a grove of oak trees. Among the lynch party was Judge Newt Morris, who had presided over the sham murder trials of Ernest Knox and Arthur Daniel in Forsyth County three years earlier. Several of the lynchers would be present a few months later at Stone Mountain, Georgia, to take part in the rebirth of the Ku Klux Klan. Tom Watson, the former Populist who was now a political kingmaker in Georgia, heartily approved of Leo Frank's murder. "The voice of the people," he wrote, "is the voice of God." Watson gave his endorsement to Hugh Dorsey, the prosecutor in the Frank case, who was elected governor in a landslide.

⁂

After a lull, German U-boats resumed their attacks on American merchant and passenger ships. Then an encrypted telegram, intercepted and deciphered by British intelligence, revealed a stunning German plot. If Mexico agreed to join its cause, Germany promised to help Mexico regain territory lost to the United States during the Mexican-American War, which included parts of present-day Texas, Arizona, New Mexico, California, Colorado, Nevada, and Utah. Americans were outraged by the prospect of German soldiers pouring across the Rio Grande. No anti-war activist could sway public opinion any longer, and the inevitable finally happened on April 6, 1917, when Congress granted President Wilson's wish and declared war on Germany. A draft was instituted, and soon hundreds of thousands of American soldiers were crossing the Atlantic to be fed into the meat grinder of the trenches.

Houses in Athens and the rest of the country sprouted banners bearing blue stars and gold stars—blue to represent a family member in the armed services, gold to commemorate one who'd died. As gold stars proliferated—26,000 Americans died in the month-long Meuse-Argonne campaign—anti-German sentiment swept the country. Headline writers routinely referred to the enemy as "the Hun." School boards banned the teaching of German in public schools. Propaganda posters portrayed the German soldier as a spider, a serpent, a skeleton drinking a goblet of blood, a yellow-fanged, club-wielding gorilla. German-inflected names of buildings, streets, even towns were Anglicized. The American Protective League came together, a quarter of a million citizens intent on harassing German sympathizers, anti-war activists, and anyone suspected of disloyalty—and, for good measure, union organizers, socialists, and "slackers" who failed to register for the draft. The Espionage Act of 1917 made it a crime to obtain information related to national defense and use it to harm the United States or help any foreign nation. The sweeping law also made it a crime to obstruct enlistments or cause insubordination or disloyalty among the armed forces. When the socialist Charles Schenck was convicted of violating the Espionage Act for circulating a flyer that opposed the draft, the US Supreme Court upheld the conviction. Justice Oliver Wendell Holmes wrote for the majority: "The question in every case is whether the words used . . . create a clear and present danger that they will bring about the substantive evils that Congress has a right to prevent. . . . When a nation is at war many things that might be said in time of peace are such a hindrance to its effort . . . that no court could regard them as protected by any constitutional right."

This law was soon followed by the Sedition Act, an attempt to tamp down growing public disapproval as the carnage in Europe worsened. It was now illegal to write or say anything that could be construed as disloyal to the government, the war effort, the draft, or the flag. John was appalled that the government would abrogate such fundamental rights—and that the herd was so willing to forfeit those rights. And yet John realized that expressing his opposition to the war was risky. It could land him in prison. So he didn't resist when he and a friend from the faculty, M. D. DuBose, were asked to go to Camp Gordon in Atlanta to teach rudimentary grammar to illiterate draftees. Refusing the request would have been unwise.

The spread of anti-German sentiment caused a sense of unease to settle in the house on Mell Street, where the father was a known lover of the German language and culture, the mother was named Gretchen, and the firstborn child was named Margarethe. The unease turned to dread in October when the news arrived that a Dutch dancer and courtesan had been captured by the French and convicted of spying for Germany. Her stage name was Mata Hari, but her birth name was Margaretha Zelle. She had slept with numerous German and French officers since the outbreak of war, and there was some suggestion in the newspapers that the French were afraid that this free spirit/loose cannon might reveal damaging secrets. When they hastily sentenced her to death by firing squad, John was among those who sensed that if Leo Frank's crime was being a prosperous northern Jew in the South, Mata Hari's crime was her unwillingness to take sides in an insane war. On the day of her execution, stylish to the end, she wore a black velvet cloak over a silk kimono, silk stockings, and high-heeled slippers. She perched a black felt hat on her head. After declining the offered blindfold, she stared unflinching at the twelve Zouaves as they raised their rifles and fired.

This chilling story riveted John and Gretchen, and it convinced them that the names Margarethe and Margaretha were too close for comfort. For the duration of the war, as the story came down to my father, they took to calling their eldest child "Margaret" in the presence of strangers. Gretchen became the generic "Darling." The faraway war had come home.

Carswell Grove Baptist Church in Millen, Georgia.

HELL IN OUR OWN LAND

I n just a year and a half of fighting, more than 110,000 Americans would lose their lives to wounds and disease on the Western Front. But they helped repel the final German spring offensive of 1918 and secure a Pyrrhic victory for the Allies that November. The bloodbath had overshadowed the stunning news out of Russia that Czar Nicholas and his family had been executed and the country had slid into civil war. The West was too shell shocked to notice or care. Along with their broken bodies and shattered psyches, American soldiers brought an unexpected gift with them when they returned from Europe: the Spanish flu, which would prove an even more prolific killer than the Great War.

The first cases were detected in March at an Army base in Kansas, where a hundred soldiers fell ill. Within a week the number of infections increased fivefold, and soon the virus was galloping across the nation. By the fall, seven cities—San Francisco, Oakland, Sacramento, and Pasadena in California, plus Seattle, Denver, and Indianapolis—had passed ordinances requiring all residents to wear masks in public. Violators faced fines or jail time. One headline stated: "'OPEN FACE' SNEEZERS TO BE ARRESTED." Despite these measures, 195,000 people died nationwide in the month of October. When cases subsided in San Francisco, the unpopular mask mandate was lifted, which triggered a second wave of infections. When the Board of Supervisors began debating a new mask mandate, the public outcry was vehement. A bomb was found and defused outside the office of the city's chief health inspector. The jails were packed with violators of the decree, which sped the spread of infections. An Anti-Mask League was formed, driven by the belief that there was a dearth of scientific evidence that masks prevented infection, along with the conviction that forcing people to wear masks was a violation of their constitutional rights. John was nonplussed. People who had willingly forfeited their constitutional rights to help fight a war in Europe were suddenly unwilling to forfeit their putative rights to fight a far deadlier war at home. For them, freedom of speech was less prized than the freedom not to wear a mask. The medical had become political. After the second mask mandate expired, San Francisco was swept with a third wave of infections. In Pasadena, sixty violators were arrested on the day the local mask ordinance went into effect. "It is the most unpopular law ever placed on the Pasadena records," the chief of police told the *Los Angeles Times*. "We are cursed from all sides." At the meeting of the Illinois Equal Suffrage Association, no one wore masks but attendance was limited to one hundred and chairs were placed four feet apart. By the end of the year, the flu had killed nearly a quarter of a million Americans. And it was just getting started.

In Athens, meanwhile, city officials acted decisively but stopped short of mandating masks. "Board of Health and Mayor Take Steps Against Spread of Influenza" read a headline in the *Athens Banner*. The university and all schools, theaters, churches, amusement tents, and billiard rooms were closed. All public assemblies were prohibited, with the exception of necessary war work. A scheduled carnival was cancelled. Spitting in public was banned. Doctors or heads of households were ordered to report all confirmed cases within twenty-four hours, and infected people were ordered to quarantine at home. Posters urged cooperation. One showed a man in a bowler hat offering a handkerchief to a boy on the verge of a sneeze. The man tells the boy, "Use the handkerchief and do your bit to protect me!" The poster adds a capitalized warning: "COLD, INFLUENZA, PNEUMONIA AND TUBERCULOSIS ARE SPREAD THIS WAY."

There were skeptics, of course. During the month-long quarantine order, one headline offered some wishful thinking: "Spanish Flu—Just Grip Camouflaged Under a New Name." An advertisement claimed there was a simple home cure: "Sterilize your nose with eucalyptus salve." But such contrariness was the exception. Most citizens complied with the measures, and they proved effective. More than a thousand people were infected in Athens, but only seventeen died—compared to more than seven hundred in Atlanta.

Everyone in the Morris family except Gretchen contracted the virulent virus. With the domestic help locked away in their homes, Gretchen was pressed into duty as nurse, cook, and maid. It must have been a harrowing time—the house, once so full of life and activity, suddenly stricken silent as John and the children suffered alone in their rooms and Gretchen fought off the terror that the sick house could turn overnight into a charnel house. She was a big believer in the power of prayer, and her fingers must have made many laps around the beads on her rosary.

The Angel of Death passed by the house on Mell Street. Everyone in the Morris family survived and recovered. By the time the pandemic ran its course—a vaccine would not arrive until twenty years later—more than 675,000 Americans were among the fifty million who died worldwide.

Peace in Europe did not bring peace to the United States. Black soldiers had served with distinction on the battlefield, and they came home expecting a warm welcome and new opportunities. They got neither. More than a million Black people had emigrated from the Jim Crow South, seeking better jobs and better treatment in cities of the North, Midwest, and West. The competition for jobs in those cities, worsened by the wave of returning veterans and a postwar economic contraction, led to friction. But it was in Georgia, predictably, that the match was lit on what would become known as the Red Summer of 1919.

The first violence was triggered not by competition for jobs but by the familiar racial meanness. The Carswell Grove Baptist Church in tiny Millen, Georgia, a venerable Black institution founded shortly after the Civil War, was hosting an anniversary celebration on a cloudless April Sunday when two White police officers spoiled the party by arresting one of the celebrants, supposedly for possessing a concealed weapon. Joe Ruffin, a prosperous Black farmer who had known the handcuffed suspect all his life, stepped toward the police car, took out his checkbook, and offered to pay the man's bond. The officers refused the offer, demanding cash. When Ruffin tried to pull the prisoner from the police car, one of the cops struck Ruffin with his gun, which went off. Ruffin, wounded in the head, fell to the ground. Now the familiar narrative took an unfamiliar twist. The Black congregants of Carswell Grove fought back. One of Ruffin's sons wrestled the gun from the police officer and shot him dead. A gun battle ensued with the surviving cop, who was wounded, then beaten to death by the crowd. The handcuffed prisoner also died in the gunfire. For this there would be hell to pay.

A gun-toting White mob soon descended on Carswell Grove Baptist Church, firing as they came. The wooden building was set on fire, forcing women and children to jump out of windows and flee into the woods. Two of Ruffin's sons were beaten by the mob, then thrown into the flames. One of Ruffin's two cars was burned—a telling symbol of White resentment over a Black man's prosperity. Soon three Black Masonic lodges in Millen were torched, more cars were burned, and a man who had helped Ruffin at the scene of the original violence was wrested from the jail, tortured, and shot to death. The violence went on for days.

And then it spread. Soon there was rioting in Washington, DC, and Chicago, two cities with solid Black middle classes and thousands of recent arrivals from the South—plus sizable contingents of war-hardened Black veterans. Mobs chased more than a thousand Black families from their homes in Chicago. The violence swept towns and cities from Connecticut to California, and it visited every southern state except North Carolina. There were more than two dozen riots. Though Blacks suffered the heaviest losses in life and property—more than fifty were killed—they did not lie down. Inspired by returning veterans, they put up resistance, not always successful, but noteworthy—and much praised by Black leaders. Remembering his epiphany during the Atlanta riot thirteen years earlier, when he vowed to spray the guts of White intruders on the grass, W. E. B. Du Bois wrote in *The Crisis* that May: "But by the God of Heaven, we are cowards and jackasses if now that that war is over, we do not marshal every ounce of our brain and brawn to fight a sterner, longer, more unbending battle against the forces of hell in our own land."

There were signs that Blacks were now willing to fight that long fight. As the historian Cameron McWirther put it: "The white attacks, and importantly the black reaction to them, emboldened blacks across the country and made 1919 a turning point in American race relations."

Those relations had nowhere to go but up. Years later, the historian John Hope Franklin would call that bloody summer "the greatest period of interracial strife the nation has ever witnessed." President Wilson, that unapologetic racist, saw to it that the federal government followed the lead of his predecessors McKinley and Roosevelt and did nothing to thwart the violence.

All summer long and into the fall, John read the dispiriting newspaper accounts. He was able to glean one ray of good news from the gloom: the bloodshed proved to be a powerful recruiting tool for the NAACP, as its membership swelled from 9,000 before the war to more than 100,000. And John would have seen that killing season as a perverse vindication of his decision to remain in the South. There was no longer any way to deny the fact: racism was not a southern sickness; it was an American sickness, and it had infected every corner of the country. John had begun to believe it was incurable.

At the peak of the Red Summer, Andrew Carnegie died at the age of eighty-three. If he was disappointed that he fell about $30 million short of his goal of giving away his entire fortune before his death, he was devastated by the Great War and the utter failure of his efforts to avert it. He believed the Simplified Spelling Board had been another failure—and a colossal waste of money. Carnegie poured more than a quarter of a million dollars into the cause, but late in life he disparaged the board as "a useless body of men." He vented his frustration in a letter to them: "I think I hav been patient long enuf." He proved his loss of patience by failing to provide any additional funds in his will, and the Simplified Spelling Board soon faded away. After working for a dozen years and spending hundreds of thousands of dollars, all these august scholars and intellectuals had to show for their effort was the now-forgotten *Handbook on Simplified Spelling*. *Through* was not destined to morph into *thru*.

Two months after Carnegie's death, the Volstead Act became law. Overnight, the making, distributing, selling, and, above all, the drinking of alcoholic beverages became illegal. Puritans everywhere rejoiced. Tipplers panicked. Crime syndicates rushed to take advantage of the lucrative business opportunity the government had handed them. For John and Gretchen, who neither drank liquor nor served it in their house, nothing changed. Years later, toward the end of Prohibition, my father asked Gretchen why she and John were so different in this respect from other neighborhood parents. Her answer suggests that there had been some problem drinkers in the Gallagher and McCurdy clans, her ex-con uncle, Jim Gallagher, most certainly among them. "Well, Richard," she told my father, "I don't want to be the first person to give an incipient alcoholic his first drink. And if I don't have it in the house, I won't have that on my conscience."

While Gretchen was not involved in the temperance movement, she was a strong supporter of women's suffrage—she would eventually become active in the local chapter of the League of Women Voters—and she was elated when the Nineteenth Amendment became law the following summer after decades of agitation. She also shared in John's elation that women were finally being admitted to the university. Their elation was tempered by the news that Gretchen's mother, Sarah McCurdy Gallagher, had died from injuries suffered in a minor automobile accident. Tom Gallagher had become prosperous enough to afford a chauffeur by then, and Sarah was forever ordering him to drive faster, faster. The woman was in step with the spirit of the times.

That fall's presidential election would present Gretchen with unappetizing options when she went to the polls for the first time. Theodore Roosevelt, hoping once again for a comeback, had died in early 1919, and the Progressive Era had died with him. Americans had grown weary of people who wanted to fix things, despite the era's impressive improvements in food safety, child labor, compulsory education, and overall wages and working conditions. Woodrow Wilson was hoping for a third term, but he suffered a debilitating stroke in the fall of 1919 and was also hampered by the lingering trauma of the war and his support for the League of Nations, which went against the war-weary public's desire to exit the international stage.

The Republicans nominated a bland senator from Ohio named Warren G. Harding, who was paired on the ticket with the equally bland governor of Massachusetts, Calvin Coolidge. The Democrats nominated Ohio governor James M. Cox, who had disqualified himself in the Morris household when he came out in support of a ban on the teaching of German in Ohio public schools, proclaiming that the language was "a distinct menace to Americanism, part of a plot formed by the German government to make school children loyal to it." Cox's running mate was assistant Navy secretary Franklin Delano Roosevelt, the only passable candidate on either ticket. Gretchen must have thought: Women have spent more than half a century fighting for the right to vote for *this*? She and John wound up voting for the socialist Eugene Debs. While Harding campaigned from his front porch in Marion, Ohio, and Cox crisscrossed the country giving hundreds of speeches, Debs campaigned from a cell in the federal penitentiary in Atlanta, where he was serving a ten-year sentence for urging resistance to the draft during the First World War—a violation of the Sedition Act. The election results were announced on the first commercial radio broadcast, emanating from Pittsburgh. Debs won 3 percent of the vote. Harding, promising "a return to normalcy," won 61 percent, nearly twice Cox's total. The coming years, despite Harding's campaign promise, would turn out to be the roaring opposite of normal.

It might have been his up-to-date neighbor and friend, R. P. Brooks, who alerted John to a provocative essay in a new collection called *Prejudices: Second Series* by the Baltimore writer H. L. Mencken. Everyone on the faculty was reading it. Titled "The Sahara of the Bozart," the essay was a slashing attack on the South, which, in Mencken's eyes, "is almost as sterile, artistically, intellectually, culturally, as the Sahara Desert." John could see that Mencken's coinage "Bozart"—a phonetic mash-up of *beaux-arts*—was not meant as an homage to the Simplified Spelling Board but was, quite the opposite, his way of mocking the coarseness that had come to dominate every aspect of life in the South. "In all that gargantuan paradise of the fourth-rate," Mencken wrote, "there is not a single picture gallery worth going into, or a single orchestra capable of playing the nine symphonies of Beethoven, or a single opera-house, or a single theater devoted to decent plays. . . . When you come to critics, musical composers, painters, sculptors, architects and the like, you will have to give it up, for there is not even a bad one between the Potomac mud-flats and the Gulf. Nor an historian. Nor a sociologist. Nor a philosopher. Nor a theologian, Nor a scientist. In all these fields the south is an awe-inspiring blank—a brother to Portugal, Serbia and Esthonia [*sic*]." It was a "stupendous region of fat farms, shoddy cities and paralyzed cerebrums."

Mencken reserved his tartest venom for the two poles of John's world, Virginia and Georgia, the former for having fallen so far from its glory days as a breeder of Founding Fathers, the latter for never having risen above its tooth-and-claw origins. "Georgia," Mencken wrote, "is at once the home of the cotton-mill sweater and of the most noisy and vapid sort of chamber of commerce, of the Methodist parson turned Savonarola and of the lynching bee. . . . The Leo Frank affair was no isolated phenomenon. It fitted into its frame very snugly." Mencken then quotes Fanny Kemble Butler, the nineteenth-century British actress and abolitionist who married the owner of rice plantations worked by slaves on the Georgia coast. The state's poor Whites, she wrote, are "the most degraded race of human beings claiming an Anglo-Saxon origin that can be found on the face of the earth—filthy, lazy, ignorant, brutal, proud penniless savages." John was likely relieved that Mencken had not claimed there were no lexicographers or philologists between the Potomac and the Gulf, and he surely disagreed with a few of the articles of Mencken's indictment. Fred J. Orr, for example, was a gifted architect, and he was living right there in Athens. Howard W. Odum, after his brief stint on the Georgia faculty, was producing major works of sociology at the University of North Carolina. And John knew native Georgians, including R. P. Brooks, who were descended from refined and enlightened families.

Then, late in the essay, John came to a passage that must have carried a vicious sting. Mencken noted that most of the "first-rate southerners" had departed in the half-century since the Civil War. Most decamped to the North, a few to South America, Egypt, or the Far East. But the first-rate southerner who stayed on—and here John could not have failed to see an uncannily accurate portrait of himself—finds himself a stranger in his own land. "He throws up his hands," Mencken wrote of such a man. "It is impossible for him to stoop to the common level. He cannot brawl in politics with the grandsons of his grandfather's tenants. He is unable to share their fierce jealousy of the emerging black—the cornerstone of all their public thinking. He is anesthetic to their political and theological enthusiasms. He finds himself an alien at their feasts of soul. And so he withdraws into his tower and is heard of no more."

The closing words delivered the sting. Everything before them rang inarguably true—John had thrown up his hands. Unwilling to participate in the prevailing boosterism and racism, unable to kneel before the Democratic Party and the Protestant God, he had indeed withdrawn into his tower to work on obscure scholarly articles and his dictionary. But did this make him a cipher, an invisible man destined to be heard of no more?

The essay infuriated Brooks and just about everyone else on the faculty. Not John. It stung him, yes, but it also amused him. He was a regular reader of *The Nation* and the *New Republic* and the *New York Times* and other periodicals, including Mencken's *American Mercury*, and he was aware just how barbaric the South appeared to the rest of the nation, just what a plump target it had become for satire and ridicule. Despite the unsettling question Mencken had raised, John found much to admire in his bombast and flaming prose. As a polemicist, he was brilliant. And very funny. And, to John's mind, very astute in pointing out that the emperor was stark naked. After years of torpor and race hate, after years of shunning outsiders and outside ideas, after years of sleepwalking through the mists of a tainted and imperfectly remembered past, the South had succeeded in turning itself into a cultural desert. Mencken had performed a personal favor to John. He had reminded him how grateful he was to be secure in a tower of his own making, in the desert but not of it, safely immersed in his research and the writing of his dictionary. Mencken had also pointed out an imperative: John must not allow himself to disappear inside his tower and be heard of no more.

American innocence was among the many casualties of the First World War. In his novel *Ragtime*, E. L. Doctorow painted a beguilingly gauzy portrait of the twilight of that American dreamtime. The novel is populated with a vivid blend of imagined characters and historical figures from the prewar era, including Henry Ford and J. P. Morgan, Emma Goldman and Sigmund Freud. The action is set in motion on a sultry summer Sunday afternoon, when a well-to-do family in New Rochelle, New York, is jolted from its comfortable routines. A Pope-Toledo Runabout has crashed into a phone pole in front of the house. The owner of the car is the famous escape artist Harry Houdini, who is invited into the house and served lemonade. "As it happened," the scene concludes, "Houdini's visit had interrupted Mother and Father's coitus."

That scene from *Ragtime* comes back to me when I try to imagine the circumstances of my father's conception. It happened on a sultry summer afternoon in 1921, shortly *after* American innocence had been forever pulverized by the Great War. But no matter. John was fifty-eight that summer and Gretchen was forty-three, hardly prime childbearing years. Their eldest child was then sixteen, their youngest seven. It's unlikely they were planning on having more. And yet, they were upstairs in their bedroom on that steamy summer afternoon, and their coitus was obviously not interrupted by a car crash or anything else, because Gretchen soon learned that she was pregnant for a fifth and final time.

My father was born in St. Mary's Hospital in Athens on May 8, 1922. He was named Richard, in honor of Great Richard, and like John he was not given a middle name. My father told me, with a laugh, that he was known within the family as "the Afterthought." He tried to sound amused by the moniker, but I imagine it must have stung. Who wants to be seen as the runt of the litter, an accident, a straggler, a trifle—an *afterthought*?

Soon after giving birth, Gretchen did something that revealed the depth of her devotion to Margarethe's career. She arranged for a wet nurse named Miss Whitlock to come to the hospital and tend to her newborn son; then she boarded a train alone and made the long trip to Chicago, where Margarethe was getting ready to graduate from the American Conservatory of Music. Polite Athens was shocked: a mother leaving a newborn child in the hospital and boarding a train alone to travel to Chicago! Unthinkable.

While in school in Chicago, Margarethe, billed as "Songbird of the South," performed regularly as a pianist and vocalist on local radio broadcasts, which made her a pioneer in a medium then in its infancy but poised for explosive growth. She also accomplished something unheard of in the American Conservatory's thirty-six-year history: she won gold medals on piano and violin, as well as first place in student competitions on both instruments. Misspelling her first name "Margaretha"—shades of Mata Hari—*Music News* reported that she was to appear, on June 20th, with the Chicago Symphony Orchestra as violin soloist on Bruch's Concerto in D Minor and as piano soloist on Saint-Saëns' Concerto in G Minor, a pair of surefire crowd-pleasers. It was a star turn Gretchen would not have dreamed of missing.

When she returned from Chicago and a taxi deposited her in front of the house on Mell Street, R. P. Brooks happened to be on his porch next door. As Gretchen came up the walkway, he stepped to his porch railing and called out: "Welcome home, Gretchen! Have you seen the baby yet?"

Headline announcing the lynching of John Lee Eberhardt.

RUBATO

On a raw winter morning the year before my father's birth, Ida Lee, the pregnant mother of an eighteen-month-old child, left her white clapboard farmhouse south of Athens. She was carrying a bushel of oats to the barn, prepared to feed the family's cows. Before she reached the barn, someone emptied a double-barreled shotgun into her back and head, killing her instantly. The overturned bushel of oats was found some fifteen feet from Ida Lee's lifeless body, suggesting she might have tried to flee her attacker.

Hundreds of citizens soon joined police in their hunt for the killer, believed to be John Lee Eberhardt, a Black man with a criminal history who lived nearby. John would have heard the rumors that were soon swirling on the Athens campus—that a Black man had raped and murdered a White girl somewhere outside of town. The rumors grew more lurid with each telling, and within hours the campus and the entire county were in an uproar.

After an extensive manhunt, Eberhardt was arrested that afternoon at the Lambda Chi Alpha fraternity house near the Athens campus, where a friend of his worked. Upon his arrest, according to one newspaper report, the suspect made a "clean-cut confession" of Ida Lee's murder.

As news of the arrest spread, people from Clarke and several surrounding counties began descending on the courthouse in downtown Athens. Soon a vengeful mob, swollen to more than three thousand, swept up the front steps of the "mob-proof" courthouse. They forced the locked doors open, smashed through plate glass, then climbed to the fourth-floor jail, where they overpowered the sheriff and, using acetylene torches and sledgehammers, broke into Eberhardt's cell. The mob hustled him out a back door of the courthouse and drove him out to the Lee farm, followed by a mile-long line of cars.

Eberhardt was chained to a pine tree, and kindling and firewood were piled around him. Given a chance to confess, the suspect denied his guilt. A torch was touched to the woodpile. When Eberhardt's clothes caught fire, the crowd beat down the flames and gave him another chance to confess. "Neither gasoline nor kerosene was used," an eyewitness reported, "in order that the job might not be done too fast." Eberhardt repeated his claim of innocence, and the fire was relit. This was in keeping with the pattern of lynching that had become well established across the South. Even here, near the line separating Clarke and Oconee Counties, where there had not been a lynching in living memory, people just *knew* how to do it, possibly because they had witnessed or participated in lynchings elsewhere—or, more likely, because they had read the dozens of detailed accounts of lynchings that had become a staple of the state's newspapers. Yes, the mob hoped that by letting Eberhardt feel the sting from the flames and then dousing them, they might get him to confess. But relighting the fire again and again had the added advantage of prolonging the victim's agony and feeding the bloodlust of the mob. It was no longer enough to kill a man without benefit of a trial; now retribution could be attained only through a spectacle of escalating torture and cruelty. In addition to being an extralegal quest for speedy justice, lynching had turned into a popular spectator sport.

This had been brought home in a particularly grotesque drama that had unfolded at the turn of the century in the town of Newnan, forty miles southwest of Atlanta. There a Black man named Sam Hose was accused of splitting the skull of his White employer with an ax during a dispute over wages. A dubious, nearly pro forma charge was added that Hose then raped his employer's wife before disappearing. Eventually he was captured and returned to scene of the crime, where a lynch mob was waiting. The local *Herald and Advertiser*, one of dozens of newspapers that covered the story in nearly pornographic detail, offered a simple explanation for the mob's thirst for speedy justice: "The people cannot be expected to wait with patience on the laggard processes of the courts."

On the Sunday of the execution, two packed excursion trains brought spectators out from Atlanta. More than two thousand people were on hand as Hose was chained to a tree and stripped of his clothing while kindling and firewood was piled around him. Before the fire was lit, executioners cut off Hose's ears, fingers, and toes, then severed his genitals and held them aloft. The torturers were in no hurry. As the historian Philip Dray put it: "The mob's act of retribution would be considered something of a failure if Hose did not die a prolonged, painful death." A can of kerosene was dumped on Hose's blood-slicked body. Finally, after these lavish preliminaries, the fire was lit.

Thrashing in agony, his eyes bulging and his blood sizzling, Hose almost managed to escape his bonds. The executioners extinguished the fire, retied Hose, splashed more kerosene on him, and relit the fire. Hose's last words were "Sweet Jesus!" Before his corpse had cooled, his heart and liver were cut out, his bones crushed. Souvenir pieces of bone sold for twenty-five cents, pieces of cooked liver went for a dime. These ghastly souvenirs were soon on display in shop windows in Atlanta.

While there is no record that the lynching at the Lee farm outside Athens reached such a rococo level of savagery, it was plenty brutal and there's no doubt that John Lee Eberhardt suffered unbearable agony each time the fire was relit after he was given another chance to confess. He continued to profess his innocence until the flames were allowed to consume him. Members of the crowd came forward to cut off Eberhardt's fingers and toes. When their souvenir harvesting was complete, a woman emerged from the crowd with a pistol and asked for permission to shoot the charred corpse. Permission was granted. Finally the mob melted away, satisfied at last that Eberhardt's death had been sufficiently prolonged and painful.

The lynching shocked John and Gretchen and many of their friends and neighbors. Chancellor David Barrow publicly denounced the crime, and the Athens Ministerial Association condemned it as an act of "barbarism." The bulk of the mob, according to newspaper reports, came from outside Clarke County. Gov. Hugh Dorsey, whose successful prosecution had led to the lynching of Leo Frank, now offered a $3,000 reward for information leading to the arrest and conviction of members of the mob that murdered John Lee Eberhardt. These expressions of outrage allowed John to console himself that Athens was still, just barely, an island of civility in a sea of backwardness. The sea had come close, but it had not quite managed to swamp the island.

How did John react to this atrocity? I would get a surprising answer to that question half a century after the torture and murder of John Lee Eberhardt.

It happened in 1972. I had dropped out of college after my sophomore year, and that fall I set out to drive cross-country with my dog in a wheezing old pickup truck, on a mission to harvest experiences that I hoped to turn into an apprentice novel. I took the southern route, intent on skirting the looming Midwestern winter, and I paused for a few days in Athens to visit Aunt Margarethe. She was seventeen years old when my father was born, literally old enough to be his mother, and I always thought of her more as a grandmother than an aunt. Her husband, Charlie Parrott, had died a year earlier, and she seemed glad for company, for anything that would distract her from her grief. She also seemed smitten by my sketchbooks and my footloose life and my dream of becoming a writer. Sensing a fellow creative spirit—and a captive audience—she developed a daily ritual while I lingered as her houseguest, enjoying the free room and board, in no rush to begin the grueling drive to the West Coast. At midday Margarethe would have her uniformed Black maid serve us a lavish lunch—such southern staples as fried chicken, collard greens, biscuits, and sweet tea—always on the best china and crystal. The maid's starched uniform and yes-ma'am, no-ma'am obsequiousness gave off a scent of the Old South that unnerved me, but the food was so delicious and Margarethe was so charming that it was easy for me to relax and enjoy the elaborate production.

As we ate, Margarethe fleshed out her past. After her spectacular graduation in Chicago—the high point of her life?—she taught music at the University of Miami for a while and performed as a piano soloist with various orchestras, including the Atlanta Symphony Orchestra. But eventually she arrived at that cold day of reckoning familiar to her mother and to all artists, that moment when it becomes necessary to weigh one's talent and will against the available professional prospects. And what were those prospects? Surely Margarethe's calculations were influenced by the arid cultural atmosphere in the South at that time—the Sahara of the Bozart—by the scarce opportunities available to all artists, especially to a classically trained musician who was disinclined to forfeit the warm comforts of home for a life of struggle in, say, frosty Philadelphia or Chicago or New York. If she was not willing to suffer for her art, the obvious course was to figure out a way to live in the style to which she intended to become accustomed.

Enter Charlie Parrott, a go-getter from the cotton and peanut flatlands of Americus, Georgia, who had attended Emory University in Atlanta and exhibited such a sharp nose for business that the University of Georgia chapter of his fraternity, Alpha Tau Omega, summoned him to Athens to straighten out their books and save them from financial ruin. Charlie, a sharp dresser, was soon cleaning up in the insurance game, and to Margarethe he must have looked like a safe bet, even if he had never heard of Max Bruch or Camille Saint-Saëns. They were married in the summer of 1930, with the stock market in tatters and the Great Depression looming. Charlie's businesses flourished—he also "made money by lending money," as one relative put it, a recipe for fostering resentment at least as old as the Bible—and after the birth of a son and two daughters, the couple could afford to set about building the handsome brick house on Rutherford Street in Athens where they would spend the rest of their lives and where Margarethe and I were enjoying our lavish lunch. As the couple settled into their new home, Margarethe's artistic dreams faded away, no match for the demands of motherhood or the abundant prerogatives enjoyed by White royalty in a small southern college town.

After lunch Margarethe would order me to stretch out on the sofa. Then, with the curtains drawn against the midday sun, she would play hours of Chopin and Brahms and Beethoven on her walnut Steinway grand, sometimes humming, frequently pausing to explain the subtleties of working the pedals, the bending of time with rubato, how Chopin requires the player's fingertips to touch the keys as softly as a cat's paws. I was in heaven, and so was Aunt Margarethe.

One day she ended her performance with a surprise announcement: she was taking me for a drive. We climbed into her car, which I remember being something big and plush and Detroit-made, probably a Buick, definitely the ride of someone who wasn't worried about the price of gas at a time when just about everyone was worried about the price of gas. We floated south out of town on Watkinsville Road, into the scoured late-autumn countryside, a world of orange dirt and kudzu and stands of loblolly pines. The sunlight was cold and yellow. Margarethe said nothing about our destination, or even if we had one.

She brought the car to rest on a hilltop overlooking rolling pastureland. She cut the engine. The single ancient pine tree in the middle distance looked like it had been etched on the sky. A white clapboard farmhouse stood on the other side of the road. As the engine ticked, Margarethe started talking. She told me that her father drove her to this spot because something horrific had happened here while she was away at school in Chicago, something he wanted her to know about and think about and never forget.

"Father told me they lynched a Black man right there," she said, nodding toward the pine tree. Her voice was quavering.

I couldn't speak. The only sounds were the ticking of the engine and the moaning of the wind. The lordly pine tree suddenly looked monstrous as I pictured a Black man with a rope around his neck swinging from one of its high branches, his feet twitching as the torch-lit mob beneath him looked skyward and howled in ecstasy. In that moment the past suddenly became close enough to taste and touch. William Faulkner got it exactly right when he said the past isn't even past. My grandfather was the son of a slave owner, and he banished racial slurs from his house and he brought his eldest child to this spot to impress upon her that evil was alive in the world and she was to have nothing to do with it. This was a revelation. Growing up in the North after the Second World War, I'd thought of lynching as a distant abomination, a relic from another century, another world. But the woman sitting beside me in the autumn of 1972 was alive during the peak years of lynching. I had always equated lynching with hanging. Unable to think of anything else to say, I asked Margarethe, "Did they hang him?"

"No," she replied. "They burned him alive." She told me the story as her father had told it to her: the murder of Ida Lee, the hunt for her killer, the arrest of Eberhardt at the Lambda Chi Alpha fraternity house, the mob's assault on the jail, the horrific torture and murder.

When Margarethe finished telling the story, she reached into her purse for a tissue and patted her cheeks. Finally, with the sunlight leaking away, she fired up the car and headed back up Watkinsville Road to Athens. I remember feeling exhausted by the day's history lesson, and on the drive to the elegant house on Rutherford Street, where her Black maid was preparing supper, Margarethe and I didn't exchange a word. We didn't need to. We understood that her father had taught her a lesson about racism that she would never forget, and she had taught me a lesson about her father that I would never forget.

PART THREE
THE WORLD BROKE IN TWO
1922–1955

A Ku Klux Klan march in Washington, DC.

A NEW LANDSCAPE OF THE MIND

Willa Cather's novel of the Great War, *One of Ours*, was published in 1922. The book sold well and won the Pulitzer Prize, but critics were divided. Edmund Wilson called the novel "a pretty flat failure." H. L. Mencken said the battle scenes were fought "not in France, but on a Hollywood movie-lot." Ernest Hemingway, who would produce a very different kind of Great War novel at the end of the decade, suggested that Cather lifted her battle scenes, chapter and verse, from D. W. Griffith's *The Birth of a Nation*. In a letter to Mencken, Cather candidly admitted to having misgivings about her novel: "It may be a complete mistake." Years later, she opened a book of essays with another frank admission—that *One of Ours* appeared at a moment that rendered it instantly obsolete, a relic from a vanished era. It was a moment when, as the literary historian Bill Goldstein put it, "the form of storytelling she prized, and had excelled at, was no longer of signal importance." Or as Cather would put it in the opening to her later book of essays: "The world broke in two in 1922 or thereabouts."

On one side of that broken world were writers like Cather, products of the nineteenth century and masters of its literary conventions; on the other side were younger writers, a generation whose hunger for new modes of storytelling was driven by the dislocations and aftershocks of the Great War. Disillusionment with discredited patriotic rhetoric led in a direct line to disillusionment with outdated and inadequate literary conventions. These writers understood that their broken world needed new voices, and they were not alone. After fighting on the Italian front, the German architect Walter Gropius summed up the era for Germans, but he could have been speaking for the entire Western world: "This is more than just a lost war. A world has come to an end. We must seek a radical solution to our problems."

Four years after the truce, radical voices began to be heard. The year 1922 began with the publication of James Joyce's novel *Ulysses* in February and ended with the publication T. S. Eliot's book-length poem *The Waste Land* in December. Joyce and the war were hovering over D. H. Lawrence, who was in Australia writing his novel *Kangaroo*, an experiment that he thought went further than *Ulysses* and would please just about no one. "Even the Ulysseans will spit on it," Lawrence predicted. Meanwhile, the first volume of Marcel Proust's masterwork, *In Search of Lost Time*, was published in English, which spurred Virginia Woolf to embark on her novel *Mrs. Dalloway* and compelled E. M. Forster to revive an abandoned manuscript that would become his own masterwork, *A Passage to India*. Sinclair Lewis published his blistering satire of the American middle class, *Babbitt*, which was formally less audacious than *Ulysses* but nonetheless remarkable for its psychological acuity and dark wit. It also would have been more accessible to a man of John's age and temperament than Joyce's volcanic outpourings.

John and Cather were contemporaries, and he shared her dismay that the fractured world was leaving people like them in its dust. In Goldstein's view, the war and its aftermath had impelled this new generation of writers "to confront and pin down on paper the texture and vitality of a new landscape of the mind." In a word, it had given birth to modernism.

While this literary vanguard was exploring new landscapes, a political rearguard was revisiting battlefields of the past. Just as the Red Summer had turned into a recruiting tool for the NAACP, *The Birth of a Nation* now turned into a recruiting tool for a second incarnation of the Ku Klux Klan. Though it adopted much of the iconography of the original Klan, including the white robes and insignia and sharp pointed hoods, this new version was a very different animal. Under the leadership of an Atlanta physician named William Simmons and the promotional wizardry of two seasoned public relations operatives, Elizabeth Tyler and Edward Young Clarke, the new Klan grew into a national organization with a much broader agenda than the subjugation of the Negro. In addition to racism, the members espoused ethnic bigotry and Anglo-Saxon Protestant morality, and their web of enemies now expanded to include Jews and Catholics, immigrants and city dwellers, union organizers and socialists, anyone who was not "Nordic" and "100% American" and sought to seduce Americans with those ubiquitous staples of the Roaring Twenties—sex, alcohol, and jazz. Or, as Klan literature described those enticements, "sensuality and sewage." The membership soon mushroomed to as many as four million men and women, most of them outside the South. Indiana and Oregon had the highest per-capita membership, and recruits tended to come from the middle and upper classes—craftsmen, businessmen, bankers, the clergy. Despite its portrayal of cities as cesspools of vice, the new Klan had tens of thousands of members in Chicago, Indianapolis, Philadelphia, Detroit, and other cities. The Klan was now a vast fraternal organization operating not in the night shadows but out in the sunshine. It hosted family-oriented outdoor carnivals that doubled as recruiting drives. It staged elaborate parades. The Klan had become immensely profitable by becoming impeccably *respectable*. And it was powerful. By the middle of the decade, the majority of the congressmen elected in Indiana, Texas, and Colorado were Klansmen. It's likely Supreme Court justices Hugo Black and Edward Douglass White were members. So was Georgia governor Clifford Walker. The Klan controlled many city councils, including the one in Anaheim, California, where police officers were allowed to patrol the streets dressed in Klan robes and symbols. At the 1924 Democratic convention, the Klan succeeded in derailing the presidential nomination of New York governor Al Smith—a Catholic, and thus a tool of that "dago priest on the Tiber."

The new Klan did have a presence in the South. In Athens, for instance, a thriving Chapter #5 opened, with headquarters downtown and some three hundred members, including prominent officers of the Chamber of Commerce, plus Masons, Odd Fellows, Elks, Shriners, Lions, and Kiwanians, four members of the Clarke County Democratic party's executive committee, and one county commissioner. The office of Grand Cyclops was held at various times by a city policeman and the pastor of the First Christian Church. There was also a Women's chapter and a Junior chapter. The cross burnings and terror rides of the original Klan now gave way to a relatively wholesome campaign to clean up vice and restore "law and order." When women wrote to complain about the objectionable behavior of a spouse or neighbor, the Klan would arrive with leather straps to flog the offenders, male and female, for such infractions as adultery or failure to support the family. John would have known many of these white-robed Protestant moralists, at least by reputation, and he was reminded yet again why he shunned all fraternal organizations. George Babbitt, he mused, would have felt right at home in Chapter #5. When John and my father walked past the Elks Club headquarters one day and my father asked what the initials B.P.O.E. on the front of the building stood for, rather than giving him the straight answer—Brotherly and Protective Order of Elks—John gave his wry smile and said: "Why, those initials stand for Best People on Earth."

The Athens Klan chapter was "average," in the estimation of the historian Nancy MacLean, but many members of the community and the university faculty, including the professor of German with the Catholic wife, were opposed to it. Their objections, however, never rose above a murmur. "The trouble with us," said the popular English teacher John Donald Wade, speaking for the faculty, "is that we have as little courage as we have voice. But with things as they are now in Georgia, *more* courage would likely mean martyrdom." Better to keep your head down and your mouth shut.

———

With the war over, John was now free to resume his periodic trips to Germany to pursue his arcane research and chip away at his dictionary. Berlin had not been touched by the war, and it was now more alive than ever, nearly manic, like a keyed-up drunk who refuses to pass out. John might have stayed in a hotel near Potsdamer Platz, a hub where street-cars, automobiles, horse-drawn carts, double-decker buses, and bicycles jostled each other in a crazy scrum, and since he was now in his sixties, he would have walked the streets slowly, drinking it all in, letting the river of humanity rush past. He admired the opulent display windows on the Kurfürstendamm, wandered past tenement blocks packed with Russian and Turkish immigrants, strolled through the Jewish quarter and past the crowded patio of the Café Josty, where he could watch the people watching him pass. The women were wearing shorter dresses and shorter hairstyles. There were prostitutes, male and female, working the streets, and those streets were the stage of nasty brawls between fascists and communists. Cocaine capsules were readily available for five marks. The inflation rate was insane. John would have visited galleries and museums showing the new expressionist painters, including George Grosz's pictures teeming with glossy businessmen, slatternly prostitutes, and wretched down-and-outs. *Der Blau Engel*, starring Marlene Dietrich, might have been the first movie with sound, the first "talkie," John ever saw. He would not have missed Fritz Lang's monumental science fiction movie *Metropolis*, two and a half hours immersed in a world broken in two—a futuristic city of gleaming spires perched above an underground hell where workers are enslaved by senseless machines. Shift change in the underground factory—thousands of faceless workers marching out while thousands more march in—brought to mind pictures John had seen of Henry Ford's new River Rouge plant in Detroit, a belching hell where tens of thousands of workers manned an assembly line that spit out a car every minute. John surely saw Bertolt Brecht's smash play set to Kurt Weil's music, *The Threepenny Opera*, and surely he applauded its cold-eyed portrait of capitalism as gangsterism, the lack of sentimentality in its pimps and prostitutes and beggars and other lowlifes. Above all, John admired Brecht for not trying to conceal the artifice on the stage, for not letting the audience forget that what it was watching and hearing was a fabrication, a life outside of life. There was something so *honest* about such art. Deep into the night the raucous bars and cabarets pulsed with jazz played by Black Americans, with performances by the sensational singer Josephine Baker and acts that catered to openly homosexual and transvestite crowds. John could feel the frenzy in the air, the urgency, the shared sense that we all have to live this free life as fast and hard as possible, right now—before it all vanishes. Mixed with the delirium was a pervasive sense of doom.

To his relief, John was still able to find refuge in the city's libraries. They were immune to the hurtling world outside, timeless and unchanging, and John buried himself there, suddenly intrigued by where Shakespeare's family name came from, increasingly pleased that the typed pages of his dictionary were now a stack nearly a foot tall.

An early radio.

THE ART AND COLOR SECTION

The upright piano and the phonograph in the living room on Mell Street were now joined by a new piece of furniture: an ornately carved cabinet that housed the latest invention, a radio. This one might have been purchased locally or ordered from the Sears catalog for $75. The year after broadcasting the results of the 1920 presidential election, station KDKA in Pittsburgh broadcast President Harding's inaugural address and the first live, play-by-play accounts of baseball and football games. Listeners were enthralled. Without leaving their homes they could witness in their minds an event taking place in real time hundreds of miles away. John and Gretchen were among the millions of Americans who embraced this innovation, and within a year there were more than five hundred radio stations in the country, and sales of radio receivers would soar from $60 million in 1923 to more than $800 million by the end of the decade. In 1926 the National Broadcasting Company became the first radio network, and it would soon link together fifty stations in two dozen states. Clear-channel stations, capable of broadcasting long distances at night, developed alongside the networks. Now a family in rural Iowa could tune in to a concert or a ball game taking place in Minneapolis or St. Louis. Programming expanded to include news, dramas, concerts, variety shows, and sudsy melodramas called soap operas. The comedy duo "Amos 'n' Andy" and Grand Ole Opry broadcasts out of Nashville attracted huge audiences. Vaudeville was doomed. Hollywood trembled that movies were doomed. The comedian George Burns would recall years later: "I knew that vaudeville was finished when theaters began advertising that their shows would be halted for fifteen minutes so that the audience could listen to 'Amos 'n' Andy.'" It was the first modern mass medium, another seductive marriage of immediacy and intimacy, far more revolutionary than the telegraph or even the telephone. There might be thousands, even millions, of people gathered around their radios listening to the president give a speech, yet each listener felt as if the president were talking directly to him or her. And in a curious way, every one of those listeners was suddenly on equal footing. "No single event in the history of invention before 1940 brought about a more striking egalitarianism." the social scientist Robert J. Gordon wrote, "news and entertainment that could be enjoyed equally by the richest baron or the poorest street cleaner."

It was most likely from the radio that John heard the bulletin that President Harding had died unexpectedly. Daily newspapers, dependent on the telegraph and printing press, were suddenly playing catch-up with this medium that could deliver the news within hours, even minutes. The initial reports said that Harding had died of a heart attack in his hotel room in San Francisco, where he had paused on a grueling western trip that was designed, in part, to put distance between himself and the spreading reports of bribes, embezzlement, and payoffs threatening to swallow his administration. Despite the strictures of Prohibition, Harding had turned the White House into the site of a rolling poker game, thick with cigar smoke and whisky fumes and the banter of cronies known as the Ohio Gang. Worse than Harding's behavior, in John's eyes, were his policies, which included limiting immigration and cutting taxes for corporations and the rich, though John surely approved of Harding's pardoning of Eugene Debs and twenty-three others convicted under the Espionage Act. But even this was too little, too late. The harsh conditions in the Atlanta penitentiary had broken Debs's health. Five years after his pardon, he died at the age of seventy.

The news bulletins of Harding's death at fifty-seven were followed by speculation that he might have died from a stroke, or food poisoning, or the incompetence of his doctors, or possibly by deliberate poisoning. His widow, Florence, blocked an autopsy, which led many to suspect she'd had a hand in her husband's death. When news surfaced of Harding's extramarital affairs and a child conceived out of wedlock—along with the cascading scandals that had been hatched on his watch—his popularity evaporated. For nearly a century he would be regarded, no contest, as the worst president in the history of the republic.

Spreading alongside the popularity of radio was the popularity of the automobile. While many of the factories were in the Midwest, the business was conducted in New York, where automotive stocks were liberally watered before changing hands. There, at a time when American corporations were extending their reach around the globe, John's younger brother Charles Ed was a rising star at the accounting firm Haskins & Sells. He was summoned, frequently by Westinghouse Electric, to perform accounting and auditing duties in London, Spain, the Netherlands, Cuba, the Philippines, New Zealand, even Russia. Back home, he handled the audits for a local outfit called the Hyatt Roller Bearing Co., which was doing brisk business with the growing herd of automobile manufacturers, most notably Ford and General Motors. Hyatt was run by a hard-nosed numbers cruncher named Alfred Sloan who, correctly assessing the future, allowed tiny Hyatt to be absorbed by much bigger United Motors, which in turn was absorbed by even bigger General Motors. The corporation may have been big and growing, but it was too loosely run for Sloan's taste. It had never been scrutinized by an auditor. Sloan, impressed by Charles Ed's work for Hyatt and determined to put GM on solid financial footing, brought in Haskins & Sells to handle GM's audits, which it would do for many years. Charles Ed was a made man.

Sloan's genius was at creating systems. As first-time buyers returned to purchase their second automobiles, Sloan, sensing the importance of install-ment buying, put together the General Motors Acceptance Corporation, which enabled buyers to pay for a new car over time—on terms that were, of course, favorable to GMAC. Sloan had already helped establish what he called the corporation's "basic price line"—its status ladder. Entry-level buyers started with a humble Chevrolet and then, as they prospered and craved new badges of their rising status, they stepped up a rung to the better-appointed and pricier Pontiac, then to an Oldsmobile, then a Buick, and finally to the sumptuous Cadillac. Aside from giving the corporation such structures and infusing it with rigorous discipline, one of Sloan's most brilliant insights was to sense that as the quality and reliability of cars improved during the 1920s, General Motors needed to offer a new selling point, something intangible, something that would capture not just the dollars but the *imagination* of the buying public. Sloan mused that car buyers were looking for more than basic transportation by then. They were looking for "comfort, convenience, power and style." He was far too dour to add the obvious topping to his list: *sex*.

With the 1920s awash in jazz and bathtub gin, Sloan was in luck. Lawrence Fisher, then head of GM's Cadillac division, made regular visits to dealers in Los Angeles, where he had discovered a young man named Harley Earl, the son of a carriage maker who was fashioning spectacular, one-off car bodies and attaching them to frames his wealthy customers shipped out from eastern factories. Many early movie stars were among his clients, including Little Mary Pickford and great big Fatty Arbuckle—in the days before Arbuckle got ensnared in Hollywood's first sex scandal. Earl, a lady's man and clothes horse in the thoroughbred class, fully grasped the sexual allure of the automobile. He built life-size clay models of his creations before he started bending sheet metal. Fisher, stunned by Earl's revolutionary methods, craftsmanship, and flair for design, made him an offer: Come to Detroit as a consultant and design the 1927 Cadillac La Salle from scratch. "We wanted a production automobile that was as beautiful as the custom cars of the period," Sloan wrote. And he got it. Earl's 1927 La Salle was longer, lower, sleeker, more *sculpted* than anything that had ever come out of an American car factory. It was also sexier, and it was a smash—"a significant car in American automotive history," as Sloan drily put it, "the first stylist's car to achieve success in mass production."

Soon Harley Earl was running GM's fledgling Art and Color Section and working up to one of the greatest moneymaking innovations in the history of American industry: the annual model change. While Henry Ford had only recently abandoned his unchanging, outdated Model T and come out with the stodgy Model A, Harley Earl set about redesigning every GM car, every year. It was the intangible Sloan had been looking for. After just a year, a car would seem hopelessly out of date—obsolete—and the consumer would be conditioned to begin thirsting for the next new thing.

John was among the millions of Americans who got car fever before Harley Earl began working his dark magic in Detroit. It is not known when John learned to drive—it must have been before 1922, the year he drove Margarethe to the scene of John Lee Eberhardt's lynching—but by all accounts he was an atrocious driver. People who rode with him describe him grinding the shift lever into first gear, then stomping on the gas pedal as he let out the clutch, pinning everyone to their seats as the car leaped forward. Then he would work through the gears as fast as possible—until a crossroads or a stop sign loomed and he would stomp on the brake pedal, sending everyone pitching forward. After the intersection cleared, he would repeat the terrifying ordeal. By the time they arrived at their destination, John's passengers were in a state of mild, rinsed-out shock. Parallel parking was beyond him. And based on his history of owning dented older models, he was immune to Alfred Sloan's and Harley Earl's seductive yearly offerings of shiny, sexy new toys.

⸺

John and Gretchen had settled into a life that was comfortable but far from opulent, at least by the standards of that manic, gaudy age, which was captured so beautifully and tragically in *The Great Gatsby*, F. Scott Fitzgerald's new novel of excess, deception, and death amid the mansions of Long Island's Gold Coast. That world must have seemed as distant as Mars to John. He and Gretchen still relied on the modest incomes from their teaching jobs, and Gretchen could always be counted on to put together a musical program for an event at the university, which brought in some extra money. John was shading into the status of esteemed senior professor, with no thought of retirement, because faculty salaries remained low and there were no fringe benefits such as health insurance or a pension fund. For John and his contemporaries, teaching late into life was a necessity, not a choice.

The neighborhood around Mell Street was now full of children, a rambunctious tribe that was largely left to its own devices. For the boys this meant daylong sandlot games of baseball and football, while the girls staged elaborate theatrical productions in the Morris's garage. When Gretchen and the children returned from Sunday Mass, there would be recitals in the house during the afternoon, children still in their church clothes singing, playing the piano and violin, reciting poetry. Margarethe was, of course, the star attraction. If the parents were entertaining or hosting a bridge game, it was understood they were not to be disturbed. At bedtime, Gretchen would sit at the piano and pound out "The Soldier's Chorus" from Gounod's opera *Faust* as the children marched upstairs to bed.

I wonder if my father, swept up in the boyhood passions of playing outdoor sports and exploring the woods and creeks and back alleys of the town, looked on his professor father the way Scout, in *To Kill a Mockingbird*, looked on her lawyer father Atticus Finch. These were southern gentlemen who always wore suits and ties and spent most of their time indoors, in stuffy classrooms or courtrooms, offices or libraries. Their hands were never dirty. When he was home, John always seemed to be seated by a lamp in the living room, peering through his owlish glasses at a book or newspaper or magazine. Scout could have been speaking for Richard when she painted this picture: "Our father didn't do anything. He worked in an office, not in a drugstore. Atticus did not drive a dump-truck for the county, he was not a sheriff, he did not farm, work in a garage, or do anything that could possibly arouse the admiration of anyone. Besides that, he wore glasses. . . . He did not do the things our schoolmates' fathers did: he never went hunting, he did not play poker or fish or drink or smoke. He sat in the living room and read."

Actually, John got out of his reading chair on a regular basis to pursue a late-blooming passion for golf. The Athens Country Club had opened on the west side of town, and though John was not listed among the charter members, friends regularly invited him to play the rolling layout designed by the renowned Scottish golf course architect Donald Ross. If no invitation came from the country club, there were other courses sprinkled around town. Of course afternoons of golf and summertime trips to German libraries were not big moneymaking ventures, and John and Gretchen, with five mouths to feed on their modest incomes, were always worried about money.

When things got particularly tight, Gretchen would assemble the children to pray novenas, nine straight nights of asking God to send money down from heaven to patch the leak in the roof or fix the carburetor in the Chrysler. When the prayers failed to produce any money, Gretchen more than once picked up the phone and called her father in Chicago.

Tom Gallagher was not thrilled to have an impecunious son-in-law who spent his afternoons on the golf course and lacked any sign of ambition, any interest in taking advantage of the opportunities that were so abundant in those boom years, any inclination to *play the game*. Why, John didn't even accompany Gretchen and the children to Sunday Mass, and of course he shunned the sorts of fraternal organizations that were oxygen to Tom Gallagher, from the Knights of Columbus to the Chamber of Commerce. Despite his misgivings, Tom, unlike the deity who ignored the children's novenas, almost always took out his checkbook and sent some money flying down the rabbit hole to Athens.

It was at about this time that Gretchen began to notice swelling in her knuckles. When the swelling subsided, she forgot about it—until it returned, a little worse each time. Soon there was redness and dull, throbbing pain, like a toothache. The worst time of day was right after she woke up, or after a long period of inactivity. She tried to walk as much as possible and began applying heat and ice to her knuckles when they hurt. Mentholated creams seemed to numb the pain. She had to visit several doctors before she got a definitive diagnosis: she was suffering from the early symptoms of rheumatoid arthritis. There was no known cure, but the doctor assured her that the pain and swelling could be managed through exercise and diet—she was to consume fish, berries, nuts, and green tea while shunning sugar, red meat, and alcohol. For a musician who relied on the dexterity of her fingers, the diagnosis must have felt like the onset of disaster.

John and John Donald Wade and other like-minded members of the faculty were delighted to learn that the second flowering of the Ku Klux Klan had already begun to wilt. The problem was that there was too much money floating around and too many people who believed they were entitled to a share of it, which led to a steady drumbeat of news stories about criminal embezzlement, bribery, grand larceny, even murders among rival factions. In Oregon, a Klansman was convicted of raping his secretary, then killing her while performing an abortion. Vigilante killings by Klansmen, usually in the South, caught the attention of J. Edgar Hoover, the newly appointed head of the Bureau of Investigation—soon to become the *Federal* Bureau of Investigation—one of Teddy Roosevelt's progressive reforms. No one in the Klan could top David Stephenson, the Grand Dragon of Indiana, who used Klan money to support a lifestyle that rivaled Jay Gatsby's, throwing lavish parties, drinking heavily, and cruising Lake Erie on his yacht with senators, congressmen, and state politicians on board. And then there were Stephenson's sexual shenanigans. Complaints from women began to surface, including one who claimed Stephenson locked her in a room during a party at his house, hit her, bit her, and tried to rape her. On another occasion he pleaded guilty to a charge of indecent exposure after he was caught with a woman in his Cadillac, his pants around his ankles. He attacked a woman during a train ride to Chicago, and the distraught woman wound up poisoning herself. By the time Stephenson was convicted of second-degree murder for his role in her death, Klan membership had dwindled from several million to just 350,000. Soon it would vanish from the scene, a victim of its own excess.

The radio and papers were offering a news story that was a welcome diversion from Klan atrocities and political scandals. In the spring of 1927 it's likely that the Morris family, like families across the country, gathered around the radio to hear the news that Charles Lindbergh had landed safely at Le Bourget airport outside Paris after a grueling thirty-three-hour solo flight from New York. *"Vive l'Americain! Vive l'Americain!"* thousands of

Frenchmen cried as they rushed the taxiing Spirit of St. Louis. When an exhausted Lindbergh crawled out of the cockpit, the first global superstar was born.

Less welcome to John was the news, three months later, of another dubious trial. Based on faulty evidence, two Italian immigrants, Nicolo Sacco and Bartolomeo Vanzetti, were convicted of murdering a guard and a paymaster at a Massachusetts shoe factory. Reading news accounts while their appeals dragged on, John would have had trouble deciding if the pair's greater crime was being avowed anarchists or being "undesirables" from southern Europe, to use the language of the restrictive Immigration Act of 1924. And John was not alone in believing that the trial was flawed. Albert Einstein, George Bernard Shaw, and H. G. Wells, among many others, signed a petition calling for the Massachusetts governor to order a new trial. Protests erupted from New Zealand to Dubai. None of it mattered. Sacco and Vanzetti died in the electric chair that summer, triggering strikes and violent protests from Paris to Tokyo. In trying to stamp out anarchism—and the immigration of "undesirables"—America had succeeded in creating a pair of international martyrs.

Shortly after the executions, John published a long two-part essay in *The Georgia Historical Quarterly* called "The Name of Oglethorpe." There's no denying the article's erudition, just as there's no denying that its audience would have been small. It drew on Old Norse, Middle English, Scandinavian sagas, Viking names, and the English Dialect Dictionary to argue that the family name of Georgia's founder had a Scandinavian provenance, which can be explained by the fact that the family originated in the north of England in an area intensively settled by Danish Vikings before they crossed the Atlantic a thousand years ago. Researching and writing such an article, at the very least, helped John briefly forget Gretchen's worsening arthritis, the executions of Sacco and Vanzetti, the Klan, and his constant money worries.

John's brother Sylvanus retired as dean of the university's law school that year. By now Sylvanus had become something of a local legend, a great wit known to his many friends as Syvlie, far more colorful than his younger brothers—the sober Episcopalean missionary Jim, the reserved and bookish John, the stiff accountant Charles Ed. My father told a story that was intended to capture Sylvanus's outsize personality. One day, the story goes, Sylvanus walked from his house on Dearing Street to catch the streetcar at Milledge Avenue. He was chewing on an unlit cigar. When he boarded the streetcar and paid his fare, the conductor said, "Um, Professor Morris, don't you know that we don't allow smoking on the streetcar?"

"Well," Sylvanus replied, "I'm not smoking."

"No sir, but you have a cigar in your mouth."

"I know that. I also have a penis in my trousers. But I'm not having sexual intercourse, am I?"

The story strikes me as a bit too redolent of the men's locker room to be wholly plausible. I have a hard time believing a southern gentleman of the old school would make such a remark in mixed company in a public conveyance. But it doesn't matter if the story is literally true. What matters is that it has been passed down through generations and accepted as part of the family myth. It may not be factual, but I do believe it touches on a truth about Sylvanus.

Despite his raffish charm and his popularity with students, faculty, and much of the town's populace, Sylvanus left behind a law school that was, in the words of one historian, "a deplorable mess." A candidate to succeed Sylvanus as dean claimed that the law school had fallen twenty-five years behind the times. Small wonder. In his twenty-seven years as dean, Sylvanus had continued practices begun after the Civil War. The faculty consisted of two local lawyers besides himself, and the school operated in cramped quarters on a shoestring budget funded by tuition and fees, with a yearly subsidy of just $500 for library purchases and salary supplements. This self-sufficiency seemed to be a point of pride with Sylvanus.

As the university tried to modernize during the 1920s, he resisted calls for the law school to put itself in shape to be accepted as a member of the American Association of Law Schools and win accreditation from the American Bar Association. When alumni and administrators pointed out that the law schools at Mercer College in Macon and Emory University in Atlanta had won ABA accreditation—and the prestige that came with it—Sylvanus countered that their accreditation reflected the size of their budgets, not the quality of their legal education. Sylvanus's resistance was no isolated act. It was part of a long-established pattern, a manifestation of the ancient southern distrust of outsiders and outside ideas, and it branded him a relic, an avowed enemy of the modern university. His attitude seemed to be: "We've always done it this way, and it has always been good enough. Why change now?" The answer was simple: because the world was changing by the hour, and it had passed him by.

The law school's alumni mounted an aggressive fundraising drive, and five years after Sylvanus's retirement, the law school moved into a new building on the north campus designed by the Atlanta architect Philip Schutze. A handsome two-story brick-and-limestone structure topped by a cupola, Harold Hirsch Hall was named after a law school alumnus who was then general counsel and vice president of the Coca-Cola company and the owner of very deep pockets. The building's ground floor was devoted to classrooms, and its second floor housed an extensive law library. At the dedication ceremony, in the fall of 1932, Hughes Spalding, chairman of the Board of Regents, praised Sylvanus for his dedication to the law school and for raising the funds to buy a small building to house classrooms and the bare-bones library in 1919. "But," Spalding said, "in the course of a few years the law school was again cramped for room." He added a telling aside: "Dean Morris was the only man in the department who gave all of his time to it. . . . The other professors came over from town to teach their classes, if they could get there." That *if they could get there* hints at a striking lack of rigor. Spalding concluded with an understatement: "You can see that our facilities were very limited." Those days were past. After Hirsch Hall opened, the faculty was expanded and the law school was soon accepted as a member of the American Association of Law Schools with accreditation from the American Bar Association. Sylvanus, who died in 1929 at the age of seventy-four, did not live to see the changes he had resisted.

Sylvanus's innate southern distrust of outside ideas had recently been on far more antic display in the hamlet of Dayton, Tennessee, where a teacher named John Scopes was put on trial for daring to teach Charles Darwin's science of evolution in a public school. This was a breach of the state's new Butler Act, which made it a misdemeanor to "teach any theory that denies the story of the Divine Creation of man as taught in the Bible, and to teach instead that man has descended from a lower order of animals." So much for the separation of church and state. And so much for the primacy of proven scientific fact over religious superstition.

For H. L. Mencken, this was open season, a license to lampoon the fundamentalist demagogues who, he believed, were largely responsible for reducing the South to a cultural and intellectual desert. He showed up in Dayton in the scorching summer of 1925, along with more than a hundred American and European reporters, to cover what he famously dubbed "the Monkey Trial." It was more like a circus. Preachers set up revival tents in town. The judge, a devout Baptist, opened each day's courtroom proceedings with a prayer. Outside the courthouse, vendors hawked Bibles and toy monkeys while a chimpanzee named Joe Mendi, a veteran of vaudeville and Broadway, entertained crowds on the courthouse lawn dressed in a fedora, plaid suit, and spats.

Mencken was in hog heaven. In his syndicated daily dispatches, he derided the "simian imbecility" of the Butler Act and portrayed the people packed into the sweltering courtroom as "morons" and "gaping primates." His preferred target was the lead prosecutor, William Jennings Bryan, three-time presidential candidate and hero of the fundamentalists who scorned the science of evolution as "absurd and harmful to society." Bryan, in Mencken's eyes, was nothing but an "old mountebank" spouting "fundamentalist buncombe" and "theological bilge." Mencken was delighted when the defense attorney, Clarence Darrow, called Bryan to the stand as an expert witness on the Bible, then eviscerated his religious beliefs, cornering Bryan into conceding that the words of the Bible should not always be read literally. The press reported their testy encounter as a bruising defeat for Bryan, whose beliefs were made to appear "mindless." But Mencken knew that Darrow's victory in this skirmish would do little to change the preordained verdict. "The net effect of Clarence Darrow's great speech yesterday," Mencken wrote, "seems to be precisely the same as if he had bawled it up a rainspout in the interior of Afghanistan." The jury deliberated nine minutes before reaching a guilty verdict. Scopes was fined the minimum $100. Five days after the trial ended, Bryan lay down for a nap and died in his sleep. For all its brimstone and loony drama, the trial had failed to address the central question Darrow had tried to raise, the legal question that interested John, a question that had nothing to do with the validity of the science of evolution: Isn't it unconstitutional to teach a religious doctrine in a tax-supported public school? The question went unasked and unanswered. The Butler Act would remain on the books for four more decades.

Georgia vs. Yale, the first game at Sanford Stadium, October 12, 1929.

CATFISH SMITH

The galloping popularity of radio was an unexpected but welcome boon to the already popular University of Georgia football team. Now it was possible for fans from the Appalachian foothills to Atlanta to the Atlantic Coast to hear live broadcasts of the games without leaving their homes. This naturally fed a hunger to witness the contests in person, and soon Athens was clogged on Saturday afternoons with the cars of fans pouring in from all corners of the state. The town fathers began debating the need for additional parking and wider streets to handle the influx. The weekend of the annual Georgia-Auburn game devolved into a spectacular bacchanal marked by the pursuit of such popular pastimes as "dissipation, licentiousness, even lawlessness," in the words of one alarmed critic.

Then there was the violence—and the growing professionalism—of the game itself. Way back in 1897, when gang tackling, flying wedges, and other vicious tactics began to dominate play, a Georgia player died from injuries sustained during a game against Virginia. In addition to the violence, there was the ugly little secret that some of the Georgia football players were not even registered as students while others were so academically deficient that they had gained admission by enrolling in the law school, where admission requirements were minimal. "Effectively," the historian Thomas G. Dyer wrote, "a double standard operated well before the turn of the century." It was destined to enjoy a long life.

During the 1905 season, eighteen college football players died from injuries incurred on the field. The following year, President Roosevelt convened college administrators to discuss ways to limit injuries, which led to the formation of the Intercollegiate Athletic Association, soon renamed the National Collegiate Athletic Association (NCAA). It standardized rules with an eye to reducing violence and injuries but showed little interest in stemming the flow of money into intercollegiate sports, a flow lubricated by the advent of radio. By the Twenties, players had become paid mercenaries, accepting cash under numerous tables and repeatedly switching schools, sometimes mid-season. At Georgia, the answer was not to clean up this "amateur" sport and purge it of money; the answer was to build a bigger football stadium that would bring in even more money.

John had played on the university's very first sports team, which was little more than an informal club, and he surely disapproved of these developments. It galled him that after thirty years on the faculty he was earning less than the school's football coaches, and it just as surely delighted him that there were voices, including a student publication called *The Iconoclast*, that spoke out strongly against the lopsided and growing emphasis on athletics, the existence of separate academic standards for athletes, and the campaign to build a massive, and expensive, new football stadium. The student editors pointed out that no athlete ever flunked out of the University of Georgia. For this heresy they were expelled from the University of Georgia.

Such iconoclasts were no match for the exposure, rabid fan loyalty, and revenue the Bulldog football team was generating. And so plans were unveiled for a $360,000 stadium to be built in the ravine carved by Tanyard Creek, where as boys John and his brothers had given wide berth to the vicious dogs guarding the Irishmen's tanneries. Part of the money came from a loan from the Trust Company of Georgia backed by the newly formed Georgia Athletic Association, made up of fans and alumni. This independent fiefdom would become, to the chagrin of generations of chancellors, a magnet for money and the power that comes with it—and, eventually, for the abuse that always comes with unbridled power.

———

A local celebrity had moved in next door to the Morris family. His name was Vernon Smith, but everyone called him Catfish because, according to legend, at his high school graduation in Macon he had won a twenty-five-cent bet by biting the head off a live catfish. His celebrity came from his stellar play on the Georgia football team as both an offensive end and a defensive mayhem artist. At six-foot-two and 190 pounds, he was a giant to my seven-year-old father, who trailed after him like a lost puppy. "He would take me around the neighborhood for walks," my father recalled, "and he sort of befriended me. He said to me once, 'Richard, you can call me Vernon.' I was the only one in town who got to call him Vernon." With a laugh, my father added, "What a role model!"

Built by convict laborers, Sanford Stadium opened on October 12, 1929 in a game against mighty Yale, which was led by its quicksilver halfback, Albie Booth. My father and his buddy Dan Magill, unable to afford three-dollar tickets, slipped under a fence and spent the game snaking through the throng of 30,000, always on the lookout for an usher who might demand to see their tickets. Catfish Smith scored the first touchdown by falling on a blocked punt in the Yale end zone. He then kicked the extra point. He scored again on a pass reception. By halftime the Connecticut Yankees, dressed in blue woolen jerseys, were melting in the ninety-degree heat of an Indian summer afternoon. Smith completed the scoring when he cornered Booth, eight inches shorter and fifty pounds lighter, and flattened him in the Yale end zone for a two-point safety. Booth popped up and barked, "That shit doesn't go around here!"

Smith, nose-to-nose, barked back, "Neither do you!"

Dan Magill and my father had worked their way down close to the field by then, and Dan cried, "Richard, look! You see that? Catfish is jawing with Albie Booth!"

The final score was Catfish Smith 15, Yale 0. It was, for better and for worse, the birth of big-time college football in the South. Georgia would eventually bring in a football coach named Wally Butts, who would win the school's first national championship and help solidify the fervor of fans and the power of the alumni-dominated Georgia Athletic Association.

John, meanwhile, was left to wonder what the $360,000 spent on Sanford Stadium could have done for faculty salaries and health insurance and pensions, for new libraries, for a campus that was run on such a tight budget that everything from routine maintenance to stadium construction was performed by convict laborers. The university had made a Faustian bargain, as John saw it, and Goethe had taught him long ago that one day there would be hell to pay.

A half-century later, by weird happenstance, I got to watch John's premonition come true. In 1983, with no qualifications other than a deep voice and a great face for radio, I talked my way into a job as a disc jockey at a Top 40 station in Savannah. As the new man, I was given the thankless graveyard shift, which meant I was on the air from midnight till 6:00 A.M., playing endless rotations of the current hits from Prince and ZZ Top and Michael Jackson's *Thriller* album while the city around me slept. Since the station broadcast University of Georgia football games, my duties also included assembling each Saturday's taped hour-long pregame show. As an added bonus, I was ordered to travel up to the campus in Athens for the annual preseason Media Day.

It was an experience I'll never forget. Georgia had won another national championship in 1980, and Bulldog running back Herschel Walker had been awarded the Heisman Trophy in 1982 before skipping his senior year and going to work for the New Jersey Generals of the fledgling United States Football League, a team that would soon be sold to New York real estate developer Donald Trump. When I arrived on the Athens campus for Media Day, there was an armada of TV trucks parked outside the athletic complex, bristling like giant insects with antennae and wires and satellite dishes. Nearby loomed Sanford Stadium, which, after four expansions, could now accommodate 82,000 fans. (Today it seats more than 92,000.) Inside the complex, an army of broadcasters, sportswriters, and nobodies like myself bustled around, interviewing coaches and players. It was a preposterous dance. The interviewers approached their subjects with great deference, especially the star players and the coach, Vince Dooley, a guy with a gingery comb-over and machined teeth who looked like he belonged on a used-car lot. All utterances from such wise men were written down or tape-recorded or videotaped as though they were holy writ, soon to be disseminated to the waiting faithful in the farthest outposts of Bulldog Nation. It was amazing to watch grown men kowtow to mumbling teenage boys, even if those boys happened to be chiseled, 250-pound slabs of beef. The same question was on all lips: Will there be life after Herschel?

Eventually I broke away from the dance and noticed . . . the girls. Some were Black, most were blonde, all were impossibly glossy and fit, as though they'd been raised on a diet of yogurt, sunshine, and Jane Fonda aerobics videos. *Co-eds don't look like this up North*, I thought, remembering my college years in New England. These girls were lurking along the walls in sundresses, bouncing up and down—the word *jiggling* came to me—and I realized they were waiting impatiently for all the old men with the microphones and notebooks to get out of the way so they could get a shot at those beautiful slabs of beef, prime boyfriend material, maybe husband material, maybe even NFL meal-ticket material. The air in that room was a hormonal cocktail, so potent, so thick, so musky that I was surprised those girls hadn't already come out of their sundresses. All in due time, I told myself.

As I drove back home to Savannah that evening, I realized I had gotten an up-close glimpse of the big-time college football business model. It was built on an infantile news media feeding pap to infantile fans while the university raked in millions of dollars off the unpaid labor of pampered teenagers who, in more than a few cases, could barely read and write. The formula had it all: get the media to feed celebrity and sex to a die-hard audience, and you'll wind up sitting on top of a very big pile of money.

Though I was unaware of it at the time, some people felt the pile was not nearly big enough. The University of Georgia had just joined forces with the University of Oklahoma to file a lawsuit seeking to end the NCAA's monopoly on negotiating college football TV contracts. The NCAA had decreed that no team could appear on national television more than six times in two years, and it picked the games to broadcast regionally and nationally. The administrators and athletic directors at Georgia and Oklahoma understood that Catfish Smith and Wally Butts and their successors had bred a blue-ribbon cash cow. And now they were determined to be the ones to milk it.

The year after I attended Media Day, the US Supreme Court ruled 7–2 in favor of the plaintiffs, freeing schools to negotiate their own TV contracts. Today, CBS pays the Southeastern Conference $55 million a year to broadcast its football games. Under a new contract that takes effect in 2024, ESPN will begin paying the conference *$300 million* a year. That is some serious milk.

Three years after I attended that Media Day in Athens, the president of the University of Georgia resigned after the Board of Regents implicated him and Vince Dooley, who by then was athletic director as well as football coach, in a pattern of academic abuse in the admission and advancement of student-athletes. The abuse was brought to light by Jan Kemp, an English professor who had the temerity to complain when higher-ups intervened to give nine football players a passing grade for a remedial English course they had failed. The passing grades enabled the players to compete in the Sugar Bowl on New Year's Day 1982. So, as it turned out, things had not progressed much in the nine decades since John began teaching remedial English to nearly illiterate country boys wearing their first pairs of shoes—only now a lot of money was at stake. For her trouble, Kemp was demoted, then fired. She sued the university, claiming she had been ousted because she had spoken out, a violation of her constitutional right to free speech. At trial, one of the university's attorneys justified the favorable treatment of a hypothetical football player this way: "We may not make a university student out of him, but if we can teach him to read and write, maybe he can work at the post office rather than as a garbage man when he gets through with his athletic career." Despite such shrewd lawyering, Kemp won the case and was awarded more than $1 million for lost wages, mental anguish, and punitive damages. She was reinstated to her job.

If John had lived to see this circus, he would have been appalled but hardly surprised. This, he'd sensed way back in 1929, was where things were inevitably headed once "amateur" sports were turned into a gushing revenue stream. The university would be powerless to turn down the money, and the money would acquire the power to pervert the mission of the university. Yes, it was a deal with the devil, as John had predicted. A losing deal. It was also John's idea of the American way: ruin a perfectly good thing by trying to turn it into money.

In the weeks after the opening of Sanford Stadium, the New York Stock Exchange went into a swoon, culminating in Black Tuesday, October 29, 1929, when sixteen million shares changed hands and the market lost 12 percent of its value in a single day. The hemorrhaging had just begun. By mid-November the market had shed half of its value, and the slide continued until the summer of 1932, when the market hit bottom after losing 90 percent of its pre-bust value. By then the nation was grinding through the Great Depression.

Kudzu.

MIRACLES

For John, the end of the boom years was marked not by the stock market crash but by the 1930 publication of a little-noticed book by a dozen southern writers based in Nashville, including John's former colleague John Donald Wade, who had left Georgia in a salary dispute and taken a teaching job at Vanderbilt University. The book, *I'll Take My Stand: The South and the Agrarian Tradition*, was a manifesto, a plea for southerners to embrace their agrarian past instead of mindlessly pursuing the "American industrial ideal." What spoke to John, especially in light of the recent crash, was the book's timely warning of the cost of worshiping material progress as an end in itself. His admiration was not dented by H. L. Mencken's dismissal of the essays as a string of "soap bubbles."

These twelve writers, each in his own way, placed humanism over materialism. John found Wade's essay, "The Life and Death of Cousin Lucius," to be the most readable in the book, a strangely dreamy tale of a man, based on an actual uncle of Wade's, who preferred to teach at the local academy rather than pursuing fame and fortune in the nearest city. John must have seen something of himself in this character. Uncle Lucius, like John, "felt that people were going too fast." His city friends, like John's, saw him as "one who had not justified the promise of his youth." His unwillingness to worship at Henry Grady's altar gave him a nobility that was far more valuable than mere wealth. In the end, despite his modest accomplishments and lack of laurels, Wade concludes that Uncle Lucius lived a significant life and that the sum of what he became was far from negligible. I believe John found comfort in this portrait.

Another essay that would have impressed him was "Reconstructed but Unregenerate" by John Crowe Ransom, which contained this dissection of the brute engine that drives Progress: "Our vast industrial machine, with its laboratory centers of experimentation, and its far-flung organs of mass production, is like a Prussianized state which is organized strictly for war and can never consent to peace." The key word here, the one that spoke directly to John, was *Prussianized*. It was the perfect word to describe a machine that has forgotten why it's running, if it ever knew. It was the perfect word to describe the dehumanizing mechanization in the underground factory in *Metropolis*, or in Henry Ford's real-life River Rouge plant, or in the roaring textile mill right there on the banks of the Oconee River near downtown Athens: unthinking, unrelenting, unable to stop once it got started. Prussianized.

Oases were blooming in the Sahara of the Bozart. Small but earnest literary magazines were struggling gamely to survive across the South. James Branch Cabell and Ellen Glasgow were publishing distinctly southern fiction that had no use for moons, magnolias, or any other Lost Cause pieties. Even H. L. Mencken approved. The year of the crash saw the publication of Thomas Wolfe's *Look Homeward, Angel* and William Faulkner's *The Sound and the Fury*, two novels that used the southern vernacular and southern history to create a new kind of myth, stark and free of delusion. These writers were the opposite of apologists, and they paved the way for a parade of serious southern writing—not a renaissance, as it has been called, but a spontaneous explosion, a literary Big Bang. Soon, seemingly out of nowhere, came Katherine Anne Porter, Robert Penn Warren (who had contributed to *I'll Take My Stand*), Carson McCullers, then Eudora Welty, Richard Wright, and Ralph Ellison, on down through Flannery O'Connor, Harper Lee, and many others.

One afternoon in the spring of 1932, as this explosion was just beginning to be heard, the Morris family's dinged-up Chrysler left Athens and headed for Atlanta. At the wheel was one of Gretchen's star pupils, Lou McGarity, with Gretchen sitting beside him on the front seat and my father in back. A dozen years after Mencken had claimed that there was not a single orchestra in the South capable of playing the nine symphonies of Beethoven, this group from Athens was on its way to hear the Atlanta Symphony Orchestra perform Edward Elgar's "Violin Concerto in B Minor" accompanied by the fifteen-year-old violin prodigy Yehudi Menuhin, whose growing fame had recently landed him on the cover of *Time* magazine.

Gretchen had resigned from Lucy Cobb by then because of her worsening arthritis. She was no longer able to play the violin—she couldn't finger the strings—and she was beginning to have trouble walking and climbing stairs. But she hadn't slowed down. She still welcomed select violin and piano students into her home, and Lou McGarity was one of her favorites, a natural talent who was willing to put in the work, two virtues that didn't always go together. He had begun studying violin with her at the age of seven and now, at fourteen, he had developed a new passion. On the ride to Atlanta, expecting a chilly reaction, Lou screwed up his courage and made a confession to Gretchen: "I don't think I'm good enough to make a living playing classical music on the violin, Mrs. Morris. Besides, I prefer the trombone. And jazz."

She surprised him. "That's just fine, Louis," she said. "You're a very fine musician, you have perfect pitch, and I know you'll master the trombone."

That evening's concert was a revelation. Menuhin, blond and chubby, waddled onto the stage dressed in short pants and knee socks. All snickering died the instant his bow touched the strings of his Stradivarius. Gretchen was transported to a place she had never visited before—she was witnessing the miracle of perfection—and Lou McGarity and my father, both students of the instrument, understood for the first time just how magical the violin could be in the hands of a genius. On the drive back to Atlanta, there wasn't much talk, but Lou McGarity must have felt convinced he had made the right career choice.

Thirty years later, I would learn just how right his choice had been. On my first trip to New York City, my father took my mother, my brother, and me to Eddie Condon's nightclub on the East Side. We got a table right next to the bandstand, where a Dixieland group was merrily jamming away. During a break, the trombone player strolled over to our table, and our father introduced us to his boyhood friend from Athens, Lou McGarity. Like my father he was a big guy, gracious, impeccably dressed, still speaking with a syrupy Georgia drawl. He joined us and I listened, slack-jawed, as my father got him to reminisce about playing with Benny Goodman and Ben Bernie and Eddie Condon's All Stars, about leading his own bands and touring Japan and playing Carnegie Hall. Nowadays, he told us, he was mostly staying close to home, relying on a regular gig with the Arthur Godfrey radio show and occasionally sitting in on jam sessions like tonight's.

When the music kicked back in, I realized I wasn't witnessing perfection. I was witnessing something even more thrilling—the ecstasy of improvisation, musicians traveling to uncharted, unpredictable places, the essence of jazz. We stayed through the last set and wound up standing in front of the club in the small hours of the morning, the latest I'd ever stayed up, while my father flagged a cab and Lou McGarity said his goodnights. I watched him and the bass player move down the sidewalk. Lou was carrying his trombone in a leather case, and the bass player was rolling his enormous instrument on a little wheel. I kept watching as they receded into the gloom. They were two workingmen heading home with the tools of their trade, but they didn't work in a garage or in the PR hive of a vast corporation like my father, and they didn't punch a time clock. They worked all hours of the day and night all over the world. They were artists. To my ten-year-old eyes this was a revelation, much as *The Gilded Age* had been a revelation to John's ten-year-old eyes. As the two musicians disappeared into the New York night, I realized I wanted a life like theirs—not making music, necessarily, but pursuing the ecstasy of improvisation at all hours all over the world. Not a humdrum workaday life. An open-ended *creative* life. Just as Yehudi Menuhin had opened Lou McGarity's eyes to his true path, Lou McGarity had opened my eyes to mine.

⸙

The year after Yehudi Menuhin's performance in Atlanta, John's son Jack, the hardiest of the three boys, responded to the worsening Depression by signing on with the Civilian Conservation Corps. This was one of President Franklin D. Roosevelt's earliest New Deal initiatives, and Jack spent his last two college summers bunking with other unmarried, unemployed young men from across the country, tasked with planting a fast-growing vine that would combat the erosion that had left the Georgia soil exhausted and rutted with red gullies, the price of the South's fealty to King Cotton.

Even though the camps, like everything else in the South, were to be rigidly segregated, Georgia's new race-baiting governor, Eugene Talmadge, refused to allow eligible Blacks to enlist in the program, claiming it was a dangerous federal incursion into state sovereignty. Only when the US Labor Department threatened to withhold the state's entire allotment did Talmadge, grudgingly, relent. When he tried to block Social Security payments to Georgians, President Roosevelt, to John's relief, intervened. It was not the last time the governor with the trademark red galluses would touch John's life.

The vine Uncle Jack and his crew planted was called kudzu, and it was said to be a miracle. This Asian plant had first been introduced to America in the Japanese exhibition at the Centennial Exposition in 1876, and now it was touted as cheap forage and the perfect way to slow erosion and rejuvenate the depleted soil with nitrogen. There was one small problem. Kudzu was so aggressive that soon it was carpeting acres of land, choking out indigenous plants, climbing power poles, mummifying trees. It was such a notorious, ubiquitous, unkillable scourge that it eventually became the title of a popular comic strip, proof that laughter is the best medicine for folly.

These were distant problems. The immediate benefit of Jack's job was his $30 monthly pay, $25 of which he was required to send home to help support his family. At a time when cooks were paid two dollars a week, the money was a godsend. It helped keep the household together and also helped finance an odyssey of raw desperation: John acquiesced to Gretchen's desire to take a 1,500-mile drive from Athens to rural Ontario, Canada, to attend a revival conducted by faith healers who modeled themselves on Aimee Semple McPherson. My teenage father was the designated driver. He told me he had to pile pillows on the driver's seat so he could see over the steering wheel, and his erratic driving in strange northern towns caught the attention of more than a few traffic cops. Faith healing was associated with Pentecostal and Charismatic denominations, people who handled snakes and twisted feet and talked in tongues, who supposedly had the power to make the lame drop their crutches and spring from their wheelchairs. For a devout Roman Catholic like Gretchen, resorting to the quackery of faith healers was a sign of just how desperate she had become. Somehow she, John, and my father survived the trip. Of course when they made it back to Athens, exhausted and bleary-eyed, Gretchen's arthritis was as bad as ever.

There was another health crisis in the family. John's and Gretchen's eldest son, Charles, was showing alarming signs of mental instability. He had married a woman named Charlotte Maurice, and while Charles was on a fellowship at Oxford, doing postgraduate work in English, she gave birth to a son, another John Morris—John *Nelson* Morris—who would grow up to become an acclaimed poet. From Oxford the couple paused in Charlottesville, Virginia, on the way to another fellowship at Iowa City. These fellowships were never renewed. Charles became erratic and couldn't seem to get his life in gear. One summer Charlotte was summoned, from a vacation in the Adirondacks, to Washington, where Charles had landed another short-lived job at the Library of Congress. She arrived at St. Elizabeth's Hospital to find her husband in a bare room, straitjacketed and delusional. She was soon joined by her father-in-law, for John had rushed to his ailing son's side. Charles, barely coherent, wanted to confess to a murder he clearly had not committed. While he recuperated in a Richmond hospital, Charlotte and young John spent the winter at Taylor's Creek, where they slept on mattresses stuffed with corn husks and survived on salty ham and tomatoes from the ranks of jars that lined the pantry shelves. A cold and lonely season.

In time Charles was released from the hospital, and John arranged a job for him with the Georgia relief agency. The family moved into an apartment in Madison, thirty-five miles south of Athens, close enough for John and Gretchen to keep an eye on them. As Charles's young son would later recall, "Professor Morris was reading Freud, hurrying through him . . . as if doing so would help his son, believing as professors do that books will save us."

Charles took up the cello in Madison, which proved to be excellent therapy. He got better, but this was not to be his last rendezvous with madness.

⁂

John responded to these crises not only by taking quixotic road trips and speed-reading Freud but also by burrowing into research that was arcane even by his standards. In the October 1931 issue of *The Journal of English and Germanic Philology*, he published an essay called "The Name of Shakspere" [*sic*]. It's a much shorter version of his earlier parsing of the Oglethorpe family name, and it ends on this light note: "My argument therefore leads to the conclusion that Shakspere is from Saxbáer (Saxi's farmstead), a place-name equivalent to Saxby, and has no more to do with drawing a sword than with shaking a spear." And in the April 1934 issue of the same journal, he published an even knottier piece, eleven illustrated and densely worked pages called "Ring-Mail." It arrives at this ringing conclusion:

> To recapitulate. Interlocked, riveted ring-mail byrnies—all admittedly of Roman workmanship—occurred in a Swedish grave-find and in the Thörsbjerg and Vimose peat-bog finds. No mail of any kind appears in Scandinavia until ca. 900 (Fig. 6), and no such ring-mail as that of the bog-finds occurs anywhere in Western Europe until we obtain such full descriptions of it in Bēowulf and *Heimskringla*, and hear of Byrhtnoth wearing it at the battle of Maldon (991). . . . Through contacts with the outside world—probably in öster-viking—the Scandinavians in the tenth century learned the art of constructing the interwoven ring-mail corselets in their own workshops, and through the Danes the knowledge of them reached England.

Many years after this was published, John's grandson John N. Morris, a poet and no intellectual lightweight, admitted to being overwhelmed by it: "I could as soon bridge the Susquehanna as imitate it." (His mother's forebears had built bridges, including one across the Susquehanna River near Harrisburg.) The feeling is mutual. I believe John's willfully obscure research and writing can be seen in one of several ways—as an outpouring of pure passion, as a form of mental calisthenics for an academic mind, or as simple escapism, a way of sealing off a modernizing world that was never terribly appealing and was now growing increasingly senseless and sinister.

The news out of Germany may have been the most sinister of all. John had seen fascists and communists brawling on the streets of Berlin in the 1920s, and now he read that the misnamed National Socialist Party—or Nazis, fascists, the right-wing opposite of socialists—were tightening their grip on power. Their leader, Adolf Hitler, had been named chancellor in early 1933, and within months the Enabling Act had been passed, solidifying his power to pass laws without the approval of parliament or the decrepit president of the Weimar Republic, Paul von Hindenburg. Soon Germans were required to prove their "Aryan" ancestry back to 1800, and non-Aryans—Jews, "Negroes," Roma—were purged from civil service jobs. After Hindenburg's death in the summer of 1934, Hitler became president. John had read Hitler's prison memoir, *Mein Kampf,* and regarded it as a river of drivel and bilge. How was it possible that the Germans were allowing this megalomaniacal nobody to take over their glorious country?

News came from Cincinnati in early 1936 that Tom Gallagher had died at the age of eighty-seven. He'd quit working a year after his wife's death, then spent his retirement as an in-demand public speaker in Chicago, regaling the luncheon and banquet circuits with the misadventures of his fictional sidekick, Casey. Tom had gone to Cincinnati to celebrate the 1935 Christmas holidays with his growing brood of grandchildren and great-grandchildren. Feeling weak, he checked himself into Good Samaritan Hospital, where he fell from his bed on Christmas Day and broke his hip. After he died a month later, the eulogies came in torrents. He was remembered as "an underwriter of the old school" and "a successful handler of men" who was also "a hard fighter," "exceptionally clean in heart and mind," and possessor of "an inexhaustible supply of good anecdotes." John and Gretchen traveled to Chicago for the funeral, which was held in Old St. Mary's Catholic Church and attended by hundreds of Tom Gallagher's relatives, former business associates, and closest friends—proof that he was "one of the beloved personalities of fire insurance." I imagine John looking around the packed church and thinking, *So this is how you wind up if you're willing to play the game. You can have it.*

John, Gretchen, and Richard in Europe, 1937.

CORONATION TELEVISION

I n the spring of 1937, John and Gretchen sailed again for Europe, sensing this was to be their last trip. John was nearly seventy-four, well past the traditional retirement age but still teaching because the university's perpetually low salaries meant he couldn't afford to stop working; Gretchen's pain never let up, constant throbbing in her knuckles and knees. She was spending more time in the wheelchair, and she had begun receiving Holy Communion standing up because kneeling and then rising was too much for her. Despite her declining mobility, she was game for one last adventure. Gretchen was always game.

Further complicating matters was the turbulent political weather in Europe. This was John's first return trip since the Nazis had taken over in 1933. Hitler's popularity and power continued to expand, the Germans continued to re-arm, Jews were beginning to flee the Continent. What was coming? John believed it could only be bad, which added to his urgency to get back to Berlin and finish researching his dictionary. He was close and he didn't want to get locked out again, as he had been during the Great War. Gretchen had a very different motive for taking the trip.

They did not travel alone. The more imposing of their two companions was Marion Foster Washburne, a renowned writer and activist who had fought for women's suffrage, was active in the American Civil Liberties Union, and helped establish schools for deaf children in her native Chicago. She was John's age, and in her long busy life, she had rubbed up against the famous and the high-minded, among them Alexander Graham Bell, John Muir, and the muckraking journalist Ida Tarbell. There was something mannish about the woman that intimidated John. She was taking the trip because she was, as always, on a mission. She wanted to revisit Estonia, a country she had seen for the first time the previous summer, the place she regarded as the fairest and finest in the world. She was hoping to write a book that would sing its many virtues. Her working title was *A Search for a Happy Country*.

Also along on the trip was the last child still living at home, my fifteen-year-old father, the Afterthought, who had not yet reached puberty and had only recently graduated from short pants to a double-breasted suit. A picture taken in Europe reveals an odd menagerie. John, grinning, dressed in a jaunty fedora and three-piece suit, looks like a septuagenarian Clyde Barrow. He's standing beside Gretchen, who is seated, wearing an elaborate floral hat and a radiant smile while Richard, brimming with mischief, rests a hand (lovingly? protectively?) on his mother's shoulder. Richard may have been an unworldly small-town Southern boy, but he had heard enough talk around the dinner table to understand that the money for this trip had come flying in through the window—maybe some of the inheritance from Gretchen's father, or possibly a check from John's youngest brother, Uncle Charles Ed, whose accounting work for Alfred Sloan at General Motors, among other corporations, had made him immune to the depredations of the Depression. Uncle Charles Ed may have been on the stiff side, but he was rich and had always been a soft touch when he passed through Athens in his Cadillac on the way from New York to Sea Island or Palm Beach or wherever it was that rich people vacationed in wintertime. Richard didn't even have to drop all that many hints before Uncle Charles Ed would peel off a five-dollar bill and tell him to go on into town and buy that pair of crepe-soled shoes he wouldn't stop yakking about.

While these visits from Charles Ed and his wife, Ethel, were always warm, I imagine they were also a cold shower for John, a reminder of the cost of the path he had chosen. Charles Ed, like Tom Gallagher, was willing to play the game, and he played it with enough zeal and skill to grow rich off it, living in an apartment on Fifth Avenue, driving that burgundy Cadillac, vacationing in Florida and Europe. Likewise Charlie Parrott, John's new son-in-law, who was growing so rich from selling insurance and trafficking in slot machines that he could afford to build that elegant house on Rutherford Street. *Accounting, Insurance. Slot machines.* In a way, John felt grateful that he didn't care about amassing a fortune or keeping up with the current standards of luxury since he could not have brought himself to do the sorts of grubby things that were necessary to make it happen. And so he kept drawing his peevish professor's salary and working on his dictionary, and he had no trouble accepting Charles Ed's offer to buy three boat tickets to Europe.

Atlantic crossings were John's idea of heaven—sleep late, no telephones, nothing to do but read and eat and loaf, take long walks on the deck, maybe a few rubbers of bridge or a game of chess. He spent hours intoxicated by Sinclair Lewis' latest novel, *It Can't Happen Here*, a frighteningly plausible fantasy about a fear-mongering nobody named Burzelius Windrip—what a name!—winning the presidency from Franklin Roosevelt and imposing a ruthless totalitarian state. Wasn't it already happening in Germany? And in Italy and Spain? And hadn't the South produced its own crop of Windrips, from Pitchfork Ben Tillman of South Carolina to William Vardaman of Mississippi, Georgia's Eugene Talmadge and, until his recent assassination, Huey Long in Louisiana, the self-proclaimed Kingfish? If he wasn't lost in Lewis's novel, John was poring over the scholarly papers he'd picked up at the recent South Atlantic Modern Language Association conference in Atlanta. He had been appointed to the executive committee of this regional offshoot of the national organization, only the second professional group he had deemed worth joining. He found, to his surprise, that he enjoyed the camaraderie of the annual conferences.

When Gretchen managed to flush John out of their cabin or the ship's library, there was always that time-killing machine, Marion Foster Washburne. Her years on the lecture circuit had turned her into a polished raconteur, and she spent hours regaling John and Gretchen and Richard with stories about her trip the previous summer. One of the highlights had been the Olympics in Berlin, which had a deeply personal resonance for Marion. Her daughter Dorothea was married to Herman Stegeman, the track coach at the University of Georgia and an old friend of John's. Herman's prodigy was a lanky high-hurdler named Forrest "Spec" Towns, who got his nickname from the freckles speckling his nose and cheeks. The gaiety was gone from Berlin, to hear Marion tell it, the buildings so drab and shabby they reminded her of the North Side of Chicago in the 1880s. Nazi flags were everywhere—that sinister black swastika on a white circle in a blood-red field—as were soldiers in brown shirts. Whenever a group of them marched past, the people threw up their right arms in the Nazi salute and cheered. All anti-Jewish posters had been removed from the streets before the Olympics, Marion reported, and the people had been on short rations of butter for months so there would be an ample supply for the foreign visitors. She did not find the German people particularly warm, but they were visibly hot for American dollars. Taxi drivers confided to her that unemployment was down under Hitler, but wages were so low that even people with decent jobs were suffering. Businessmen who had originally supported Hitler now grumbled about high taxes and onerous regulations. All such criticisms of the regime were spoken in a whisper, after a glance over the shoulder. Marion said she could taste the fear. When he heard this, John thought immediately of Lewis's diabolical creation, Buzz Windrip.

In the Olympic Stadium, which seated more than 100,000, Marion saw no litter, no rowdyism, no drunkenness. "I must admit, there's something electrifying about being in such a throng—the sheer animal power of it," she said. "On our second day at the games, we got a surprise. While we were drinking cider and eating hot dogs, I spotted Adolf Hitler seated in a nearby box."

"What's he look like?" asked Richard, who had heard about Hitler on the radio and had seen his picture in magazines.

"Not terribly impressive, to tell you the truth. He looked exactly like his pictures—a middle-sized, middle-aged man in a brown uniform, with a little black moustache and a lock of black hair falling over his forehead. But he had something, some sort of charisma. Whenever he entered the stadium, or whenever a German athlete won an event, everyone stood and stretched their rights arms toward him and sang the national anthem and that hideous Horst Wessel hymn. I could see their fingers trembling with emotion. It was almost like they worshiped the man."

Horst Wessel, as John knew, was a street-brawling storm trooper who'd been murdered by communists and then turned into a revered Nazi martyr by Joseph Goebbels' propaganda machine. John couldn't resist belting out the opening bars of the hymn: *"Die Fahne hoch, die Reihen fest geschlossen . . ."*

"Thank you, dear," Gretchen said, patting John's arm. She could not abide bad music, especially bad martial music, even when it was performed passably well. John was grinning. She studied his profile—the square jaw, the full head of white hair. He was still a handsome man, with good years ahead of him. More than I've got, she thought, without sorrow or self-pity.

Marion went into a rhapsody describing the thrill of seeing Spec Towns set a world record in the 110-meter high hurdles during qualifying, then watching him win the gold medal with ease. "That boy seemed to fly!" she said. But the big news of those Olympics was that Jesse Owens, an American Black man, won four gold medals, a humiliating blow to Hitler's pronouncements on the supremacy of the Aryan race. Infuriated, Hitler refused to congratulate Owens.

"I didn't learn till later that Owens is the grandson of slaves," said Marion, who was always on the lookout for hypocrisy. "Hitler's snub made big news at the time—but not many people know that when Owens returned to the States, President Roosevelt didn't even invite him to the White House. And when he attended an awards ceremony at the Waldorf-Astoria in New York, he had to ride the freight elevators with the hotel's Negro staff. We Americans are so sanctimonious."

Indeed we are, John thought in his dry way.

They arrived in London a few days before the coronation of King George VI and Queen Elizabeth. The city was buzzing with preparations for what was to be the most lavish coronation in the history of the empire, a transparent attempt to paper over the shock of King Edward VIII's scandalous abdication, the previous December, so he could marry that American divorcee, Wallis Simpson. Surveying the bustling streets from their hotel balcony, John mused that it obviously wasn't cheap to make things look like business as usual.

They gave Richard a small allowance and set him loose every morning, and he soon fell in with a local boy named Tom. The two hit it off "like bandits," in Richard's telling, and he followed his new companion everywhere.

Tom seemed to know every crooked street, every alleyway, even knew some of the bobbies by name. Richard had found the traveler's dream: a local who knew the lay of the land and was willing to let the dim foreigner tag along.

People were pouring into the city from across the country—and around the world—and the boys watched families setting up elaborate campsites in the parks, others unfurling bedrolls on sidewalks and benches, staking out their viewing spots along the procession route. They'd brought cooking stoves, picnic baskets, thermoses for tea. There was a carnival air to it all.

On the day of the coronation, Tom and Richard watched the parade from their perch in a sycamore tree on Whitehall. Beneath them flowed an endless stream of people from the farthest reaches of the British Empire—African princes and Scottish bagpipers and Indians in ballooning pantaloons. Richard couldn't stop thinking this was a movie, and the people passing below them were all paid actors. Tom explained to him that everyone was upset that King Edward had run off with an American woman, and a lot of people, including Tom's mum, believed she was a floozy who'd learned her tricks in a Chinese brothel. Richard didn't know what floozies or brothels were, but he guessed they were dirty and he was sharp enough not to ask.

———

Now we have to imagine a scene; it's the only way. The hotel staff has turned the lobby into an impromptu theater, setting up rows of folding chairs facing a crude wooden box with a glass screen. It rests on a high table at the end of the room, visible to all. Gretchen doesn't feel up to battling the mob scene on the streets, so John has dutifully wheeled her to a spot on the side of the lobby where, with Marion seated between them, they have a clear view of the screen.

By noon the lobby is packed, all eyes trained on the screen. For hours they watch gray people dodder like sleepwalkers up The Mall, through the

Admiralty Arch, then down Whitehall to Westminster Abbey. On and on they come for hours, moving as if they're underwater, under *muddy* water, as an announcer prattles on about the Queen of Norway and the Marquess of Anglesey, the bagpipers of Ballachulish and Prime Minister Baldwin and his handsome wife, Lucy. John hears several people gushing about the "miracle" they're witnessing. John has read about this new invention called television, but these people call the crude box a "telly," as though it were a new kind of candy or a harmless pet.

At the end of the parade is the most preposterous thing John has ever seen—eight liveried white horses pulling a carriage with three cherubs on the roof, ropes of what appears to be gold dripping from the corners, huge wheels with wooden spokes. It looks like a wedding cake on wheels. The crowd begins roaring as the coach draws closer, and John can see a small man and a small woman sitting side-by-side in its cocoon of velvet. They're being jostled and they're trying to smile, but they both look like they're about to be sick . . .

John wakes up slumped in his chair. The lobby is deserted. The glass screen is the color of a sidewalk, all the sleepwalkers gone, the announcer silenced. John has a foul taste in his mouth, and he needs a bath. The spectacle inside the box has revealed yet another aspect of a world he does not care to belong to, a world where people are drunk on every new contraption. This one struck him as nothing but gray ghosts and noise.

As he makes his way to the elevator, John realizes the reaction of the crowd in the lobby was even more dismaying to him than the contraption itself. The people around him hadn't seemed to notice or care how terrible the pictures were. They behaved like children watching fireworks blossom on a Fourth of July sky, cooing, gasping, cheering in unison whenever the camera zoomed in on a bagpiper or the prime minister's horsey wife. Yes, there was something childish, something nearly infantile, about such unthinking worship of novelty.

Up in the room John finds Gretchen in a steaming bath, a towel over her eyes. She tells him she asked Marion to wheel her up after he dozed off, and the hot water is doing wonders for her knees. "So," she says, "if it put you to sleep, I gather you weren't terribly impressed by the latest miracle."

"I don't believe I've ever been so bored. What is it with the British and their worship of that useless royal family?"

"Tradition, by Jove, tradition!" She laughs. "Marion thinks television's going to change everything, that it'll be the absolute death of movies."

"I'm sure she's right. Marion's always right."

"Now don't be that way. She means well."

"I'm afraid you're right. Those are the ones you've got to watch out for—the ones who mean well."

"Would you be so kind and turn the hot water back on for me?"

"Of course, dear." As he turns the knob marked H, he feels it again: the familiar dislocation, the sensation that he's living outside of time, that he's frozen in an earlier decade or even an earlier century when he, like his father, had been educated in a way that prepared a man to take part in what used to be called the learned professions. The pace of American life has been speeding up since the day John was born, and now it seems to move at the precise speed at which money changes hands, always faster, always more of it, all of it dedicated not to the acquisition of learning but to the acquisition of the latest thing. A man's worth used to depend on family and education and the merit of his work, but it's coming to depend more and more on how well he keeps up with the current standards of luxury. He thinks again of Charles Ed and Charlie Parrott. During the Atlantic crossing John discovered a magazine in the library called *LIFE*, and as he flipped through the pictures, he felt he did not live in the country he was seeing: a monstrous hydroelectric dam in Montana, a new suspension bridge in San Francisco, movie star weddings, beach fashions, trout fishing in Pennsylvania, an oil well fire in Texas, quintuplets, polo ponies—

"That's enough, dear."

Gretchen is still hidden behind the towel. He turns off the hot water and leaves her in peace. As soon as he starts packing, Richard comes barreling into the room, spouting gibberish about watching the parade with his imaginary friend Tom, something about Windsor Greys and golden cherubs and men-fish called tritons. John doesn't catch half of what he's saying.

"Youth Serves the Führer" All Ten-Year-Olds in Hitler's Youth.

A HAPPY COUNTRY AND A DOOMED COUNTRY

The next morning's papers confirmed John's suspicions. "The picture was so vivid," the *Daily Mail* gushed about the coronation broadcast, "that one felt this magical television is going to be one of the great modern inventions." John read a half-dozen similar news accounts aboard the freighter that was carrying them from London to Estonia.

For five days the freighter crawled across the North Sea, through the Kiel Canal and up the Baltic to the Gulf of Finland. By the end of the first day, Richard had befriended the Estonian crew, who communicated with broken English and sign language. They were so amused by the plucky young American that they agreed to let him introduce them to his parents and their lady companion. Marion had already remarked to John and Gretchen that Richard reminded her of Kipling's Kim, "little friend of all the world," and once he performed the introductions, she, being Marion, took the opportunity to question the crewmen for the book she was hoping to write. They told her, in their halting English, how much they loved their free country, where their wages were enough to pay for ample food, clothing, and good times. Every one of the men told Marion they would rather live in Estonia than anywhere else in the world. She was thrilled by their fervor. It renewed her faith in the book she was hoping to write.

"Land ahoy!"

John, squinting through field glasses, had spotted the first wooded islands off the Estonian coast. Hearing his cry, everyone hurried to join him at the starboard rail. They slid past dozens of islands in the twilight, close enough to see castles surrounded by cultivated fields, harbors with gaily painted houses, piers, church steeples. John and Gretchen exchanged smiles. It was even lovelier than Marion had led them to believe.

As they drew nearer to Tallinn, they were joined by other freighters approaching the port. The sea was a sheet of indigo glass. Freighters were tied to the docks of factories and warehouses, and Marion pointed out the naval base built by Peter the Great and abandoned at the end of the Great War, when the defeated Russians made their hasty retreat to Leningrad, 150 miles to the east. John couldn't shake the feeling that the woman was in love with the sound of her own voice.

The medieval Old Town rose steeply from the water, surrounded by a massive stone wall, the skyline punctured by steeples and the domes of Greek and Russian Orthodox churches. It was nearly midnight but still not full dark, and the streets were alive with people as the taxi carried the Americans from the docks and into Old Town. The taxi deposited them at the Kuld Lövi Hotel, Marion's favorite.

While John and Gretchen got settled into their room, Richard went exploring. At the end of the hallway, a window looked out on red tile roofs, onion domes, a courtyard with a barbered lawn, and flowering bougain-villea bushes. Richard couldn't believe there was still blue ink in the sky at midnight. London had felt like a movie. This was a dream.

———⊷———

The next morning John and Gretchen hired a droshky, a Russian-style horse-drawn carriage, which Marion insisted was the only way to explore Old Town. With Richard seated between them, they spent the day clop-ping through the narrow streets while Marion stayed behind at the hotel taking care of the pile of correspondence that had been waiting for her at the front desk.

Their driver was a one-legged Estonian named Kaius Kirsipuu who smoked a meerschaum pipe and spoke excellent German. He began by telling them, with a laugh, that he had made a present of his right leg to the German army. He said there had been some sharp fighting in the forest just a few kilometers from here before the Russians and Germans were finally driven out and Estonia regained its independence. Kaius pointed out the palace where the president now lived, built by Peter the Great so he could park his wife there while he retreated to the modest stone house he'd built out in the woods, where he and his "Jolly Company" of men gambled and went hunting and drank vodka like most men drink water.

At suppertime, Kaius dropped them at his favorite sidewalk café on a square just outside the Old Town wall. The square was surrounded by modern apartment buildings and movie theaters, electric signs, bus stops and taxi stands and buzzing scooters. John felt like he'd blinked his eyes and stepped from the Middle Ages into the modern world. Behind their table, stone steps climbed a steep green hill, flowers spilling from the landings. Concert music drifted down the hill to them. John remarked that he found the Old Town even more enchanting than Heidelberg, one of his favorite cities. Gretchen barely heard him. Her knuckles were throbbing in time with the music, like a metronome. The music reminded her of Prokofiev, but not so strident, silkier. All she could think about was that tomorrow, at last, they would reach Pärnu.

—◦◦◦—

They left early the next morning for the seaside resort town, which Marion pronounced PAIR-nu. The train was crowded, mostly vacationing families headed to the beach, plus a sprinkling of Swedes and Danes and Finns. Gretchen sat pressed against a window, her knees banging against Richard's every time the train swayed or rocked, little agonies she tried to ignore. A sliver of skin was visible between the cuffs of Richard's suit pants and the tops of his socks. Was he finally beginning his first growth spurt? The train rocked and their knees banged together again. Soon, she told herself, soon this agony will end.

Their hotel was run by a member of what Marion called the "Balt nobility" and his Finnish wife, a tall woman with hair so blonde it was nearly white. Their rooms were perfumed by the sea air and flower boxes on the windowsills. While John and Richard unpacked, Gretchen left, walking with her cane, to meet Marion in the lobby.

They hired a droshky that carried them onto a long tree-lined avenue that led to a white-columned classical building—the Heilbadenstatt. Gretchen could see the Gulf of Riga shimmering through a curtain of birch trees. The beauty of the scene was overwhelmed by the throbbing in her knees. It seemed the shuffling horse would never get them to the end of the avenue.

Finally, a nun was leading them into a room made of white tiles, and the women were sinking into a vat of greenish-brown sea mud. It felt like warm, semi-liquid asphalt, and Gretchen sank but did not touch bottom. Instead, the ooze held her in suspension, and she could feel her muscles and the cords inside her joints begin to unknot. She kept as still as she could. It was bliss—except for the fact that Marion would not stop talking. She resumed the monologue she'd begun on the train from Tallinn, something about how the Estonians never truly embraced Christianity . . . all those steeples and domes were somebody else's idea . . . a pagan streak . . . worshiping ancestors and talking to the trees . . . the mysterious curative powers of their sea mud . . .

Her words were coming from a great distance now as Gretchen reached a state of relaxation she had never experienced, her bones and muscles melted by the warm muck, her body weightless, touching nothing. She was a sack of skin filled with air. Marion must have succumbed, too, because she had finally stopped talking. Time stopped. Gretchen drifted into darkness where nothing happened, where she expected nothing to happen. She could no longer hear her own breathing. So *this* is what it's like to be free of pain. She had no memory of this state, and she did not ever want to leave it. She was happy and she imagined this is how we feel when we die, dissolved into something infinite, at peace, unafraid of the end. When she opened her eyes, she realized she was ready for death. More than that: she realized she welcomed the release it would bring.

John took Richard to the movies that night after Gretchen told them she needed to rest. *Saratoga*, the new picture with Clark Gable and Jean Harlow, was playing, and all the way to the theater, Richard talked nonstop about the movie's plot and the things that went on behind the scenes. It was strange, John thought, the way travel opened the boy up, made him voluble in a way he had never been at home. Kipling's *Kim* did seem about right.

"Jean Harlow collapsed on the set and died of kidney failure when the movie was ninety percent complete," Richard said, though John doubted he knew what kidney failure was. "So they had to shoot the final scenes with a double, shooting her from behind. I'll bet nobody even notices. Wanna bet?"

John was startled by the story. "How do you know such things?"

"I read all about it in the copy of *Photoplay* that was in the library on the boat from New York. She was only twenty-six when she died."

John remembered seeing the magazine alongside the copy of *LIFE* that he'd flipped through. So movie gossip was now part of the reading diet of fifteen-year-old boys, along with stories about hydroelectric dams and quintuplets and polo ponies, a new world of rapidly proliferating information that meant nothing to John.

The movie tickets cost just five cents so John splurged on ice cream made with real cream and fresh strawberries, called *jaatis*. It was delicious, and father and son stood off in a corner of the lobby, slurping away in a state of ecstasy.

They sat in the orchestra of the nearly full theater, and as soon as the house lights began to dim, John felt the familiar thrill. He thought of the television broadcast in London, and he could not imagine experiencing such a sense of communion sitting at home alone in front of a little box.

Saratoga turned out to be a garbled mess, something about Clark Gable winning a racehorse farm as payment for a gambling debt, but John was mesmerized by Jean Harlow. Her platinum hair and phosphorescent skin made her look like she'd been dipped in milk, and the knowledge that she was dead served to heighten her ghostliness. It was a disturbing thing to witness—a laughing, flirting dead woman with penciled-on eyebrows and pillowy lips, a figment who continued to radiate life and sexual allure. No other way to say it, she was immortal even though she had died of kidney failure. A thought came to John: with all the recent breakthroughs in medicine, people were still suffering and dying pointlessly from kidney failure and arthritis and polio and cancer. Why couldn't someone find a cure for such afflictions, the way they'd developed sulfa drugs and other miracle vaccines? Jean Harlow should not be dead, and Gretchen should not continue to suffer, her only relief coming from those primitive mud baths. John was rescued from these dark thoughts when the credits rolled and the houselights came back up. The spell was broken.

On the way back to the hotel, John had to admit Richard had been right—the illusion was so seamless that he hadn't noticed when the double had taken the place of poor dead Jean Harlow.

Gretchen returned to the Heilbadenstatt every day the following week. She preferred to go alone so she didn't have to listen to Marion's monologues. As she sank into the warm mud and delicious torpor, only the faint glow of the tile walls penetrated her eyelids. Each day it took less time for time to stop, for her to become emptied out, suspended in space, free of thoughts and pain and the memory of pain. Each day it was easier to become reacquainted with how it felt to welcome death.

For hours after she left the Heilbadenstatt, the pain was vanquished. While John worked in their room on arrangements for Berlin, Gretchen took long walks with Richard along the beach. She didn't need the wheelchair, barely used the cane. For the first time in years, she was able to walk briskly, gulping the salt air. She was made of rubber and felt as giddy as a girl. Richard raced ahead of her, sometimes diving into the surf but always emerging quickly with a shout, delighted by the shock of the cold water.

On their last day at the beach, they came upon a group of young people, a little older than Richard, who seemed to be of another species. They were all bronzed, as smooth as seals, with hair like polished brass. They had built a fire and were singing songs in German, taking turns darting into the water. They looked like little gods and goddesses, Gretchen thought, the most beautiful young people she had ever seen. Even Richard stared at them with awe.

Back at the hotel, Gretchen asked the owner's Finnish wife about the young Germans on the beach. "Ah, yah," she said, "these group are from I believe it is Bavaria. They call themself Hitler's Youth."

When they got back to the room, John announced that their train to Berlin would leave tomorrow at noon. Gretchen's first thought was that she had taken her last mud bath. Her second thought was that she must never let John know that she was ready to die.

⟶ ❊ ⟵

Berlin was even grimmer than Marion had led them to expect. Buildings that were once pristine had fallen into disrepair during the Depression. The streets were shabby, and with the Olympics over and the international visitors gone, Nazi propaganda posters were everywhere. John found them sickening. They promised *Work, Freedom and Bread*. They announced that *Youth Serves the Führer*. And they boasted that *We Farmers Throw Out the Manure*, with a picture of a farmer tossing a pitchfork laden with communists and Jewish bankers.

Worst of all were the formations of soldiers marching through the streets—something very different from the parades that had amused John forty years earlier. These men were armed, and whenever they entered a streetcar, all passengers rose and thrust their right hands into the air and barked, "Heil, Hitler!" It was apparent to John that the Nazis were not building up the armed forces and pumping out tanks and artillery and bullets and gas because they wished for peace; they were preparing for war because they intended to wage war.

John once again found refuge in the libraries while Richard was turned loose on the streets with a small allowance, enough to buy an ice cream cone and a six-ounce bottle of Coca-Cola, a little taste of home. Every day he went to the Reichstag to witness the changing of the guard, and every time he went into a store he got the salute and a hearty "Heil, Hitler!" He returned the salute. He found it amusing—until his father sat him down and told him that the sight of people saluting brown-shirted storm troopers and black-coated S.S. guards was the opposite of amusing. It was, John said, the behavior of a doomed country.

Many of John's acquaintances had left—for France, England, America. When he questioned those who remained, he was surprised by their insouciance. Yes, it was odd that they had to prove their Aryan ancestry, they told him, but rules are rules and it didn't do any harm and, besides, what was the alternative? If you didn't prove your racial purity, you couldn't get a decent job, or tenure, or any of a thousand benefits large and small. No one seemed to sense that there could be a dark motive behind this demand, that it could be a prelude to a cleansing like the one that had taken place in Forsyth County, Georgia, back in 1912. Remarkable, John thought. Once again, the Germans were sleepwalking to their doom.

On the boat back to New York, they heard the news that the aviator Amelia Earhart and her plane had disappeared in the South Pacific on the last leg of her around-the-world flight. Gretchen was distraught. She had always cheered pioneering women like Earhart—Harriet Beecher Stowe, Susan B. Anthony, Clara Barton, Harriet Tubman, and, in a minor key, Marion Foster Washburne. As her own body continued to betray her, Gretchen was deeply saddened by the loss of a woman as courageous and inspiring as Earhart, who had already flown solo across the Atlantic, across the continental US, and from Hawaii to California. Gretchen allowed herself to be encouraged that no trace of Earhart, her navigator Fred Noonan, or their twin-engine Lockheed Electra had been found. Maybe they'd landed safely on some remote atoll and were awaiting rescue. Maybe they'd been plucked from the Pacific by the crew of a fishing trawler. Maybe . . . but Gretchen knew better than to believe in such fairy tales. She also knew that her own death was coming, and she was ready.

Gone With the Wind *premier in Atlanta*.

FURRINERS

At the age of sixteen, Richard won a scholarship to Spring Hill College, a small Jesuit school in Mobile, Alabama. Gretchen was no longer able to climb stairs so, with the children all gone, she and John sold the house on Mell Street and moved into a ground-floor flat on Milledge Avenue.

When the family convened there for the holidays at Christmastime in 1939, everyone was amazed to see that Richard had undergone a growth spurt and was now nearly as tall as John. During the holidays, father and son went to see another Clark Gable picture in another theater—the Colonial in Athens, where *The Birth of a Nation* had had its regional premiere.

The Colonial was showing the latest skewed take on the Civil War, an extravaganza called *Gone With the Wind* that had recently had its world premiere at the Loew's Grand in Atlanta. Watching the newsreels—the airport arrivals of the stars, the ticker tape parade down Peachtree Street, the banquets, the spotlights stroking the crowd, and the night sky outside the theater—John had noted with bitter amusement that Jim Crow had prevented the movie's two Black stars, Hattie McDaniel and Butterfly McQueen, from attending the all-White premiere. No surprise there. Nothing could be allowed to gum up this opportunity for Atlanta to burnish its image as the city too busy to hate. What was surprising to John was that Margaret Mitchell's novel had won the Pulitzer Prize. He saw the book as little more than another Lost Cause apology, a melodrama Thomas Nelson Page would have loved. And the writing was dreadful.

Now, watching oily, jug-eared Rhett Butler sparring with saucy Scarlett O'Hara as the world around them burns, John found the movie was failing to provide the promised escape. His mind kept wandering from the fantasy war on the screen to the real war in Europe. He couldn't stop thinking that his dire predictions had come true with appalling accuracy—that Hitler's preparations for war had culminated in his invasions of Czechoslovakia and Poland, had finally goaded the reluctant British and French to act. After they'd declared war on Germany three months ago, President Roosevelt had gone on the radio to promise that the United States would remain neutral—an unconvincing echo of Woodrow Wilson's similar promise twenty years earlier. Roosevelt added what sounded to John like a caveat: "Even a neutral has a right to take account of facts. Even a neutral cannot be asked to close his mind or his conscience." Even a neutral, in other words, has the right to change his mind and take sides. And if that happens, John realized, *my three sons will be prime cannon fodder.*

Gone With the Wind got a standing ovation from the Athens audience. At last, the applause seemed to say, someone in Hollywood was willing to admit that White southerners were not all monsters and that they had suffered terribly for their beliefs. John knew all about that suffering, but he accepted something that the clapping people around him were unwilling or unable to admit: that suffering was self-inflicted, and there were millions of blameless Black people who had suffered—and continued to suffer—far worse.

———

Now Governor Eugene Talmadge made a fatal miscalculation. He had earned his law degree from the University of Georgia when Sylvanus was dean of the law school, but he was no fan of the university, which he regarded as an elitist incubator of race mixers, communists, religious radicals, and other undesirables. In 1941, after his reelection to a third two-year term, Talmadge was approached by Sylla Hamilton, a former instructor in the university's laboratory school who had been fired from her job. Bitter over the firing, which she blamed on Walter Cocking, the dean of the university's College of Education, Hamilton told Talmadge that Cocking was planning to build a training school for teachers that was to be "for both blacks and whites." Cocking had recently completed a study of state-supported Black higher education in the state, and while the study exposed the inherent hypocrisy of a separate-but-equal educational system, Cocking never promoted the mixing of the races in any university facility. Even so, he had enemies besides Sylla Hamilton. They began to whisper that Cocking was a homosexual, or that he was carrying on an affair with his Black female cook.

Talmadge smelled blood. At a meeting on May 30, 1941, he stunned the Board of Regents by recommending that Marvin Pittman, the popular president of the Georgia State Teachers College in Statesboro, not be reemployed. Pittman's sin? According to a disgruntled faculty member and Talmadge ally, Pittman permitted the instruction of communism and supported racial equality. Though both charges were fabrications, the regents complied with Talmadge's request. He then moved to fire Cocking and, by an 8-to-4 vote, the regents again complied. Upon hearing the news, an outraged Harmon Caldwell, the university president, said he would resign immediately if Cocking did not receive a hearing.

Talmadge relented, and after a closed-door meeting in Atlanta on June 16, at which testimony heavily favored Cocking, the regents voted 8-to-7 to reinstate him. Now it was Talmadge who was outraged. "I'm not going to put up with social equality in this state as long as I'm governor," he fumed. "We don't need no Negroes and white people taught together."

True to his word, Talmadge began a campaign to stock the Board of Regents with handpicked cronies so he could get rid of Cocking. He also vowed to purge all college faculties in the state of "furriners," which he defined narrowly not as people from foreign countries or even from outside the South, but as people from outside the state of Georgia. Suddenly John, a native Virginian, found himself in the governor's cross hairs.

John and Gretchen were spending the summer at Taylor's Creek, and now they worried not only about global events but also about John's job security. In late June a letter arrived from R. P. Brooks, who opened with a quip that living at Taylor's Creek must be "like being snowbound in Iceland." Then he got serious: "It seems clear that Talmadge has worked himself into a frenzy and is determined to wreck the University as far as it lies within his power to do so."

Brooks reported that he had spoken "strongly" in favor of Cocking at the June 16 hearing before the Board of Regents, which had resulted in Cocking's reinstatement. He also reported that Talmadge had ordered the regents to compile a list of all faculty members who were not native Georgians. Then Brooks veered back to humor: "I do not believe that Talmadge would have the effrontery to attack the older group of 'foreigners.' However, many of you are so near the boneyard anyhow that he might take the notion to buy a small farm near Athens and turn you out to graze, with an allowance of twenty-five or thirty dollars a month."

Brooks also reported that he and other native Georgians on the faculty were "trying to work up sentiment here for a protest." He got forty-three members of the faculty to sign a letter to Talmadge, supporting Cocking and Pittman and complaining that, due to anemic state support, the university's libraries and laboratories were "inadequate," faculty salaries were lower than at other state universities, and the school was constantly in danger of losing its accreditation. Talmadge was unmoved.

A few days later, John got a letter from President Caldwell, thanking him for sending a clipping from the *Richmond Times-Dispatch* about Talmadge's crusade to purge "furriners" from the faculty. "The fact that the governor is taking such an attitude toward professors born out of state is very distressing and embarrassing to us," Caldwell wrote. "I cannot believe, however, that he really intends to carry into effect some of the proposed policies about which he has talked."

Believe it. In the month after Cocking's reinstatement, Talmadge took the low road, hiring a private investigator who got a handyman to reveal that Cocking had entertained Blacks in his home. Talmadge then railed against Cocking's ties to the Julius Rosenwald Fund, a clear attempt to rouse anti-Semitic feelings, and he spoke about a vague international communist conspiracy that forced him to purge "suspect" volumes from university libraries. Talmadge was pulling all the levers: racism, anticommunism, and anti-Semitism.

It appeared to work. At the July 14 meeting, Talmadge's handpicked regents voted 10-to-5 to remove Cocking and Pittman. Emboldened, Talmadge began to fire faculty and staff throughout the university system, including an assistant professor of education at Statesboro who lost her job because she was from the North—the very worst kind of furriner—and had spoken out in Pittman's defense.

But the purge began to backfire. The General Education Board cut off all aid to the university, and the Southern University Conference, which was not an accrediting agency, voted to drop the university from its rolls.

Students began protesting on the Athens campus, and they burned Talmadge's effigy on three occasions and likened him to Adolf Hitler. At Statesboro, students walked out of classes after sending a petition to Talmadge in support of Pittman. The story was beginning to make national news.

Then came the gut punch. At its annual meeting on December 4, the powerful Southern Association of Colleges and Schools voted unanimously to strip the White schools in the University of Georgia system of their accreditation. Degrees from these schools were now virtually useless for anyone trying to get into a graduate or professional school. The University of Georgia was a pariah.

Three days after the university system lost its accreditation, the Japanese bombed Pearl Harbor and the United States entered the war. The following year's gubernatorial campaign would be dominated by Talmadge's disastrous meddling in the university system's affairs. Ellis Arnall, the attorney general, ran against Talmadge on a promise to restore the university's accreditation and reputation. But the campaign pointed out that this uproar, despite Sylla Hamilton's original accusations, was never about the possible racial integration of Georgia schools. Everyone, including Walter Cocking, knew that was out of the question. As the *Atlanta Constitution* pointed out at the height of the controversy: "Any statement that suggests that the university or members of its faculty encourage or favor racial intermingling or racial co-education is untrue and should not be believed."

Jim Crow was never in danger. This uproar was about Eugene Talmadge's misguided power grab, and in that fall's election the voters of Georgia would conduct a purge of their own. Arnall won the election handily, then lived up to his promise to make reforms that led to the university winning back its accreditation. The university would recover, but its reputation had been tarnished, and the experience left John and many others badly rattled. It *can* happen here, John realized. And it very nearly did.

Mushroom cloud from an atomic bomb.

THE DINOSAURS CLUB

Despite his pacifist views, John didn't object when his three sons decided to enlist. Unlike the pointless Great War, this was a fight, both in Europe and the Pacific, against forces of pure evil that sought nothing less than total world domination. Extraordinary times called for extraordinary action.

John agreed to teach German to officers training on the Athens campus. Jack joined the Navy and wound up as captain of a motor torpedo boat in the Philippines. My father joined the army's First Cavalry and also got shipped to the Pacific. Charles was the only one who stumbled. A brief stint in the army's Officers' Candidate School was cut short by a fresh brush with madness. There were reports of violence, imprisonment, and hospitalization, followed by an ambiguous discharge.

Then tragedy struck, unrelated to the war. John's and Gretchen's second daughter, Sarah, was living in Monroe, twenty-five miles southwest of Athens, with her husband, Albert Mobley, and their three young sons. Albert had opened an auto finance company, but with the Depression dragging on, sales were slow and the business failed. Soon after the collapse of the business, Albert committed suicide. Sarah, devastated, came to Athens with her boys and set about piecing her life back together. She didn't have the luxury of despair. She went to work in a men's clothing store, and when the Army Signal Corps came to town, she landed a job as a secretary. John and Gretchen were amazed. The woman was a warrior.

My father's experience during the Second World War was a spooky echo of his grandfather's experience during the Civil War. Like grandfather Charles, my father got attached to a general, I. P. Swift, and was given the seemingly cushy job of writing letters while stationed on New Guinea. It was certainly better than charging Japanese machine gun nests. As my father put it, he killed as many of the enemy as they killed of him. But Swift, like the martinet Alexander Lawton before him, was a perfectionist, and when he tasked my father with writing letters of condolence to the families of fallen soldiers, he gave very explicit orders. Every parent of a dead son was to get a one-of-a-kind letter above the signature of sensitive, caring I. P. Swift. "I don't want any two letters alike," Swift told my father. "I don't want any mother in Kansas City bumping into some mother in Atlanta and finding out they got duplicate letters."

My father was a lightning-fast typist—he had set a record of typing 115 words a minute during high school, a skill that would serve him well as a newspaper rewrite man after the war—but fast as he was, he could not keep up with the rate men were dying. "One day we lost several hundred men," my father recalled, "and I was writing variations on a theme until the point when I was getting punchy. I had about twenty to go—one in California and the next one in Maine—and I wrote the same damn letter. I had just run out of gas."

Within minutes, Swift called him in to his tent. "At ease, Junior," he said. "Do you remember an order I gave you when we first landed on this island? I gave you an order never, never to make two letters alike. And you've done it. You have disobeyed an order."

My father was petrified—it was an offense that could lead to a court-martial. Though Swift let it drop, he was never as cordial after that night. Fifty years after the war, my father was still bitter over the snub.

Far worse was the news from home. The Red Cross notified Richard that Gretchen was going to be operated on to remove a tumor. When he told Swift about it, in the hope that he might get a pass to go home, the general said, "Well, you're certainly a long way from Georgia. Is the tumor malignant?"

My father didn't know what the word meant. He learned fast. Then the Red Cross cabled back to say the tumor was benign, another new addition to my father's vocabulary. Two weeks later they cabled again to say the tumor was, indeed, malignant and they'd operated and she didn't have long to live. Swift was his usual warm self. "I don't see how you can possibly get there, and you may not get there in time," he told my father. "We'd have a hell of a time getting you on an airplane."

Even more revealing than the general's cold practicality was my father's naïve hope that the US military would fly him halfway around the world in wartime so he could tend to his dying mother. He was still a provincial Southern boy.

Gretchen died from stomach cancer on May 18, 1944, at the age of sixty-four. She was free of pain at last.

While Gretchen was dying, John was being lionized for a dubious achievement. He was among five professors who had taught for at least fifty years at the university, meaning that combined they had served for more than a quarter of a *millennium*. They were featured prominently on the front pages of the Athens newspapers before the university celebrated its 159th anniversary on Charter Day. "The Kind of Men Who Made Our Nation Great," one headline read. The unspoken subtext here was that each of these selfless public servants had been forced to teach late into life by the university's notoriously low pay and lack of benefits. John was now a decorated member of the Dinosaurs Club.

<hr />

The pictures of the mushroom cloud over Hiroshima stunned John. Even he had not imagined that human beings were able—and willing—to harness a destructive force of this magnitude and use it to kill fellow human beings. Three days later, his shock was doubled by the news that a second bomb had been dropped on Nagasaki. The Japanese had refused to surrender, believing, foolishly, that the Americans had only one bomb. John tried to console himself. At least this horrific news meant that his sons would be coming home from the Pacific.

When Richard got his discharge, he returned to Athens to find that John had finally retired from the university and was spending his days rattling around the empty apartment on Milledge Avenue, lost in a fog of grief. To alleviate this grim situation, Richard took John's dictionary to New York City and began knocking on doors at publishing houses, confident he would be deluged with offers. When no editor showed interest, my father grew indignant. How could they be blind to the merits of such a monumental achievement? An unlikely character was about to point me to the answer.

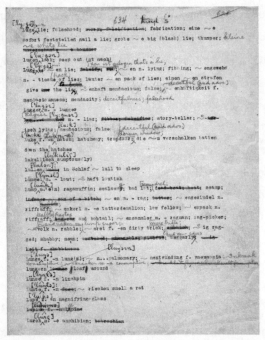

Page 634 of the manuscript of John Morris's German-English Dictionary.

WAS THE PROFESSOR A MADMAN?

t was Hugh Hefner, of all people, who finally led me to the truth about John's dictionary. While I was deep in the research and writing of this book, I accepted an assignment from The Daily Beast website to write an advance obituary of the founder of the Playboy empire. As a lifelong lover of obituaries, I found this assignment a plum—but a plum with a challenge. With someone as well-known as Hefner, I needed to find a fresh way to tell the familiar story of how a Chicago adman had turned sex into fabulous profit. Eventually it hit me: my cousin Jon Morris, eldest child of my Uncle Jack, was an All-Star center for the Boston Patriots of the American Football League back before the invention of the Super Bowl, and I knew that he'd married a woman named Gail he'd met while she was working as a Bunny in the Boston Playboy Club. Of course. Interview a former Playboy Bunny—the perfect way to get an inside take on Hugh Hefner!

I called Jon and Gail at their retirement home on the Georgia coast, not far from the site of the rice plantations where Fanny Kemble Butler had witnessed and chronicled the horrors of slavery two centuries earlier. Gail was happy to talk about working as a Bunny, first in San Francisco and then in Boston. I'd expected (hoped for?) a river of invective about Hefner's exploitation of women, but Gail surprised me. Despite the push-up bras, the brutal hours poised on high heels, and the inevitable come-ons from customers, she told me she loved the job. It was so *glamorous*. She worked in the Showroom in the San Francisco club, which she likened to "a castle." She got to introduce Frank Sinatra, Tony Bennett, Dean Martin, and Sammy Davis Jr. while making up to $400 a week, more money than she'd ever dreamed possible. I asked her if she had read Gloria Steinem's famous exposé in *Show* magazine based on her undercover job as a Bunny in the New York City club in 1963. Gail, who grew up in blue-collar Eugene, Oregon, dismissed Steinem, a Smith College grad, as a coddled East Coast liberal. For a young working-class woman, Gail told me, Hugh Hefner had provided a job that paid good money and gave her entrée to a magical world. As a bonus, she met a golden football star at a charity softball game between the Boston Bunnies and the Boston Patriots, and that man would become her husband and the father of their two children. My Hef obit had taken a U-turn.

When Jon came back on the line, I told him I was writing a book about the life and times of our paternal grandfather. Jon asked if I knew that John had been a proponent of phonetic spelling, and I said I did. Jon speculated that his father had dropped the h from his name in deference to our grandfather's devotion to phonetic spelling. Jon then asked if I knew that John had written a dictionary, and again I said I did. I thought I'd trumped him when I told him my father had tried to sell the dictionary to New York publishers after the Second World War, but nobody was buying. I assumed the manuscript was lost. Then Jon trumped me.

"I've got the manuscript of the dictionary in a bunch of boxes somewhere in my attic," he said. "John must have given them to my father, and my father gave them to me. I've been meaning to take them to the dump. You're welcome to have them if you want them." After begging him not to take the boxes to the dump, I promised to come down soon to fetch the treasure.

Jon and Gail had six cardboard boxes waiting on the floor of their garage when I showed up. I shipped them to my home in New York City, sight unseen. When I got home and opened the boxes in the presence of a native German speaker who is also fluent in English, I was in for a surprise.

The boxes contained stacks of brittle, yellowing pages—more than a thousand of them—covered with typing and crabbed handwriting and cross-outs. In addition to the dictionary, there was a bound, inch-thick "Alphabetical List of Names." The edges of its pages appeared to have been nibbled by termites, or possibly mice. This sample entry from the List of Names returns us to the thicket that produced John's essays on the origins of the names Oglethorpe and Shakspere:

ACUTT, AYCOCK, ACOCK—The basis of this name may well have been the Old Norse Saga name Aki, which appears in the Domesday Book as Achi liber homo, Achi f. Siwardi, Achi huscarle R.E., together with the compounds Achil (Akketill) and Aculfus (Akulf). The much-disputed suffix -cock is discussed under -gaut (q.v.).

The definitions in the dictionary are accompanied by pronunciation keys but no phonetic spellings. Some entries have simple one-word translations while others include rambling addenda that verge on free association. *Halb*, the German word for half, contains a full page of sample compounds, including "halftime," "half as much," "half-baked," half-breed," "half-cocked," "halfway," "half-wit," and so forth. At this point my German friend started noticing errors. *Geheftet*, for instance, is defined as "unbound," but it means the opposite, "bound." Possibly a typo, I told myself. My friend pointed out that John translated the feminine noun *Baracke* as "barracks," which my American Heritage Dictionary defines as "a building or group of buildings used to house military personnel." But my friend pointed out that the German word for military housing is *Kaserne*. A *Baracke*, according to the Pons German-English Dictionary, is a "hut, shack or hovel," clearly implying dilapidation but with no mention of the military. This was no typo. This was a bald error, and it got worse. One of the great appeals of German, besides the consistency of its pronunciations, is the precision of its meanings; there is a correct word for just about everything. But at times John seemed deaf to important nuances. For instance, he defines both *ersaufen* and *ertrinken* as "to drown." Accurate as far as it goes, but it fails to point out a crucial shade of meaning. You would use *ertrinken* to express that "a child drowned tragically in the flood." But you would use the less formal and more damning *ersaufen* to say that a drunkard "drowned his sorrows in drink." According to my German friend, if a newscaster used *ersaufen* to describe the tragic drowning of a child, he would be fired on the spot for failing to show compassion for an innocent victim.

Before my friend and I dissected those manuscript pages, I had accepted my father's implication that New York publishers rejected the dictionary because of their innate provincialism and myopia. Having been bruised more than once by that crowd, this was a charge I was ready to believe. Now I knew differently. Now I knew that they had rejected the manuscript for the very valid reason that, other than the herculean effort that went into making it, there was nothing exceptional about it—no phonetic spellings, no etymologies, no enlightening usage notes, no erudite examples of word usages lifted from literature, à la Samuel Johnson. It was little more than an assiduous catalog, a very workmanlike—and very long—list that was both disjointed and riddled with errors. It was a huge disappointment to me. After combing through the manuscript, my German friend delivered a stinging verdict: "This is the work of a crackpot." Then came a question: "Do you think your grandfather was a madman?"

Maybe so. There was certainly a history of mania in the family, and anyone who could spend decades compiling such a flawed work was, at the very least, in the grip of an obsession that blinded him both to the work's flaws and to its possible usefulness. But maybe John simply didn't care about such things. If he was indeed mad, maybe there was a method to his madness.

An artist's rendering of the Montgomery bus boycott.

THE DELUGE

After my father's failed attempt to sell the dictionary, John lived the rootless life of an octogenarian widower. He wandered "from pillar to post," in my father's words, staying sometimes at Taylor's Creek with his sister Louise, sometimes in Washington with the family of his son Jack, sometimes in Richmond at the apartment of my bachelor father, who had landed a job as a cub reporter on the *Richmond Times-Dispatch*.

While staying with my father, John frequently went to the movies at the Byrd Theatre, a palace with chandeliers, a sumptuous velvet curtain, and elaborate decorative flourishes. John loved the theater's air conditioning almost as much as he loved the movies. These were among the many good things about the modern world, things like running water and flush toilets and refrigeration and automobiles and paved roads and phonographs and radio and new drugs called antibiotics that would soon conquer pneumonia and other infections. Television he could live without.

Still unable to parallel park, John usually just pulled his car onto the sidewalk outside the Byrd Theatre and left it there. When a bemused cop would ask at the ticket booth about the car on the sidewalk, the ticket seller would say, "Oh, that's Professor Morris's." And the cop, shaking his head, would move on. The family name still counted for some small thing.

In Richmond, my father had met a sleepy-eyed young beauty named Anne Slusher, a social worker from Bluefield, West Virginia (or "West *by God* Virginia," as my father put it to his Virginian friends). A romance bloomed. Soon after they met, however, my father accepted a job as a reporter at the *Washington Post*. He found an apartment he could share with John in suburban Chevy Chase, and on his days off he raced back to Richmond to do his courting. The relationship survived this erratic launch, and Richard and Anne were married in the fall of 1949. After the newlyweds settled into a garden apartment in suburban Silver Spring, Anne gave birth to my brother Rick the following summer and, two years later, to me. Shortly after my birth, my father accepted a PR job with Ford in Detroit. It was at this time that the family snapshot mentioned in this book's prelude was taken—ancient John balancing infant me on his knee.

This was also when the United States detonated the first hydrogen bomb, an entirely new level of devastation. Technology, that benign force for good, had now been so thoroughly corrupted that it had produced weapons capable of ending all life on the planet. This was the final proof of something John had believed for many years: once humans develop a weapon, they will always use it and they will always replicate it and refine it. This was madness. I have a theory that the H-bomb was what finally broke John. As he passed the age of ninety, he began to falter.

After my family left for Detroit, John moved in with Uncle Jack and Aunt Leigh and their growing family in suburban Chevy Chase. A full-time nurse was hired and Jon, the eldest child, remembers John sitting in a chair all day, withdrawn, locked away somewhere as his memory slowly failed. It's likely this was the onset of dementia. One night Uncle Jack heard noise downstairs, and when he went to investigate, he found his father in his pajamas, merrily urinating on the living room rug.

That was it. Uncle Jack, who had resisted the move, swallowed hard and got John set up in a nursing home in nearby Olney, Maryland, where he would have round-the-clock professional care and could live out his final days in comfort and peace.

———

In the last year of John's life, a cascade of world-shaking events took place. In the spring of 1954, the US Supreme Court ruled unanimously in the landmark *Brown vs. Board of Education* case that the separate-but-equal doctrine anointed fifty-eight years earlier by *Plessy vs. Ferguson* was unconstitutional. Public schools must be integrated. The South would resist for years, kicking and screaming, but a fundamental pillar of Jim Crow had been toppled.

On a less stirring note, Vice President Richard Nixon announced that the Eisenhower administration was embarking on the biggest public works project in human history, bigger than the Panama Canal, the Hoover Dam, and the Pyramids combined. A new system of "interstate" highways, Nixon announced, would soon stretch from coast to coast. An achievement of such magnitude sent bland, bald Dwight Eisenhower into an uncharacteristic fit of poetry. As he put it in his memoirs: "The amount of concrete poured to form these roadways would build eighty Hoover Dams or six sidewalks to the moon. To build them, bulldozers and shovels would move enough dirt and rock to bury all of Connecticut two feet deep."

The following summer, a fourteen-year-old Black boy from Chicago named Emmett Till was visiting relatives in Money, Mississippi, when he had a fateful encounter with a White woman in a grocery store. The woman claimed Till had whistled at her and grabbed her—a flagrant crossing of the color line. The woman's husband and brother-in-law promptly kidnapped Till, and his naked body was pulled out of the Tallahatchie River three days later. He had been beaten beyond recognition, an eye gouged out, a bullet hole above his right ear. Barbed wire was wrapped around his neck and fastened to a heavy fan blade. But now something astonishing happened. Now the old familiar equation of White supremacy, retribution, and terror got flipped. Till's mother, Mamie Till-Mobley, insisted that her son's casket be open at the funeral so press photographers and crowds of strangers could see his pulped face. "Let the world see what I've seen," Till-Mobley said. In a single inspired stroke, she had turned terror back on itself and, in doing so, forced millions of people around the world to confront the horrors of segregation and lynching. Another pillar of Jim Crow had been toppled.

John's sister Louise died at Taylor's Creek that momentous summer. Three months later, on September 4, John died in the Olney nursing home at the age of ninety-two. The *Washington Post* obituary said he had been "seriously ill for several weeks," without specifying the nature of the illness. My father was more succinct: "He just died of old age."

Margarethe arranged to have the body transported to Athens, and the university chapel was reserved for a funeral service—with a closed casket. But the turnout was sparse. "A few people came by," my father recalled, "but Margarethe didn't realize that two generations had gone by, and the people who knew him were either dead or didn't remember anything."

Soon after John was buried next to Gretchen and his parents in the family plot in Oconee Cemetery, a Black woman named Rosa Parks refused to surrender her seat to a White passenger in a public bus in Montgomery, Alabama. After Parks was arrested and fined, the Black community mounted a boycott of city buses, getting to and from work by carpooling, walking, riding bicycles and even mules. The boycott lasted for more than a year, and it led the US Supreme Court, in an echo of *Brown vs. Board of Education*, to rule that state and local laws that separated bus passengers by race were unconstitutional.

Now, with Jim Crow on the run, the civil rights movement marched toward its full glory. It was something John would have loved to witness. It was a force of nature and nothing could stop it—not firehoses, not police dogs, not centuries of hatred. After John, the long-overdue deluge was finally unleashed.

CODA

SO BE IT

used the word "disappointment" to describe my initial reaction to John's
dictionary, and it's not inaccurate. I was disappointed that a work I'd
pictured as magisterial proved to be so pedestrian and disjointed, the
uneven outpourings of an obsessed man who had quite possibly known
moments of madness. From there my disappointment expanded to include
the fact that this lifelong project—like its author—left no discernible mark
on the world. This was not because such a project lacked merit, or because
it would have had, at best, a limited audience. This, I concluded after years
of research, was because John, like John Wade's fictional Cousin Lucius,
had no interest in fame or fortune. We're back to the Morris character
trait that was both John's blessing and his curse: his utter lack of interest
in winning the world's approval.

As I closed in on finishing this book, I found myself entering a hall of
mirrors where stray assessments of other peoples' lives kept reflecting back
on John's life. For instance, John's grandson John N. Morris, the teacher
and poet, left an unfinished memoir called *Then: Essays in Reconstruction*. In
it he offers an assessment of his father, my sometimes-mad uncle Charles,
that could, with a little tweaking, be applied to John: "In dying sane, or
almost so, though he left no slightest noticeable mark on the world, my

father was, I think, a kind of hero . . . Perhaps this view of him is melo-
dramatic or (almost the same thing) sentimental or otherwise false. But
in these autobiographical paragraphs I maintain it is the right one." And I
maintain this is the right view of both Charles and John.

In an afterword to *Then*, a colleague of John Nelson Morris's at Washington University, Wayne Fields, offered an appraisal of the author, which,
once again, could serve as a description of our grandfather. "John was a
writer in the purest sense," Fields wrote. "He wrote to make the thing he
made, not for any other reward. He, of course, hoped for approval but did
not complain about its scarcity and, if anything, seemed vaguely troubled
even by that quiet desire."

Now came a happy accident. After I'd finished combing through the
manuscript of John's dictionary and was returning it to its many boxes, I
stumbled on an exchange of correspondence tucked in among the pages,
obviously misplaced. The exchange begins with a typed note from John
on University of Georgia Department of German letterhead. It's dated
May 21, 1932, and addressed to "Dear Doctor Feise." This is Ernst Feise
(1884–1966), the German-born head of the Department of Germanic
Languages at Johns Hopkins University and an authority on German
literature, especially Goethe and Heinrich Heine. In his note, John is
seeking Feise's opinion of a list of words he calls "omissions" that were
absent from existing German-English dictionaries and that John planned
to include in his work in progress. The note closes with this revealing
admission: "I have had little encouragement from the publishers, which,
of course, in the existing condition was to be expected; but I still feel that
such a work is greatly needed, and hope, in the end, to find a publisher
who is willing to take a chance."

Feise's response, hastily handwritten on the same page (he says he's
busy packing), is that a colleague will be sending John some additional
material. "We have both read the ms. and found it very interesting, and
made very few suggestions," Feise writes before closing with an ominous

bit of advice: "If it cannot find a publisher, why not ask Röseler whether he could not print it in installments or as a *Beiheft*?"

He's referring to Robert O. Röseler, who was then on the German faculty at Ohio State University and had just published a popular book called *College German*. He and Feise were also general editors at Gateway Books, publishers of "a distinctive new series of German texts."

Though nothing came of Feise's suggestion that John approach Röseler, this exchange was a revelation. It proves that John did not lack interest in winning the world's approval, after all. Yes, he wrote to make the thing he made, but he also hoped for approval from publishers—and, therefore, readers. He did not complain about the scarcity of approval and, like his grandson and namesake, he was vaguely troubled even by that quiet desire. But he believed in the merit of his work, and he hoped to sell it.

I kept getting drawn deeper into this hall of mirrors. John's brother Sylvanus offered this assessment of their father's final years, an assessment that, I believe, could be applied nearly verbatim to John's final years: "All his children were alive, his four sons were at work, none of them had gone astray. His daughters had educational advantages and the pleasures of refined surroundings. He was blessed with 'love, honor, obedience and troops of friends.' I can safely say no man had more and warmer friends than he. In any village in the state one may go, some of his old students speak lovingly of him."

That's not nothing. John also had a long and loving marriage that produced five devoted children, he had many friends, and he had touched the lives of thousands of young people, largely for the better. He wrote obscure articles few people read—no sin there—and he spent decades toiling on a project that left no noticeable mark on the world and amounted to exactly nothing other than the fulfillment it gave him. Taking all this into account, my initial disappointment began to change into something very different. To borrow John N. Morris's word, I began to see that the way John chose to live his life was nothing short of heroic. Like his father Charles and his son Charles, he may have known seasons of madness, but he lived life on his own terms, and I doubt he died with any regrets.

Here at the end, I imagine John at another funeral, this time his own. The coffin lid pops open and John sits up and looks around the University of Georgia's empty chapel, and he thinks, *So this is how you wind up if you refuse to play the game. So be it.*

That, to me, is heroic.

ACKNOWLEDGMENTS

This book is dedicated to Anne Drayton Nelson for the simple reason that I could not have written it without her guidance, support, and deep knowledge of the history. Immense thanks to Virginia Humanities for awarding me the Emilia Galli Struppa Fellowship—and especially to Jeanne Siler for guiding me through the shoals presented by the pandemic. Thanks also to the dogged archivists at the Hargrett Rare Book and Manuscript Library at the University of Georgia—Steve Armour, Steven A. Brown, and Gilbert Head—and to Heather Riser at the Small Special Collections Library at the University of Virginia, and to Dan Abitz at the South Atlantic Modern Language Association.

Many people shared memories, documents, and leads to fresh sources as I was researching this book, and some of them also read portions of the manuscript and offered invaluable insights. They include Steven A. Brown, Phyllis McFarland Correa, Mark Costantino, Nancy McFarland Gaub, Foster Mobley, Joe Morris, Jon and Gail Morris, Rob Morris, Will Morris, Anne Drayton Nelson, David Newton, Elsa Parrott Skaggs, and Earl Swift.

Thanks, once again, to my editor, Jessica Case, and the dedicated crew at Pegasus Books, as well as Derek Thornton for his cover design. Thanks also to my godsend of an agent, Alice Martell. And last but far from least, love eternal to Marianne.

SOURCES

BOOKS

Adams, Henry. *The Education of Henry Adams*. Boston: The Massachusetts Historical Society, 1918.

Atlas, James. *The Shadow in the Garden: A Biographer's Tale*. New York: Pantheon Books, 2017.

Ayers, Edward L. *The Thin Light of Freedom: The Civil War and Emancipation in the Heart of America*. New York: W. W. Norton & Co., 2017.

Ball, Edward. *Slaves in the Family*. New York: Farrar, Straus & Giroux, 1998.

Boswell, James. *Life of Johnson*. New York: Oxford University Press, (rev.) 1970.

Brandon, Craig. *The Electric Chair: An Unnatural American History*. Jefferson, N.C.: McFarland & Co., 1999.

Brands, H. W. *The Reckless Decade: America in the 1890s*. New York: St. Martin's Press, 1995.

Buder, Stanley. *Pullman: An Experiment in Industrial Order and Community Planning*. New York: Oxford University Press, 1967.

Carnegie, Andrew. *The "Gospel of Wealth" Essays and Other Writings*. New York: Penguin Books, 2006.

Cash, W. J. *The Mind of the South*. New York: Alfred A. Knopf, 1941.

Didion, Joan. *Where I Was From*. New York: Alfred A. Knopf, 2003.

Doctorow, E. L. *Ragtime*. New York: Random House, 1975.

Dray, Philip. *At the Hands of Persons Unknown: The Lynching of Black America*. New York: The Modern Library, 2003.

Du Bois, W. E. B. *The Souls of Black Folk*. Chicago: A.C. McClurg & Co., 1903.

———. *The Autobiography of W. E. B. Du Bois* New York: Oxford University Press, 2014.

Dyer, Thomas G. *The University of Georgia: A Bicentennial History, 1785-1985*. Athens: The University of Georgia Press, 1985.

Essig, Mark. *Edison & the Electric Chair: A Story of Light and Death*. New York: Walker & Co., 2003.

Foner, Eric. *Reconstruction: America's Unfinished Revolution, 1863–1877*. New York: Harper & Row, 1988.

Foote, Shelby. *The Civil War: A Narrative*. New York: Random House, 1974.

Ford, Richard. *Between Them: Remembering My Parents*. New York: HarperCollins, 2017.

Friedel, Robert, and Paul Israel. *Edison's Electric Light: The Art of Invention*. Baltimore: The Johns Hopkins University Press, 2010.

Goldstein, Bill. *The World Broke in Two: Virginia Woolf, T.S. Eliot, D.H. Lawrence, E.M. Forster, and the Year That Changed Literature*. New York: Henry Holt & Co., 2017.

Gordon, Linda. *The Second Coming of the KKK: The Ku Klux Klan of the 1920s and the American Political Tradition*. New York: Liveright, 2017.

Gordon, Robert J. *The Rise and Fall of American Growth: The U.S. Standard of Living Since the Civil War*. Princeton: Princeton University Press, 2016.

Grant, Donald L. *The Way It Was in the South: The Black Experience in Georgia*. Athens: University of Georgia Press, 1993.

Hardy, G. H. *A Mathematician's Apology*. New York: Cambridge University Press, 1990.

Hobson, Fred. *Serpent in Eden: H.L. Mencken and the South*. Chapel Hill: University of North Carolina Press, 1974.

Hughes, Thomas P. *American Genesis: A Century of Invention and Technological Enthusiasm*. New York: Viking Penguin, 1989.

Hull, A. L. *Annals of Athens, Georgia, 1801-1901*. Athens: Banner Job Office, 1906.

———. *A Historical Sketch of the University of Georgia*. Atlanta: The Foote & Davies Co., 1894.

Hynds, Ernest C. *Antebellum Athens and Clarke County, Georgia*. Athens: The University of Georgia Press, 1974.

Irby, Richard. *History of Randolph-Macon College, Virginia*. Richmond: Whittet & Shepperson, 1894.

Isenberg, Nancy. *White Trash: The 400-Year Untold History of Class in America*. New York: Viking, 2016.

Larson, Erik. *The Devil in the White City: Murder, Magic, and Madness at the Fair That Changed America*. New York: Vintage Books, 2004.

Lee, Harper. *To Kill a Mockingbird*. Philadelphia: J. B. Lippincott Co., 1960.

Lindemann, Albert S. *The Jew Accused: Three Anti-Semitic Affairs (Dreyfus, Beilis, Frank) 1894-1915*. Cambridge: Cambridge University Press, 1991.

Litwack, Leon. *Trouble in Mind: Black Southerners in the Age of Jim Crow*. New York: Alfred A. Knopf, 1998.

MacLean, Nancy. *Behind the Mask of Chivalry: The Making of the Second Ku Klux Klan*. New York: Oxford University Press, 1994.

Macy, Beth. *Truevine: A True Story of the Jim Crow South*. New York: Little, Brown and Co., 2016.

Magill, Dan. *Bull-Doggerel: Fifty Years of Anecdotes from the Greatest Bulldog Ever*. Atlanta: Longstreet Press, 1993.

Martin, Peter. *The Dictionary Wars: The American Fight Over the English Language*. Princeton: Princeton University Press, 2019.

McCullough, David. *The Path Between the Seas: The Creation of the Panama Canal 1870-1914*. New York: Simon & Schuster, 1977.

McWirther, Cameron. *Red Summer: The Summer of 1919 and the Awakening of Black America.* New York: Henry Holt and Co., 2011.

Mencken, H. L. *Prejudices: Second Series.* New York: Alfred A. Knopf, 1920.

Mintz, Steven, and Kellogg, Susan. *Domestic Revolutions: a Social History of American Family Life.* New York: The Free Press, 1988.

Moran, Richard. *Executioner's Current: Thomas Edison, George Westinghouse, and the Invention of the Electric Chair.* New York, Vintage Books, 2003.

Morris, Edmund. *Edison.* New York: Random House, 2019.

Morris, John. *Organic History of English Words, Part One: Old English.* Strassburg: Verlag von Karl Trübner, 1909.

———. *Minimum German Grammar.* publication date unknown.

Morris, John N. *Then: Essays in Reconstruction.* St. Louis: The Press at Washington University, 2002.

Morris, Sylvanus. *Strolls About Athens in the Early 1870s.* Athens: The Athens Historical Society, 1912.

———. *Principia of Law.* Athens: The McGregor Co., 1923.

Oney, Steve. *And the Dead Shall Rise: The Murder of Mary Phagan and the Lynching of Leo Frank.* New York: Pantheon Books, 2003.

Oshinsky, David M. *Worse Than Slavery: Parchman Farm and the Ordeal of Jim Crow Justice.* New York: Simon & Schuster, 1996.

Östling, Johan. *Humboldt and the Modern German University: An Intellectual History.* Translated by Lena Olsson. Lund, Sweden: Lund University Press, 2018.

Phillips, Patrick. *Blood at the Root: A Racial Cleansing in America.* New York: W.W. Norton & Co., 2016.

Pomerantz, Gary M. *Where Peachtree Meets Sweet Auburn: A Saga of Race and Family.* New York: Scribner, 1996.

Porter, Horace. *Campaigning With Grant.* New York: Mallard Press, 1991.

Rosen, George. *A History of Public Health.* Baltimore: Johns Hopkins University Press, 1958.

Sandmeyer, Elmer Clarence. *The Anti-Chinese Movement in California.* Urbana and Chicago: University of Illinois Press, 1939.

Schlereth, Thomas J. *Victorian America: Transformations in Everyday Life, 1876–1915.* New York: HarperCollins, 1991.

Shirer, William. *Berlin Diary: The Journal of a Foreign Correspondent, 1934–1941.* New York: Alfred A. Knopf, 1941.

Skrabec, Quentin R. *The 100 Most Significant Events in American Business: An Encyclopedia.* Oxford: Greenwood, 2012.

Smil, Vaclav. *Creating the Twentieth Century: Technical Innovations of 1864–1917 and Their Lasting Impact.* New York: Oxford University Press, 2005.

Spalding, Phinizy ed. *Higher Education for Women in the South: A History of Lucy Cobb Institute.* Statesboro: Georgia Southern Press, 1994.

Talley, Dale Paige. *Images of America: Hanover County.* Charleston: Arcadia Press, 2004.

Thomas, Frances Taliaferro. *A Portrait of Historic Athens & Clarke County*. Athens: The University of Georgia Press, 1992.

Thomson, David. *A Biographical Dictionary of Film (Third Edition)*. New York: Alfred A. Knopf, 1995.

Twelve Southerners. *I'll Take My Stand: The South and the Agrarian Tradition*. New York: Harper and Brothers, 1930.

Ward, Geoffrey C. (with Ric Burns and Ken Burns). *The Civil War: An Illustrated History*. New York: Alfred A. Knopf, 1990.

Washburne, Marion Foster. *A Search for a Happy Country*. Washington, DC, National Home Library Foundation, 1940.

Weitz, Eric D. *Weimar Germany: Promise and Tragedy*. Princeton: Princeton University Press, 2018.

Wells, Ida B. *Crusade for Justice: The Autobiography of Ida B. Wells*. Chicago: The University of Chicago Press, 1920.

———. *The Light of Truth: Writings of an Anti-Lynching Crusader*. Edited by Mia Bay. New York: Penguin Books, 2014.

White, Richard. *The Republic for Which It Stands: The United States During Reconstruction and the Gilded Age, 1865–1896*. New York: Oxford University Press, 2017.

White, Walter. *A Man Called White: The Autobiography of Walter White*. New York: The Viking Press, 1948.

Wilson, Edmund. *A Piece of My Mind: Reflections at Sixty*. New York: Farrar, Straus and Cudahy, 1956.

Woodward, C. Vann. *The Strange Career of Jim Crow*. New York: Oxford University Press, 1955.

Wynes, Charles E. *Race Relations in Virginia, 1870–1902*. Charlottesville: University of Virginia Press, 1961.

Zucchino, David. *Wilmington's Lie: The Murderous Coup of 1898 and the Rise of White Supremacy*. New York: Atlantic Monthly Press, 2020.

NEWSPAPER, MAGAZINE, WEBSITE, AND JOURNAL ARTICLES

Bacote, Clarence A. "Negro Proscriptions, Protests and Proposed Solutions in Georgia, 1800–1908." *The Journal of Southern History* 25, no. 4 (November 1959): 471–98.

Benbow, Mark E. "Birth of a Quotation: Woodrow Wilson and 'Like Writing History with Lightning.'" *The Journal of the Gilded Age and Progressive Era* 9, no. 4 (October 2010): 509–33.

Du Puy, William. "Inventors and the Army and the Navy." *Scientific American*, September 14, 1912.

"Edison and the Big Fair." *The Chicago Tribune*, May 13, 1891.

"Enraged White People Are Driving Blacks from County." *The New York Times*, December 26, 1912.

Eyewitness to History. "The Execution of Mata Hari, 1917." www.eyewitnesstohistory.com.

"Far Worse Than Hanging." *The New York Times*, August 7, 1890.

Hanna, Julian. "Harmless Eden: Revisiting D.H. Lawrence's *Kangaroo*." *3:AM Magazine*, October 28, 2014.

King, Gilbert. "The Stalking of the President." *Smithsonian Magazine*, January 17, 2012.

Lechuga, Rita Isabel and Castro, Cristina. "Dramatic Effects of Control Measures on Deaths From Yellow Fever in Havana, Cuba in the Early 1900s." *Journal of the Royal Society of Medicine* 110, no. 3 (March 1, 2017): 118–20.

"The Mask Slackers of 1918." *The New York Times*, December 10, 2020.

McGuire, Peter S. "The Railroads of Georgia, 1860–1880." *Georgia Historical Quarterly* 16, no. 3 (September 1932): 179–213.

"Mob Batters Down Door at Cumming." *The Atlanta Georgian*, September 10, 1912.

Morris, John. "On the Development of Diphthongs in Modern English from O.E. *i* and *û*." *American Journal of Philology* 15, no. 1 (1894): 74–76.

———. "The Name of Oglethorpe." *Georgia Historical Quarterly* 11, no. 3 (September 1927): 216–47; no. 4 (December, 1927): 291–320.

———. "The Name of Shakspere." *The Journal of English and Germanic Philology* 30, no. 4 (October 1931): 578–80.

———. "Ring-Mail." *The Journal of English and Germanic Philology* 33, no. 2 (April 1934): 194–204.

———. "Sidney Lanier and Anglo-Saxon Verse-Technic." *American Journal of Philology* 20, no. 4 (1899): 435–38.

"Murder Suspect of Mrs. Lee Burned at the Stake." *The Athens Banner*, February 17, 1921.

Orr, Fred J. "A Country Home in a City." *Country Life in America*, November 1908.

Ross, Alex. "Willa Cather's Quietly Shattering War Novel." *The New Yorker*, July 7, 2020.

Sjursen, Danny. "America's First 'Endless War' Was Fought in the Philippines." *The Nation*, December 18, 2019.

Twain, Mark. "The Chicago of Europe." *The Chicago Daily Tribune*, April 3, 1892.

ARCHIVES AND LIBRARIES

Catalogue of Randolph-Macon College for the Collegiate Year 1883–84.

Dabney, John Blair. *The John Blair Dabney Manuscript*. The University of Virginia Library, Charlottesville, 1850.

Eugene Talmadge Papers, Hargrett Rare Book and Manuscript Library at the University of Georgia.

Georgia Biography Files, Hargrett Rare Book and Manuscript Library at the University of Georgia.

Georgia Photo File, Hargrett Rare Book and Manuscript Library at the University of Georgia.

H.W. Caldwell Papers, Hargrett Rare Book and Manuscript Library at the University of Georgia.

Miller-Morris Papers, Hargrett Rare Book and Manuscript Library at the University of Georgia.

Papers of the Morris Family, 1727–1931, Small Special Collections Library at the University of Virginia.

Pope-Carter Family Papers. Duke University. Rubinstein Library, Durham, N. C.

R.P. Brooks Papers, Hargrett Rare Book and Manuscript Library at the University of
    Georgia.
The Virginia Museum of History and Culture, Richmond.
The Wartime Correspondence of Charles Morris and Mary Minor Morris.

MANUSCRIPTS, DISSERTATIONS, ORAL HISTORIES, AND SPEECHES

Adams, Charles Francis Jr. *A College Fetich (sic): An Address Delivered Before the Harvard
    Chapter of the Fraternity of the Phi Beta Kappa.* Boston: Lee and Shepard, Publishers,
    1883.
Foye, Arthur Bevins. *Haskin & Sells: Our First 75 Years.* New York: Haskins & Sells
    Publishing, 1970.
Lipscomb, Andrew. *Substance of a Discourse Delivered Before the Legislature of Georgia on
    the Occasion of the Fast-Day.* Milledgeville, Ga.: Houghton, Nisbet & Barnes, 1860.
Morris, John. *A German-English Dictionary* (unpublished, undated).
Morris, Richard. *My Life and Hard Times* (unpublished oral history, 1995).
Ray, David Winter. *A History of Streetcar Service in Athens, Georgia, and Some Possibilities
    for Its Reintroduction.* Master's thesis, University of Georgia, 2005.
Reed, Thomas Walter. *History of the University of Georgia* (unpublished, 1948).
Spalding, Hughes. "Dedication of Harold Hirsch Hall." *University of Georgia Bulletin*
    (March 1933).

AUTHOR INTERVIEWS

McFarland Correa, Phyllis, May 3, 2017.
McFarland Gaub, Nancy, April 29, 2017.
Mobley, Foster, October 8, 2016.
Morris, Jon, September 4, 2016.
Morris, Richard, April 5–15, 1995.
Nelson, Anne Drayton, June 14, 2016.
Skaggs, Elsa Parrott, August 28, 2017.

LETTERS

John Morris to Annie L. Lewis, October 15, 1889.
John Morris to Sarah Morris, July 2, 1917.
Robert P. Brooks to John Morris, June 28, 1941.
Harmon Caldwell to John Morris, July 1, 1941.
Gretchen Morris to Sarah Morris Mobley McFarland, April 12, 1943.
John Morris to Sarah Morris Mobley McFarland, December 12, 1954.
Richard Morris to the author, November 27, 1997.

ABOUT THE AUTHOR

Bill Morris is the author of the novels *Motor City Burning*, *All Souls' Day*, and *Motor City*, and the nonfiction book *American Berserk: A Cub Reporter, a Small-Town Daily, the Schizo '70s*. His writing has appeared in *The New York Times*, *Granta*, *The London Independent*, *The Washington Post Magazine*, *L.A. Weekly*, *Popular Mechanics*, *The Millions*, and *The Daily Beast*. He lives in New York City.